THE SEALED ENVELOPE

THE SEALED ENVELOPE

Toward an Intelligent Utopia

GEORGE SCIALABBA

Yale UNIVERSITY PRESS | NEW HAVEN & LONDON

Published with assistance from the foundation established in memory of Amasa Stone Mather of the Class of 1907, Yale College.

Yale University Press books may be purchased in quantity for educational, business, or promotional use. For information, please e-mail sales.press@yale.edu (U.S. office) or sales@yaleup.co.uk (U.K. office).

Set in Sabon LT Pro, Nobel family type by IDS Infotech Ltd.

Printed in the United States of America.

ISBN 978-0-300-28239-9 (hardcover)
Library of Congress Control Number: 2025939098
A catalogue record for this book is available from the British Library.

Authorized Representative in the EU: Easy Access System Europe, Mustamäe tee 50, 10621 Tallinn, Estonia, gpsr.requests@easproject.com

10 9 8 7 6 5 4 3 2 1

In memory of Christopher Lasch, Barbara Ehrenreich, and Richard Rorty

Il buon tempo verra.

—Engraved in Percy Bysshe Shelley's signet ring

CONTENTS

THE SEALED ENVELOPE

Prelude

THE SEALED ENVELOPE

This is a book about ideas, my own and others'—ideas about politics, about culture, and about political culture. But do ideas matter, especially when it comes to politics? In theory, the outcome of elections in the United States reflects, with only minor distortions, the political preferences—the ideas—of the electorate. That's what representative democracy is supposed to mean. Only it doesn't work out that way. The range of choices over which the American electorate is allowed to exercise its preference is sharply and systematically constrained. Electoral politics is dominated by two major parties, whose programs, to the extent they differ, correspond to the needs and goals of opposing sectors of the business community. The goals and ground rules that all sectors of business agree on constitute the framework of public policy, rarely or never challenged in the electoral arena. Policy proposals—especially from the left—that fall outside this framework remain invisible and inaudible.

This is not a conspiracy theory. Business leaders do not meet in secret to decide how best to delude the public mind and thwart the public will. They don't need to. In a capitalist democracy, business control over the state is assured structurally, in two ways. First, since most people are economically vulnerable—

they depend on employment rather than on ownership or some other entitlement to survive—the best predictor of their voting behavior is likely to be the state of the economy at election time. Overall, the state of the economy is determined by the level of investment. Since investment decisions in a capitalist economy are made privately, governments must nurture that most delicate of blossoms, "investor confidence."

The second reason for business dominance is that political participation in a mass society costs a lot of money. Voting may be free, but setting the agenda is enormously expensive. To work out and put forth a detailed political program at the national level requires information, organization, and publicity, and all these require cash. Since most of the people with a great deal of spare money are capitalists, they have an effective monopoly on public political speech.

There are even finer meshes. Just as the traditional rebelliousness of Parisians depended on the city's mazelike character and was tamed by Baron Haussmann's mid-nineteenth-century renovations, the living conditions of twentieth-century American left-wing intellectuals were disrupted, as Russell Jacoby wrote in *The Last Intellectuals,* by "the restructuring of cities, the passing of bohemia, the expansion of the university." Cheap, comfortable urban space, where the temporarily marginal can congregate, no longer exists. Print or online, little magazines can rarely afford to pay their contributors more than nominally. The spectacular postwar growth of higher education sucked virtually an entire generation of intellectuals into college teaching; a contracting job market reinforced their academic socialization, which emphasized specialization and deference and subtly discouraged ideological explicitness. The panic currently raging among the young about their career prospects could not be a more effective de-radicalizing agent if it had been designed for that purpose by the U.S. Chamber of Commerce.

The foregoing, as the ideologically literate will recognize, is a précis of Historical Materialism 101. It can be compressed still further, into a sentence by Marx: "In every society, the ideas of the rulers are the ruling ideas." But though historical materialism may be true, it can't be the whole truth, or else why this book, which consists of nothing but ideas about ideas? True, "ideas are material forces," says the sophisticated historical materialist, meaning that they matter. But what are ideas, actually? Are they material or immaterial? What does that distinction even mean—how would the world look different if we decided the question in one way or the other? And do we need to answer it at all—do we really require a theory about ideas?

As the reader of this collection will discover, I prefer critics to theorists. Political theory seems to me largely—though not entirely, of course—an elaboration, as often as not unnecessary, of moral intuitions and imaginative identifications. Even John Rawls, the greatest political philosopher of the last hundred years, did not really improve on Matthew 25:18–31. Much as I respect Marx (himself as much a critic as a theorist), my theory of social change comes from Percy Bysshe Shelley's *Defence of Poetry:*

> The great secret of morals is love; or a going out of our own nature, and an identification of ourselves with the beautiful which exists in thought, action, or person, not our own. A man, to be greatly good, must imagine intensely and comprehensively; he must put himself in the place of another and many others; the pains and pleasures of his species must become his own. The great instrument of moral good is the imagination.

Imagination, sympathy, solidarity—by whatever name: this is the true engine of political progress.

Of course, imagination, too, needs criticism—it must not put reason to sleep. We know what the sleep of reason produces. It's tempting to say that imagination is the accelerator, reason the brake; that imagination supplies the force and reason the form; imagination the motive and reason the means. But the very neatness of the dichotomy should make us suspicious. If they're wholly distinct, how can passion subvert reason or reason subdue passion?

A humane politics starts with the fact of unnecessary suffering. We need a moral imagination to notice it and care about it; we need reason and knowledge to figure out what to do about it. (Though we can overdo the latter; as Barbara Ehrenreich pointed out, the one surefire way to reduce poverty is to give poor people money.) But whatever our favorite theory of moral psychology and of the relationship between imagination and reason, it's clear that noticing and minding come first. The impulse of sympathy, and the imaginative identification with another person on which it rests, are the origin of moral imagination.

Most of my subjects are exemplars of moral imagination. (The exceptions—Buckley, Kissinger, Kristol, Friedman—are exemplary failures of moral imagination.) Here I would like to say a few words in praise of my three dedicatees, whose memory, in gratitude for much enlightenment received, I would hope, in a small way, to perpetuate.

Barbara Ehrenreich came as close to my ideal of a public intellectual as anyone else in my lifetime. She earned a Ph.D. in biology but became a freelance writer, at first part-time, soon full-time. Her twenty books included an original brand of amateur anthropology (*Witches, Midwives, and Nurses: A History of Women Healers; Blood Rites: Origins and History of the Passions of War;* and *Dancing in the Streets: A History of Collective Joy*), political economy (*The American Health Empire: Power, Profits, and Politics; The Mean Season: The Attack on the Welfare State;* and *The Worst Years of Our Lives: Irreverent Notes from a Decade of Greed*), sexual politics (*Complaints and Disorders: The Sexual Politics of Sickness; For Her Own Good: Two Centuries of the Experts' Advice to Women; Women in the Global Factory;* and *Re-Making Love: The Feminization of Sex*), and two nonpareil works of social commentary and criticism (*The Hearts of Men: American Dreams and the Flight from Commitment* and *Fear of Falling: The Inner Life of the Middle Class*). She was also endlessly available to little feminist and left-wing magazines or grouplets and dependably witty and pungent in the many polemics she conducted with opponents on her right.

More popular and influential than any of Ehrenreich's other books was *Nickel and Dimed: On (Not) Getting By in America.* Sociologists and anthropologists have gone underground in order to capture aspects of life normally hidden to middle-class readers, but it's safe to say that none have turned in an account written with such verve and generosity. In 2000, after Bill Clinton's historic welfare reform had greatly expanded the ranks of the poor, Ehrenreich decided that, as a citizen, a writer, and a radical, she ought to find out, and report, what life in America is like on the minimum wage. So she spent several months in various parts of the country as a waitress, a housecleaner, and a clerk at Walmart, living (very uncomfortably) solely on her earnings. The book is full of barbed humor, aimed mostly at herself, but the conclusion is perfectly serious:

> When someone works for less pay than she can live on—when, for example, she goes hungry so that you can eat more cheaply and conveniently—then she has made a great sacrifice for you, she has made you a gift of some part of her abilities, her health, and her life. The "working poor," as they are approvingly termed, are in fact the

> major philanthropists of our society. They neglect their own children so that the children of others will be cared for; they live in substandard housing so that other homes will be shiny and perfect; they endure privation so that inflation will be low and stock prices high. To be a member of the working poor is to be an anonymous donor, a nameless benefactor, to everyone else.

Ehrenreich and the historian Christopher Lasch liked and respected each other, which might seem surprising. Ehrenreich was an outspoken feminist, while Lasch incurred much suspicion among feminists for arguing that virtually everything in modern life undermined marriage and the family, which were the only safeguards against the narcissistic, overly dependent character structure that he diagnosed as "the neurotic personality of our time." Ehrenreich understood that Lasch was fully committed to sexual equality at the same time as he insisted on the reality and importance of sexual difference, especially in the child's psychic development. He was notoriously wary of pronouncing on policy, but insofar as he did, his main suggestion was that work should be restructured to make equal childcare easier and to ensure that child-rearing did not retard a woman's career.

Lasch fused intellectual history, psychoanalytic theory, sociological analysis, and political polemic into an exceptionally intricate and wide-ranging critique, to which most subsequent commentators have, in my opinion, failed to do justice. I haven't found any short summary I like better than my own, from *Only a Voice:*

"Lasch's work is an extended quarrel with modernity, defined as the advance of an overlapping, mutually reinforcing phalanx of political centralization, mass production, expanded consumption, automation, geographical mobility, the bureaucratization of education, medicine, and family life, moral cosmopolitanism, and legal universalism. Against this barrage of abstractions, Lasch insisted on the fact of human scale. The human creature has a specific evolutionary endowment and gestational history. As a result, the human infant has a powerful and threatening fantasy life, which it can only outgrow gradually, through a range of close-up interactions, involving both authority and love, with the same caregivers over many years. The bureaucratic rationalization of work and intimate life plays havoc with this scheme of development, producing a weak self, stripped of traditional skills, tools, and autonomy, entirely dependent on large forces beyond its comprehension, much less control, and crippled by ambivalence toward remote, impersonal authority. What sustained the strong pre-modern self was the virtue of hope; what sustains the weak modern self is the ideology of progress."

This is a long way from what most people think they know about Lasch, which is that *The Culture of Narcissism,* his only bestseller, was an eccentric and bad-tempered condemnation of just about everything in modern life. There is a short and painless remedy for that distorted view: read the introduction to his most important book, *The True and Only Heaven,* and especially the sections titled "The Making of a Malcontent" and "The Land of Opportunity: A Parent's View." There he speaks, for almost the only time in his oeuvre, in the first person about his own vision of the good life. It is far from the humorless Puritanism that all too many people unthinkingly associate with him.

Lasch and Richard Rorty did not admire each other, which I always greatly regretted. Lasch thought Rorty intellectually modish—a common misjudgment—and Rorty thought Lasch an intellectual killjoy, an equally common misjudgment. Of all American philosophers, Rorty was the most up-to-date with Continental novelties, but he was also an old-fashioned partisan of enlightenment, progress, and liberation—the very ideals Lasch argued throughout his career were inadequate.

Rorty devoted the first half of *his* career to demystifying religion and metaphysics and to reformulating, wryly but rigorously, the pragmatism of William James and John Dewey. Later on, surveying the rubble and wanting to give the disenchanted something to hold on to amid the gale winds of Nietzschean and Foucauldian nihilism, he wrote an exquisite book, *Contingency, Irony, and Solidarity.* After explaining why morality cannot be grounded in either religion or reason, he goes on to explain how it might be grounded—provisionally—

> not by inquiry but by imagination, the imaginative ability to see strange people as fellow sufferers. Solidarity is not discovered by [philosophical] reflection but created. It is created by increasing our sensitivity to the particular details of the pain and humiliation of other, unfamiliar sorts of people. . . .
>
> This process . . . is a matter of detailed description of what unfamiliar people are like and of redescription of what we ourselves are like. This is a task not for theory but for genres such as ethnography, the journalist's report, the comic book, the docudrama, and, especially, the novel. [Some] fiction . . . gives us the details about kinds of sufferings being endured by people to whom we had previously not attended. [Some] gives us the details about what sorts of cruelty we ourselves are capable of, and thereby lets us redescribe ourselves.

His subtle and adventurous readings of Nietzsche, Freud, Proust, Larkin, Orwell's *1984,* and Nabokov's *Lolita* show us how such description and redescription might be done.

Here and throughout Rorty's writing, it is a little disquieting to watch him dissolve the traditional bases of morality without our knowing what, if anything, will replace them. What replaces them is contingency: our fallible moral imagination, which we must continually recalibrate and renegotiate with our moral community. It is a fragile basis for hope, but unlike the others, it is not illusory.

I am writing this introduction in the wake of the 2024 election. A (slim) majority of voters chose to vest the executive power of the U.S. government in a chronic liar and sociopath, a man denounced by two hundred of his former colleagues in government as dangerously incompetent and authoritarian, and whose party is intent on razing to the ground the social and political architecture—the New Deal—that produced the most prosperous and equitable period of American history. The disdain of Trump voters for the Democratic Party is understandable, but their inability to perceive the far worse toxicity of the Republican Party is unaccountable and will condemn millions of their fellow citizens—and themselves—to economic hardship and environmental catastrophe.

Before a disaster of this magnitude, an essay collection seems quixotic. I began writing in 1980; my entire writing life has been shadowed by the baneful ascendancy of the New Right. What sustains hope, for me, is a metaphor of Rilke's. In *Letters to a Young Poet* he writes that love is a form of knowledge, and that a single act of creation is the fruit of "a thousand forgotten nights of love." He hopes lovers will be solemn and responsible as well as joyful, but he reassures his youthful correspondent that, even when they are selfish or careless, their passion is not wholly dissipated but is passed down to the future, despite themselves, as though in a sealed envelope. That is as much as I hope for these jottings.

PART I

MODERNITY AND THE QUESTION OF PROGRESS

1

"NO, IN THUNDER!"

Christopher Lasch

I.

One of the bittersweet pleasures of American intellectual life in the late twentieth century was to follow the curious evolution of Christopher Lasch, one of America's most important social critics. It was not, however, a widely shared pleasure. A lot of people simply stopped paying attention. Lasch's comradely hectoring alienated much of the left, while the right suspected (correctly) that however much he scolded leftists, his most fundamental opposition was to capitalism's ravages. His antipathy to liberalism, in both its "compassionate" and "pragmatic" versions, to feminism and other varieties of cultural radicalism, and even to the new "communitarianism" has been unflagging. By now, virtually every political and cultural tendency in recent American history has smarted under Lasch's criticism. But the philosophical foundations of those criticisms became clear only in 1991, a few years before his death, with the publication of *The True and Only Heaven: Progress and Its Critics,* a landmark work of social and cultural criticism. The scope and complexity of its central argument, and the ingenuity with which a vast range of evidence is brought to bear, are phenomenal. Even if you remain, as I do, unconvinced—"unconverted" might be more appropriate—you cannot be unimpressed.

In the first phase of his career, Lasch published three collections of historical and political essays: *The New Radicalism in America* (1965), *The Agony of the American Left* (1969), and *The World of Nations* (1973). Though clearly a product of the New Left, with its attractive but unstable blend of Marxist analysis and anti-authoritarian impulse, Lasch differed from other radical historians in at least two respects. Most of them studied American foreign policy, labor movements, or slavery, while Lasch's interests were mainly cultural and psychological. And perhaps as a consequence, he had a far more ambivalent attitude toward authority. Militant, unqualified opposition may have been an adequate response to imperialism, economic exploitation, and slavery, but mass culture and the rise of "the intellectual as a social type" (the subtitle of *The New Radicalism in America*) inevitably evoked more complicated judgments and diagnoses.

By the mid-1970s the civil rights, antiwar, and antipoverty movements within the New Left had largely faded from public view, leaving behind only the counterculture. The personal became virtually the whole of the political. Lasch always had reservations about the New Left's cultural politics; and as the carnival turned into a riot, his disenchantment deepened.

But instead of turning rightward, like many other disaffected intellectuals, he turned inward. Under the influence of Max Horkheimer, Theodor Adorno, and the rest of the Frankfurt School, who combined a philosophically sophisticated Marxism with psychoanalytic theory, Lasch produced three studies of "the socialization of reproduction": *Haven in a Heartless World* (1977), *The Culture of Narcissism* (1979), and *The Minimal Self* (1984). He tried to show that the pressures of competition and commodification had gradually transformed education, medicine, psychotherapy, social work, entertainment, journalism, and even scholarship into agencies for the formation of a specific character type, one that fit the requirements of twentieth-century capitalism. This character type—"the narcissistic personality of our time"—is morally pliant, emotionally and aesthetically voracious, ingratiating but wary of intimate, permanent relationships, in contrast with its nineteenth-century "bourgeois" predecessor, which was rigid, self-righteous, austere. To simplify: the bourgeois character suited a culture of production; the narcissistic character, a culture of consumption. These two types, in more general form, as the "ethos of production" and the "ethos of consumption," are the twin suns around which Lasch's conceptual system revolves in *The True and Only Heaven.*

Lasch's last two books, *The Revolt of the Elites and the Betrayal of Democracy* (1994) and *Women and the Common Life* (1997), were essay collections. Each included entertaining oddities: for example, "The Comedy of Love and the *Querelle des Femmes:* Medieval and Early Modern Aristocratic Satires of Marriage" in *Women and the Common Life.* But each was also thematically unified: in the first case by Lasch's belief that scientific humanism, technological progress, and addictive consumerism had undermined America's civic culture, and in the second by his contention that feminism had gone astray in demanding for women equal participation with men in the intellectually and spiritually bankrupt world of contemporary work. "Mainstream feminism is now concerned almost exclusively with a single goal—to 'empower' women to enter business and the professions on an equal footing with men." But unfortunately, "professional careers are no more liberating for women than for men if those careers are governed by the requirements of the corporate economy." In this essay, "The Sexual Division of Labor, the Decline of Civic Culture, and the Rise of the Suburbs,"

Lasch came as close as he ever did to proposing a sexual politics. But death intervened.

II.

The ur-text of modernity, in Lasch's account, is Adam Smith's *The Wealth of Nations,* which argues that the creation and satisfaction of new needs in the course of economic development is a process potentially without limit. From this claim flows nearly every belief and value at the core of the modern outlook: the primacy of efficiency and economic growth, the perception of nature as resource, the ethical priority of individual welfare, the definition of the good life in terms of leisure and abundance, and most important, the image of history as continuous moral and material progress, made possible by the spread of scientific and social rationality. This is the worldview of the Enlightenment, Marx's no less than Adam Smith's. The quarrel between democratic socialism and liberal capitalism is not over whether these values should be realized, but how.

Adam Smith's originality lay in grasping the implications of what was then a relatively new development: the division of labor. So persuasively did he argue its advantages that it came to be considered, along with secularization, the sovereignty of the individual, and the Scientific Revolution, one of the essential preconditions of modernity, a cornerstone in the ideology of progress. True, the costs of progress were soon enough evident. Secularization frequently threatened psychic stability and morale. Enhanced individual freedom meant diminished social cohesion and solidarity. The predominance of science diverted imaginative energies from non-quantifiable forms of inquiry and expression and made possible a purely instrumental view of the natural (eventually also the human) world. But for all these ills the defenders of modernity had a plausible diagnosis: growing pains. As Kant remarked on the French Revolution, one learns to exercise freedom by exercising it, and in no other way.

The disadvantages of the division of labor (about which Smith was candid, even eloquent, unlike subsequent champions of capitalism) were famously summed up by Marx in a single word: alienation. The division of labor meant the concentration of production, and this meant the loss of economic autonomy, of the freedom to work where one lived, to choose one's own materials, style, rhythms, customers. Wage labor meant forced mobility, the decay of local communities and loyalties, monotonous and unhealthy work, and economic vulnerability. All of which Marx (like all subsequent champions of socialism) accepted as a necessary evil. Through the sheer immensity of its wealth-creating powers, mass production would at length bring into being a population capable of rationalizing and humanizing it. As with other historic innovations, so too with this one: through many trials, tears, and woes, Progress will lead us home.

III.

I hope this description of the modern *weltanschauung* sounds banal. It's meant to. However inchoately, the ideology of progress is as obvious to most of us as the shape of the earth. Whether radical, liberal, or conservative, we would no more think of denying the necessity of industrialism or the eventual triumph of reason and science over traditional dogma and local prejudice than the desirability of a rising standard of living or the right of everyone to plan her own life. Wars, depressions, and other typical local and global disasters may retard progress but cannot ultimately reverse it. Even what is to count, fundamentally, as progress—a fuller, freer, more mobile and abundant, leisured and cultivated life for more and more individuals—is generally agreed on.

To all this, the spirit of the age, Lasch replies (like Thomas Carlyle, one of the heroes of *The True and Only Heaven*), "No, in thunder!" Modernity is a mistake. Progressive ideology in all its aspects—optimism, individualism, rationalism, humanitarianism, internationalism, efficiency, growth, centralization—rests on a misunderstanding of history and human nature. Of course no single book, however ambitious, could fully argue such a claim. So diffuse and pervasive is the progressive outlook that merely to gesture at a critique of it would be an achievement. But Lasch's critique cuts deep.

It is, first of all, historical. According to progressivism, capitalist development created an increasingly educated, militant, unified working class, whose challenge to wage labor and private ownership of the economy became more and more radical. The Russian and Chinese Revolutions derailed this socialist dynamic, which is currently in historical limbo. But whatever radical opposition to capitalism there's been has come from industrial workers, together with a few professionals and intellectuals, and has been oriented to the future—to the fulfillment of capitalism's stunted potential by new, non-capitalist institutions.

Wrong on all counts, Lasch replies. The working class and its socialist or social democratic leaders have fought hard, but never over fundamentals. The only challenge to capitalism per se—to wage labor, the factory system, and the concentration of credit—came from movements of independent small producers threatened with extinction: farmers, craftsmen, shopkeepers, and others usually disparaged by Marxists as politically naive or reactionary "populists." Socialist struggles were about wages and working hours. Only the "reactionary" populists, rooted in a vanishing way of life, raised questions about self-management, the effect of work on the worker, or the control of investment.

The historical scholarship of the past two decades supports this claim of Lasch's, along with another: that the political philosophy of the American Revolution was not Lockean liberalism or "possessive individualism," an ideological precursor of liberal capitalism, but an older, "republican" philosophy of civic virtue. The Revolution was less about property rights than about citizenship. And once again, it was small producers and proprietors who were the main bearers of this ideology and the source of the most effective and radical opposition.

These historical reinterpretations lead Lasch on toward a deeper moral and psychological revisionism. The ideology of progress assumes that maturation involves moving away from narrow and particular affections toward abstract and universal ones. Family, ethnic, regional, and religious loyalties are things we are supposed to grow out of, or at least subsume in a wider sympathy. When such loyalties are exclusive, we call them "chauvinistic" or "fanatical"; and we usually assume that the more intense one of these particularistic commitments is, the more likely it is to be dangerously exclusive.

For Lasch, this devaluation of the local and traditional is a radical error. It is not enlightenment but memory, not breadth of sympathy but intensity of identification, that makes for inner strength. In *The Culture of Narcissism* and *The Minimal Self,* Lasch argued that to achieve secure selfhood an infant must experience love and discipline from the same source; otherwise the child, and eventually the adult, will feel for everyone in authority the same combination of rage and terror that the infant feels for whoever it depends on. And more: it was the advent of wage labor and mass production, which removed the father's work from the child's experience, thereby drastically altering his role in the child's psychic development, that has produced the characteristic neurosis of our time, along with a culture of consumption.

In *The True and Only Heaven* he takes a further step. What does it mean, he asks, that the democratic movement of the eighteenth century and the anti-capitalist movement of the nineteenth, like the civil rights movement of the 1960s, were wrought not by the "universal class" of Marxist theory, not by enlightened rationalists liberated from local attachments and traditional beliefs, but by people very much committed to such attachments and beliefs, people loyal to the "archaic" creeds, crafts, and communities under attack from the forces of "progress"? Not, that is, by people looking toward the future, but by people looking toward the past?

It means, he answers, that "the victory of the Enlightenment," with its unwillingness to accept limits on human aspiration and its promise that in a rational society the traditional virtues would be obsolete, "has almost eradicated the capacity for ardor, devotion, and joyous action." On moral even more than environmental grounds, "the basic premise of progressive thought—the assumption that economic abundance comes before everything else, which leads unavoidably to an acceptance of centralized production and administration as the only way to achieve it—needs to be rejected." Not rational optimism but supra-rational hope is true wisdom and succor:

> Popular initiative . . . has been declining for some time—in part because the democratization of consumption is an insufficiently demanding ideal, which fails to call up the moral energy necessary to sustain popular movements in the face of adversity. The history of popular movements . . . shows that only an arduous, even a tragic, understanding of life can justify the sacrifices imposed on those who seek to challenge the status quo.
>
> The idea of progress alone, we are told, can move men and women to sacrifice immediate pleasures to some larger purpose. On the contrary, progressive ideology weakens the spirit of sacrifice. . . . Hope does not demand

> a belief in progress. . . . Hope implies a deep-seated trust in life that appears absurd to those who lack it. It rests on confidence not so much in the future as in the past. It derives from early memories . . . in which the experience of order and contentment was so intense that subsequent disillusionments cannot dislodge it. Such experience leaves as its residue the unshakable conviction, not that the past was better than the present, but that trust is never completely misplaced, even though it is never completely justified either.

IV.

These passages probably make clear why it has proved so easy to dismiss, even ridicule, *The True and Only Heaven.* Scorn for an errant people, its rulers, and its false gods, and stern insistence on a complete change of heart and mind—this is the tone of a prophet. In fact, Lasch does declare his allegiance to "the tradition of Judeo-Christian prophecy." The "heart" of that tradition is belief in "the power and majesty of the sovereign creator of life; the inescapability of evil in the form of natural limits on human freedom; the sinfulness of man's rebellion against those limits; the moral value of work, which at once signifies man's submission to necessity and enables him to transcend it."

This "tragic understanding of life" Lasch also finds, more or less secularized, in the thought of Carlyle, Emerson, Orestes Brownson, William James, Georges Sorel, and Reinhold Niebuhr, as well as in eighteenth-century republicanism, nineteenth-century Populism, and the Southern black culture from which Martin Luther King Jr. emerged. Lasch's reconstruction of this sensibility, the "ethos of the small producer," proceeds in step with, and as a kind of counterpoint to, his critique of progressivism and its ethos of abundance. As intellectual and social history, it is a tour de force.

Lasch is of course less interested in historiographical virtuosity than in civic virtue. He wants his critique and reconstruction to contribute to the transformation of our culture. But toward what? Populism "has generated very little in the way of an economic or political theory," he admits. "Its advocates call for small-scale production and political decentralization, but they do not explain how these objectives can be achieved in a modern economy."

Neither has anyone else, so populists should not be faulted too harshly. There is, though, another, more plausible objection to Lasch's radical antimodernism. At one point he attributes William James's chronic ambivalence about modernity to "the difficulty of carrying on an essentially theological controversy without its theological context." But surely this is Lasch's difficulty, too? Or does he propose to resurrect "the theological context"—the existence of God, the freedom of the will, the immortality of the soul? The Covenant and the Incarnation? Must we believe in order to be saved? If so, then we are lost. We cannot believe the unbelievable, even to salvage our culture.

V.

Critics have complained, and readers will demur, over the length of *The True and Only Heaven*. But the change to small-scale production and political decentralization is so drastic, so urgent, and so unlikely that the case needs to be made decisively. It is hard to imagine a more rigorous and comprehensive argument than Lasch has made over the decades. Even so, he will probably remain, like other critic-prophets, a voice crying in the wilderness.

Throughout history, the pain of everyday life has elicited a promise of happiness: first of Paradise, then of Progress. To have shown that Paradise is a myth, that supernatural religion is the opium of the people, is the enduring legacy of the Enlightenment. To show that Progress is a myth, that historical optimism is the opium of the intellectuals, is the aim of the Enlightenment's critics. About which a chronically ambivalent modern reviewer might say that these critics, from Carlyle and Emerson to James to Niebuhr to Lasch, have in a sense carried on the Enlightenment's own work: opposing the displacement of our hopes and the distancing of our fulfillment, forcing humanity's attention back to the limits and glories of our un-ideal world, reminding us that the kingdom of heaven is within.

2

REQUIEM FOR THE ENLIGHTENMENT?

John Gray

From time immemorial the prime agency of individual and social reproduction has been inertia, the biological form of which is instinct and the cultural form, tradition. That is to say, things were done one way because they had been done that way before—an efficient, though not infallible, way to achieve organismic and societal stability. Modernity is, in one of its numerous definitions, the progressive attenuation of inertia by consciousness. Where tradition was, there shall reason be.

In the classical account, science, democracy, market relations, and ethical individualism were born and grew up together. The first modern generations looked upon what these phenomena had wrought, pronounced them good, and called for their indefinite continuation and extension. But subsequent developments have not been altogether satisfactory: environmental spoliation, advanced weaponry, totalitarian social organization, the destruction of peasant societies and folk cultures, widespread anomie, and an altered rhythm of daily life that has arguably produced toxic levels of stress and epidemic psychopathology. Many writers, from Pascal to Lasch, have rehearsed these ills and proposed that modernity be reconsidered. *Enlightenment's Wake: Politics and Culture at the Close of the Modern Age,* a collection of recent writings by the English political philosopher John Gray, takes its place in this antimodernist tradition.

Gray defines the Enlightenment project as a combination of rationalism, or the criticism and reconstruction of morality and politics by means of reason alone; universalism, or the supercession of fundamental cultural differences, which will eventually dwindle and disappear; humanism, or the technological subjugation of nature for human purposes; and scientism, the neglect or disparagement of informal, tacit knowledge. Each of these beliefs and hopes is, he argues, an illusion. Reason cannot resolve fundamental conflicts among values. It cannot define a universal human identity, or specify a universally valid set of rights, or formalize all local knowledge. Following Michael Oakeshott and Isaiah Berlin, Gray maintains that rights and values are frequently incompatible. Our identities are inherited rather than created, the product of contingency and circumstance rather than choice. Much of our knowledge is embedded in traditions, in whole ways of life, and cannot be judged or even understood apart from them. This pluralism, powerfully and insistently stated, frames Gray's historical and political arguments. In particular it motivates his rejection of contemporary liberalism, especially the Rawlsian, rights-based variety predominant in the United States.

Because political philosophy in the Anglo-American mode remains for the most part animated by the hopes of the Enlightenment, above all by the hope that human beings will shed their traditional allegiances and their local identities and unite in a universal civilization grounded in generic humanity and a rational morality, it cannot even begin to grapple with the political dilemmas of an age in which political life is dominated by renascent particularisms, militant religions, and resurgent ethnicities.

So far we may imagine Gertrude Himmelfarb and Irving Kristol nodding approvingly, perhaps with a murmured reservation or two. What lifts Gray's work far above neoconservatism in intellectual and moral seriousness is his forthright acknowledgment that unregulated market relations may ultimately be destructive of everything worth conserving. It is not that Gray underrates the merits of the free market. On the contrary, his previous book, *Beyond the New Right*, contained a strongly affirmative account of the moral foundations of market institutions, and his essay in *Enlightenment's Wake* titled "Post-Communist Societies in Transition" is withering in its depiction of the legacy of central planning. But Gray understands, as many British and American conservatives do not, that the market is merely a means of promoting human welfare, one that must be adapted and modified by each community, not an immutable ordinance of suprahistorical Reason. It is true that self-reliance, self-restraint, and the other virtues fostered by market relations are indispensable; and that markets are far superior epistemically to any alternative yet proposed. It is also true that humans flourish only in the shelter of families, neighborhoods, tribes, traditions, and well-known and well-loved places, and only with a minimum of economic security; and that all these things are threatened by the spread of market relations. To hold these discordant truths in tension, as Gray does, is an uncommon and valuable achievement.

In opposition to "market fundamentalism," which countenances unemployment, forced mobility, de-skilling, urban real-estate speculation, and so on at levels that are destructive of stable, healthy communities, Gray proposes a "social market" perspective. First elaborated in post–World War II Germany, social market theory views the market not as an ideal type that each society should strive to approximate but as one element in a society's ensemble of institutions and folkways, which it is policy's job to harmonize. The market should not command automatic legitimacy. Instead, as Gray puts it in a formulation that discloses vast common ground with democratic socialists: "In all those cultures where democratic institutions are themselves elements in the common conception of legitimacy, market institutions will be stable and flourishing only in so far as their forms and workings are acceptable, ethically, culturally and economically, to the underlying population."

What's heartening about this proclaimed subordination of abstract economic efficiency to actual human well-being is that he means it. In *Enlightenment's Wake* and in even more detail in *Beyond the New Right,* Gray argues that although competition, risk, and inequality are inevitable and in fact desirable, many people will nonetheless be entitled to public help. He proposes an "enabling welfare state"—a happy phrase, which strikes exactly the right note. His principle is that those who have fallen out of the market economy or never been part of it should be helped to enter it, and that such assistance should, whenever feasible, be provided through the market (though funded publicly, for example, with vouchers). Education, health care, day care, job training are all on the table and must, he insists, be funded not grudgingly but generously. Moreover, "enablement" (a decided terminological advance over "empowerment") mandates not only individual entitlements but also public goods (again, provided to the extent feasible through a market): clean streets, parks, urban transport, the arts, noncommercial scientific research, and so on. With gratifying impatience Gray waves aside objections from the doctrinaire libertarian right. The proper goal of policy is to preserve healthy—according to our admittedly fallible and changeable contemporary judgment—communities, not to maximize economic freedom and economic growth, abstractly conceived.

On similar grounds Gray waves aside objections from the doctrinaire libertarian left to state action in defense of traditional morality. Although a self-described "ultra-liberal" in this area, he is scathing about the invention of "fundamental rights" by defenders of abortion, homosexuality, and pornography. All such controversies should be resolved through debate, negotiation, compromise—in short, politics—rather than by defining new and presumably unalterable constitutional rights. In the essay "Toleration: A Post-Liberal Perspective," Gray argues persuasively that the core proposition of rights-based liberalism—that the state should be neutral among all ways of life or ideas of the good—is mistaken. The right attitude for the majority in a morally divided community is tolerance, which is a solicitude for social peace arising in equal measure from self-confidence and self-doubt. Peaceableness and humility are not, however, the same thing as a refusal to make moral judgments.

In "The Undoing of Conservatism" Gray mounts a harsh critique of free-market extremism—from the right. The post–World War II social compact in Britain and America provided for full employment and a welfare state financed by the proceeds of economic growth. Faced with stagflation in the late 1970s, conservative parties scrapped the social compact but retained the assumption that political legitimacy depends on economic growth. The resulting feverish pursuit of growth has, predictably, generated social instability. Now, Gray writes, "the dystopian prospect . . . is of a highly dynamic but low-growth economy in which a permanent revolution in technologies and productive arrangements yields large-scale structural unemployment and pervasive job insecurity." The stability of communities and families—the highest conservative value, one would have thought—has been sacrificed to "microeconomic flexibility, productivity, and low labour costs." GATT (General Agreement on Tariffs and Trade) and global free trade are pernicious policies, likely to entail "costs in human suffering that may come to rival those of twentieth-century experiments in central economic planning." Gray's summary indictment is powerful:

> The social and cultural effects of market liberalism are, virtually without exception, inimical to the values that traditional conservatives hold dear. Communities are scattered to the winds by the gale of creative destruction. Endless "downsizing" and "flattening" of enterprises fosters ubiquitous insecurity and makes loyalty to the company a cruel joke. The celebration of consumer choice, as the only undisputed value in market societies, devalues commitment and stability in personal relationships and encourages the view of marriage and the family as vehicles of self-realization. The dynamism of market processes dissolves social hierarchies and overturns established expectations. Status is ephemeral, trust frail and contract sovereign. The dissolution of communities . . . weakens, where it does not entirely destroy, the informal social monitoring of behaviour which is the most effective preventive measure against crime. . . . The incessant change promoted and demanded by market processes nullifies the significance of precedent and destroys the authority of the past. Indeed it is not too much of an exaggeration to say that market liberal policy delivers the *coup de grace* to practices of authority and of subscription to tradition already severely weakened during the modern period.

This should be tattooed on Newt Gingrich's forehead.

"Enlightenment's Wake," the book's last and longest essay, is a masterly attempt to think through the problem of modernity. The problem is that critical rationality, as propagated by the Enlightenment and modeled on the natural sciences, has (along with market rationality) undermined the cultural authority of virtually all moral values, norms, customs, and beliefs in virtually all modern societies. The moral foundations of Western culture have been hollowed out. To the question "Why be good?" there is now no philosophically compelling answer. The name of this condition is nihilism: the eventual result may be spiritual paralysis or, worse, a war of all against all and of all against nature.

Trenchantly and lucidly, Gray canvasses our alternatives. One course, advocated uncritically by religious fundamentalists and with great subtlety and rigor by philosophers like Alasdair MacIntyre, is to return to premodernity. The Enlightenment, according to MacIntyre, was not merely a misfortune but a mistake: about moral theory, Aristotle and Aquinas were right all along. Gray disagrees and argues cogently that modernity represents not the abandonment but the consummation of classical and Christian thought. Together they form one tradition, which is now exhausted; no return is possible.

It is not, of course, everyone's tradition. Gray alludes frequently to the East Asian industrial nations, especially Japan, who appear to have achieved economic modernization without undergoing cultural Westernization. He hopes fervently that they never do Westernize, lest they suffer our nihilist fate. I think he underestimates the vulnerability of East Asian cultural traditions to the inroads of individualism and the blandishments of consumer culture. To paraphrase Freud: the voice of appetite is a soft one, but it does not rest till it has gained a hearing. In any case, as Gray recognizes, Western liberal societies can no more import the Confucian ethos than they can re-create the Christian one.

Perhaps we can muddle through? Why not retain liberal values but abandon the hope of giving them a philosophical justification? Why not, as Richard Rorty has suggested, affirm "Enlightenment humanism without Enlightenment rationalism"? That makes good sense to me, and Gray allows that Rorty's is "perhaps the most powerful attempt we are likely to see to reformulate liberalism in explicitly post-Enlightenment terms." Nevertheless, he rejects it as parochial and excessively sanguine. Public and private cannot be kept separate, as Rorty recommends. Political institutions are the expression of a culture and a cosmology. The institutions of bourgeois liberal democracy are no exception, and the culture they express is, Gray repeats, ephemeral and exhausted.

Well then . . . what? Gray's reply is unflinching and not in the least melodramatic: The human race, he concludes, may very well destroy itself or suffer increasing, and finally irreversible, cultural entropy. Even more likely, and no less tragic, we may deplete and disfigure the nonhuman world beyond recovery.

Unless . . . here Gray's accustomed lucidity fails him, or at any rate fails me. He finds some saving intimations in the later Heidegger, particularly the notion of *Gelassenheit,* or "releasement," derived from Meister Eckhart and other German mystics. "Releasement," according to Gray, is a disposition to "wean ourselves from willing and open ourselves to letting things be"; to attend calmly "to beings, to the things of the earth, in all their contingency and mortality"; to embrace "the groundless contingency that makes and unmakes the world." In Heidegger's words: "Releasement toward things and openness to the mystery belong together. They grant us the possibility of dwelling in the world in a totally different way. They promise us a new ground and foundation upon which we can stand and endure in the world of technology without being imperiled by it."

Out of respect for Gray, I will suppress my usual shallow, logocentric exasperation with Heidegger and merely observe that I don't find the above very helpful. I wish that Gray had, at the crucial juncture, not ascended into philosophical mysticism but instead descended into social criticism. I wish he had gotten down to cases, had said to his readers, humbly and prosaically, citizen to citizen: “Look, we can’t all—all human beings, that is—have air conditioning, safari vacations, automatic dishwashers, cars that go faster than forty or fifty miles an hour, meat every day (or every week), high-definition television with scores of channels, and bulgeless, odorless, wrinkle-free bodies. We’ll spoil the planet if we try; and besides, those things are not all that important. What’s important is [my own list follows; I would have liked to see Gray’s]: singing in harmony at least once a week; having a body practiced in graceful movement; taking part in frequent and lively political (or aesthetic or metaphysical) arguments; knowing many poems and prose passages by heart; having wilderness nearby or at a moderate distance; and, above all, having useful and (at least part of the time) stimulating work. What’s more, everyone could have all these things without spoiling the planet.”

There’s something to “releasement”; I don’t deny it. But I suspect we’ll get a better sense of it by hearkening to Wallace Stegner, Wendell Berry, or Seamus Heaney than to Heidegger. Philosophy as practiced by Gray and Rorty can lead us out of the modern wilderness; only imagination and social criticism can lead us (if anything can) into the postmodern promised land.

3

THE HEDGEHOG AND THE FOX

Alasdair MacIntyre vs. Richard Rorty

Fifty years ago, William F. Buckley Jr. vowed not to read another book about liberalism until his mother wrote one. Liberalism was riding high then, and Buckley was probably annoyed by its champions' triumphalist tone. He would feel differently now. You can hardly walk around the block today without tripping over a critique of liberalism. There are critiques by wild-eyed Randians, free-market libertarians, neoclassical economists, neo-Burkean conservatives, Catholic integralists, critical race theorists, postmodernists, and, of course, Marxists.

Criticizing liberalism is a venerable American tradition, arguably beginning with Tocqueville. But a few figures in recent decades stand above the flood. Michael Sandel began as an academic critic of John Rawls with *Liberalism and the Limits of Justice* (1982) but with *Democracy's Discontent: America in Search of a Public Philosophy* (1996) and *What Money Can't Buy: The Moral Limits of Markets* (2012) became America's leading communitarian public intellectual. Robert Nozick's *Anarchy, State, and Utopia* (1974), though based on an obvious fallacy that even Nozick later acknowledged, became the bible of adolescent libertarians of all ages. Christopher Lasch criticized liberalism from both the left and the right—he was a socialist in political economy, a conservative in culture. The year before his death in 1992, he produced an ambitious synthesis, *The True and Only Heaven: Progress and Its Critics,* which attempted to transcend liberalism and conservatism.

Perhaps the most unexpectedly popular book of political theory in this period was Alasdair MacIntyre's *After Virtue* (1981), which paired an Aristotelian critique of liberalism with a sweeping diagnosis of the ills of modernity. No one, including MacIntyre, could have expected such a difficult, abstract book to be so influential. Otherwise fractious conservatives were unanimous in their reverence, while even most liberals and leftists—at least those who pay any attention to philosophy—accorded it a grudging respect.

In the early 1980s, after a prolonged study of Thomas Aquinas, MacIntyre joined the Roman Catholic Church. Among the American Catholic intelligentsia—a growing presence in American intellectual life—MacIntyre is now a superstar. A research professor emeritus at Notre Dame, he is still, at ninety-three, very active. The formerly steady stream of his publications has ebbed, but Notre Dame's Center for Ethics and Culture organizes a regular procession of conferences, colloquia, and lectures in which he features prominently. Now Notre Dame University Press has brought out *Alasdair MacIntyre: An Intellectual Biography* by the French Catholic philosopher Émile Perreau-Saussine, which is actually less an intellectual biography than an essay on MacIntyrean themes. Though derivative and a little meandering, it's engaging and accessible, and it does sometimes clarify MacIntyre's arguments, which can be knotty.

MacIntyre has had an unusual trajectory. Born in Glasgow to a working-class family, he grew up in London and attended the University of Manchester and later Oxford. He taught philosophy at Manchester, Leeds, Exeter, and Oxford and at no fewer than a dozen universities in the United States beginning in 1970, and his academic honors are legion. He started out on the left: in the late 1950s he joined E. P. Thompson's legendary journal *The New Reasoner*, which along with *Universities and Left Review* became the *New Left Review* in 1960. He was a contributor to *Out of Apathy* (1960), an influential manifesto edited by Thompson, and shared the latter's disenchantment with both Stalinism and the Labour Party. But while Thompson settled on "socialist humanism" to describe his position, MacIntyre was moving in a different direction: not away from socialism but away from humanism. Across the Channel, a new generation of Parisian Marxists led by Althusser were also moving away from humanism, toward a structuralism that dispensed with human agency altogether. MacIntyre affirmed human agency, but only subject to the norms of a community or the will of God.

Throughout the 1960s, Marxism continued to fascinate MacIntyre as both an ethics and a philosophy of history. Stalinism, though hideous, did not discredit Marxism, he insisted: "The barbarous despotism of the collective Czardom which now reigns in Moscow is as irrelevant to the question of Marxism's moral substance as the life of a Borgia pope was to Christianity's moral substance." Eventually he renounced Marxism, citing "the impotence of Marx's economic theory." But he retained much respect for its moral and intellectual seriousness. Concluding the "Marxism and Religion" chapter of *Marxism and Christianity* (1968), his farewell to the New Left, he offered this qualified tribute:

> Both liberals and Christians are too apt to forget that Marxism is the only systematic doctrine in the modern world that has been able to translate to any important degree the hopes men once expressed, and could not but express in

> religious terms, into the secular project of understanding societies and expressions of human possibility and history as a means of liberating the present from the burdens of the past, and so constructing the future. Liberalism by contrast simply abandons the virtue of hope. For liberals the future has become the present enlarged.

Liberalism is notoriously hard to define. For MacIntyre the political radical, liberals were those who, while professing concern for the less advantaged, have no intention of allowing them significantly greater social power. Judging from scattered hints in his later works, those egalitarian sympathies remain alive. (When asked by an interviewer in 1996 what values he retained from his Marxist days, he answered: "I would still like to see every rich person hanged from the nearest lamp post.") But as MacIntyre's immersion in and commitment to premodern philosophy deepened, liberalism increasingly seemed at the root of everything wrong with the modern world: rationalism, secularism, individualism, and materialism. Unifying his extraordinarily broad political and philosophical interests, *After Virtue* grew into a critique of an entire civilization.

For MacIntyre, the ascendance of liberalism is seen most starkly and ominously in the evolution of moral reasoning from Aristotle to the present. The classical tradition of Aristotle and Aquinas rested on a shared conception of cosmic or social order, derived from Aristotle's metaphysics and Aquinas's theology. Both thinkers—like most other human beings until a few hundred years ago—believed in a hierarchy of causes and of authorities, culminating in a Supreme Being, that is, God. But the Scientific Revolution of the sixteenth and seventeenth centuries undermined Aristotle's metaphysics, and the Protestant Reformation introduced several new and heterodox theologies. In response, moral philosophers in the eighteenth and nineteenth centuries, including Hume, Smith, Diderot, Kant, Bentham, and Mill, tried to provide a rational but non-metaphysical justification for morality. All of them, MacIntyre argues, failed.

In the twentieth century morality was severed from rationality altogether. The dominant form of moral theory, MacIntyre claims, is now "emotivism," the idea that evaluative statements are nothing more than expressions of preference. "X is good" simply means "I like X," but disguised as a factual statement in order to manipulate the hearer. Emotivists naturally see things differently. For them, "I like X" means "I like X. This is my overall standpoint, and this is how X fits in with it. Maybe if we talk awhile, you might come to like X too." But MacIntyre would have none of it. Not imaginative rapprochement but "rational justification"—a rigorous deduction from the human *telos*—is the only honest way to conduct a moral argument. For MacIntyre, emotivism has made honest communication impossible; we can only inveigle one another.

The initial chapters of *After Virtue* set out the cultural consequences of this philosophical impasse. The absence of a cosmic order, with its associated *telos* or purpose, condemns modern society to widespread anomie, superficiality, and narcissism. Modern culture, MacIntyre claims, has evolved several representative character types, notably the manager, the therapist, and the aesthete. All are profoundly manipulative. The first two deploy fictitious expertise to achieve goals foreign to the employee or patient; the third treats other persons as interesting sensations to be consumed. Modern moral life is a series of interminable quarrels and subtle conflicts of will which, for lack of a recognized moral authority, can never be resolved.

So what is this *telos,* which alone can redeem us? *Telos,* like "Being" and "dialectic," is one of the most important and mischievous terms in the history of philosophy. It means, roughly, "essential nature, ultimate end, purpose, goal, fulfillment."

According to MacIntyre, moral philosophy is futile unless it starts from a correct understanding of our *telos*. Only with a grasp of our true end can we judge what our duties are and what virtues will enable us to fulfill them.

For MacIntyre, the human *telos* is what Aristotle called rational happiness. That sounds unproblematic, even banal. But why is reason more essential to humans than, say, love or beauty? Why is it more universal than suffering or nobler than sympathy or courage? And what is an essential nature, anyway? Is it something every member of the species has? But then, isn't a person who is temporarily or permanently deprived of reason still human?

The concept of *telos*, so central to MacIntyre's philosophy, is fatally flawed. He insists that the end or purpose or goal of human life is objectively discoverable and is the same for every member of *Homo sapiens*. But our purposes are not a matter of fact or deductive reasoning; they are a matter of choice. We don't discover our goals as a result of scientific or philosophical inquiry; we work them out, with much imaginative and emotional effort, and they often change as we change. Human nature is compatible with any number of *teloi*.

There are other, better ways—our usual ways, actually—of reaching moral consensus than by metaphysical arguments about a *telos*. Two people arguing about whether something is good may offer factual reasons, in case one thinks the other is misinformed, or may suggest that the other's reasoning is faulty. If that doesn't produce agreement, they may canvass principles and values relevant to the dispute, and if they share one and can agree on how it applies to their disagreement, then they've reached agreement. In the most difficult case, however, facts and logic will not suffice: the disputants will have to reveal to each other the whole scaffolding of beliefs, experiences, and hopes underlying their positions, each one trying to see the issue with new eyes—or, more precisely, with an enlarged moral imagination.

This is a better way to describe our moral life than as a search for "rational justification." The supposedly interminable and irresolvable disagreements MacIntyre laments should instead be seen as *conversations:* long-lasting, society-wide conversations, which sometimes (as with slavery), but by no means always, issue in violence. Our national conversations about Jim Crow and interracial marriage ended in the 1960s. Our conversation about the full humanity of women seemed to have ended in the 1980s and 1990s, though Republicans and evangelicals seem bent on re-opening it. Our conversation about homosexuality ended happily; our conversation about legalizing marijuana—maybe also psychedelic drugs—looks promising. Our conversation about economic inequality and reviving the New Deal is unfortunately going nowhere—but there *was* once a New Deal, which is perhaps grounds for hope. Our conversation about global warming has, alas, barely begun. But despite the persistence of conflict, MacIntyre's insistence that modern pluralism makes moral and political progress impossible is at odds with our history.

Contra MacIntyre, moral judgments incorporate both reason and emotion. Hume formulated that truth provocatively, saying that reason is always the servant of emotion. It's what pragmatists like James and Dewey meant by identifying the imagination as our key moral faculty; and it's why Richard Rorty wrote that we should expect moral progress chiefly from the work of novelists, journalists, ethnographers, and other purveyors of thick descriptions rather than from philosophy.

It is not only the dark side of modernity—the alleged manipulativeness, shallowness, aimlessness, and fragmentation—that MacIntyre deplores. Even liberalism's finest achievements are hollow. Natural rights and human rights, he scoffs, have no more reality than witches or unicorns; the Bill of Rights, the

Declaration of Independence, and the UN Universal Declaration of Human Rights are "fictions," with no objectively rational justification. But those great documents are not philosophical arguments, nor do they depend on philosophical arguments. The Bill of Rights, for example, means: "Where this document's writ runs, no one shall be prevented from voting or running for office or starting a newspaper or any other political activity merely because he is not a gentleman." It does not mean, as MacIntyre appears to assume, "There are wraithlike entities called rights subsisting in a shadowy metaphysical realm, from which we must deduce how best to organize our polity."

And how do we today, who believe even less in those wraithlike metaphysical entities than the Founding Fathers did, rationally justify our affirmation of these truths? Our justification is simply this: We trust ordinary people, governed only by persuasion, with ultimate political power. We could explain further, but it wouldn't satisfy MacIntyre, for whom the absence of an abstract, nonhuman authority is a decisive defect in liberalism. Liberalism is purely negative, he complains, a matter of setting limits on authority. Liberal principles, MacIntyre writes, "set before us no ends to pursue, no ideal or vision to confer significance upon our political action. They never tell us what to do." Maybe not, but they do tell us why we are no longer bound by those immemorial hierarchies and metaphysical chimeras that crushed so many people before the modern age. We can never be grateful enough for that.

In the foreword to *Alasdair MacIntyre: An Intellectual Biography,* the distinguished French philosopher Pierre Manent approvingly notes MacIntyre's fifty-year-long "steady core of antiliberal anger" but then wryly observes, in Tocquevillian accents, that "the alternatives to liberalism have lost all credibility.

Never has a principle organizing human association been more criticized while triumphant, or more triumphant while discredited." MacIntyre would probably agree, even if not in the same jaunty tone. He too thinks liberalism will be around a long time, though not because it's resilient or the least bad alternative. Rather, liberalism is a blight, a toxic fog that has settled permanently on our cultural and political landscape. "What matters at this stage is the construction of local forms of community within which civility and the intellectual and moral life can be sustained through the long dark ages which are already upon us."

For a little light in this gloom, we may turn to a posthumous book from MacIntyre's lifelong antagonist Richard Rorty. *What Can We Hope For? Essays on Politics* is a miscellaneous collection, unified only by Rorty's humane passion for democracy and equality. The title echoes Kant's "What can I hope for?"—supposedly one of the essential questions philosophy exists to answer. The change from "I" to "we" is significant: solidarity was the alpha and omega of Rorty's political philosophy.

Richard Rorty (1931–2007) was MacIntyre's polar opposite in all ways except one: both men liked and respected the other. Rorty was an anti-foundationalist, while MacIntyre grimly insists that philosophy without metaphysical foundations is the merest fiction. Rorty thought our paramount moral and political obligation was to reduce suffering and increase happiness. MacIntyre thinks it is to follow the path of virtue marked out by the traditions of our community, guided by that community's view of the *telos* or purpose of human life. Rorty thought the Enlightenment, and the spirit of criticism it bequeathed, inaugurated a new and fortunate period in history, an epoch in which personal and social liberation are at least possible. MacIntyre thinks we will be lucky to survive that liberation. Rorty was fond of drawing a distinction between Enlightenment rationalism and Enlightenment liberalism. He agreed with MacIntyre that

Enlightenment rationalism—the attempt to ground morality in reason—had failed. But he thought Enlightenment liberalism—egalitarianism, free speech, universal suffrage, the separation of Church and State—had succeeded gloriously and was humanity's best hope. MacIntyre holds out little hope, except in Catholicism, where he has come to rest.

Rorty seems to have felt that his philosophical celebrity entailed an obligation to comment on contemporary political issues, while MacIntyre seems to feel that *his* philosophical celebrity entails an obligation not to. As a result, Rorty was pretty much a model public intellectual in the twenty years before his death, while MacIntyre may as well have been writing from inside a monastery.

Rorty was an ecumenical leftist; he called himself a socialist, social democrat, or liberal—whatever term he thought least likely to derail the conversation. Though he was an early and strong partisan of feminism, gay rights, and racial justice, he was distressed by the schism between identity politics and class-based politics in the 1980s and 1990s. *Achieving Our Country: Leftist Thought in Twentieth-Century America* (1998) urged a united front between the Old and the New Left, the reformist left and the academic left—in effect, an alliance between all (non-DNC) liberals and all leftists. They needed to unite, he warned, to prevent the following all-too-likely scenario:

> Members of labor unions, and unorganized unskilled workers, will sooner or later realize that their government is not even trying to prevent wages from sinking or to prevent jobs from being exported. Around the same time, they will realize that suburban white-collar workers—themselves desperately afraid of being downsized—are not going to let themselves be taxed to provide social benefits for anyone else.

> At that point, something will crack. The non-suburban electorate will decide that the system has failed and start looking for a strongman to vote for—someone willing to assure them that, once he is elected, the smug bureaucrats, tricky lawyers, overpaid bond salesmen, and postmodernist professors will no longer be calling the shots.

Twenty years later, with Trump's election, this imagined scenario came true. The passage went viral, and Rorty was briefly, posthumously hailed as a prophet.

Rorty's other political book, *Contingency, Irony, and Solidarity* (1989), was perhaps his best. Embracing Proust, Nabokov, and Orwell, Nietzsche, Heidegger, and Derrida, it argues that for political purposes, philosophical agreement with others is unimportant, while imaginative identification with them is all-important. For Rorty the pragmatist, there are no universally valid and binding moral or political truths. One cannot be argued into solidarity or any other virtue. There is no "human essence," no "nature of things," on which to ground a morality or a political order. The liberal theory of justice, he writes, is based on "nothing more profound than the historical facts which suggest that without the protection of something like the institutions of bourgeois liberal society, people will be less able to work out their private salvations, create their private self-images, reweave their webs of belief and desire." This affirmation of solidarity based on the acceptance of contingency is the scaffolding of Rorty's politics. It could hardly be farther from MacIntyre's politics. Curiously, MacIntyre reviewed the book, not ill-humoredly, concluding with the puckish suggestion that "inside [these pages] there is perhaps a novel pleading to be let out." I suspect Rorty took that as a compliment.

What Can We Hope For? rounds up a last selection of topical pieces from Rorty's archive. Each of the eighteen pieces collected here discusses an essay-sized topic—economic inequality ("Making the Rich Richer" and "Back to Class Politics"), globalization ("Can American Egalitarianism Survive in a Global Economy?"), cultural politics ("Demonizing the Academy"), international affairs ("The Unpredictable American Empire" and "Half a Million Blue Helmets?")—humanely, incisively, and elegantly. Perhaps the most memorable is "Looking Backwards from the Year 2096," a review of the preceding (that is, twenty-first) century by a nameless speaker at the century's end. Increasing misery and resentment gave rise to increasingly uncontrollable civil strife, he or she tells us, resulting in a military dictatorship in mid-century. Eventually the Democratic Vistas Party restored civilian rule, but everyone was much chastened and American exceptionalism much weakened. "Compared with the Americans of a hundred years ago [that is, 1996], we are citizens of an isolationist, unambitious, middle-grade nation." The speaker concludes that "everything depends on keeping our fragile sense of American fraternity intact." The piece's allusions to Whitman's *Democratic Vistas* and Bellamy's *Looking Backward* underline this moral.

In this last book—in all his writings—Rorty had two purposes: first, to show how little traditional philosophy mattered; and second, to show how little that fact mattered—how little, that is, our moral life rests on deductions from principles and how much, instead, on sympathy, solidarity, and moral imagination. The poet Shelley said as much two centuries ago in *A Defence of Poetry:* "A man, to be greatly good, must imagine intensely and comprehensively; he must put himself in the place of another and of many others; the pains and pleasures of his species must become his own. The great instrument of moral good is the imagination." The imagination—not moral philosophy, not conformity with the *telos,* but the capacity to be moved by the sufferings of others. A surprisingly simple message from so sophisticated a philosopher as Rorty, but to judge by the state of the world, not a superfluous one.

4

CAN WE BE GOOD WITHOUT GOD?

Charles Taylor

There seems to be a connection, historical and perhaps even logical, between metaphysics and morality; that is, between views about the nature of being or knowledge and views about justice and the good. A vague sense (which is all that most of us have) of this connection is one thing, however; an original, rigorous, and comprehensive historical account is something else again—an immense achievement. Yet this is only one feature of Charles Taylor's monumental book *Sources of the Self: The Making of the Modern Identity* (1989). Here Taylor bears out, to some extent at least, a seemingly extravagant compliment proffered by Richard Rorty in reviewing Taylor's *Philosophical Papers:* "He is attempting nothing less than a synthesis of moral reflection with intellectual history, one which will do for our time what Hegel did for his." Here is Taylor's own statement of his aims:

> To write and articulate a history of the modern identity . . . to designate the ensemble of (largely unarticulated)

> understandings of what it is to be a human agent: the senses of inwardness, freedom, individuality, and being embedded in nature which are at home in the modern West . . . to show how the ideals and interdicts of this identity—what it casts in relief and what it casts in shadow—shape our philosophical thought, our epistemology and our philosophy of language, largely without our awareness.

Not quite so grand as Hegel's, perhaps, but ambitious enough. What is the "modern identity"? Whatever else may characterize it, at least three elements do. First, inwardness, or the understanding of our selfhood not as externally defined, by the privileges and duties of our station or our relation to the overall order of being, but as something attained through turning inward, taking a reflexive stance, exploring our inner structures, resources, or depths. Second, the belief that ordinary life—work, friendship, marriage and the family—is our proper sphere and an adequate source of meaning and fulfillment rather than the ignoble lot of those not up to the ascetic, contemplative, or military virtues of saint, sage, and warrior-aristocrat. Third, expressivism, or recourse to nature and the feelings it evokes in us as a spiritual and moral counterweight to analytic, instrumental reason.

Taylor narrates the history of philosophy (in some cases also of theology, literary theory, and modern literature) in relation to the gradual emergence of each of these elements. For example: According to Plato, correct perception of the cosmic order makes possible self-knowledge and control of the passions; reason is the source of morality and happiness. Augustine modifies Plato's conception: rather than employing dialectic to arrive at the Idea of the Good, the soul reflects on its activities and powers and recognizes God as their source. Descartes turns inward, looking not for God but for intellectual certainty and moral dignity. In Descartes' successors, especially Locke and Kant, this reflexivity or inward turn is further radicalized and secularized. By the end of Taylor's account, what had seemed merely a sequence of philosophical positions now appears as a vast drama whose upshot is us.

Here's another narrative. The triumph of Enlightenment rationalism meant an increased sense of individual autonomy and dignity, of what Taylor calls "self-responsible freedom." But at the same time, the decline of belief in Divine Providence and the new scientific view of nature as inert matter, a mechanism subject to rigid laws, threatened the loss of perennial spiritual and moral resources. According to Taylor, Kant's concept of morality as an aspect of human rational agency, a "secularized variant of *agape* implicit in reason itself," and the Romantic "notion of an inner voice or impulse, the idea that we find the truth within us, and in particular in our feelings," were both responses to this threatened loss, attempts to supply the defects of the culture's newly forming identity. In Taylor's tale of Western intellectual history as the evolution of an identity, in his ability to bring the most diverse cultural developments into his story line, there really is something reminiscent of Hegel. And fortunately, unlike Hegel, he writes lucid prose.

The scope, complexity, and ingenuity of Taylor's arguments make them difficult to summarize except in drastically compressed form (like my last two paragraphs). Detailed discussions of ancient and seventeenth-century philosophy, Renaissance Neoplatonism, Reformation spirituality, Montaigne, Kant, Deism, the Enlightenment, the German Romantics, Schopenhauer, Baudelaire, Dostoevsky, Nietzsche, Rilke, and Pound, among other topics and writers, are carefully woven into the narrative tapestry. And Taylor fully acknowledges that the history of ideas cannot by itself explain the large shifts in outlook he is tracking; several brief but sensible observations about historical causation dispel any misgivings on this score.

Sources of the Self is a work of scrupulous but not at all detached scholarship; it is intensely purposeful. Like virtually everyone else nowadays, Taylor is worried about modernity. The core of the modern identity, the essence of modernity, is scientific rationality. The application (in Taylor's view, the misapplication) of the axioms and methods of the natural sciences to epistemology, ethics, psychology, and the social sciences—a tendency he calls "naturalism" and claims is standard procedure in those fields—has, he believes, obstructed our access to our traditions and depleted our moral resources.

This is a common enough theme, to which Taylor brings uncommon philosophical skills. His earlier writings, particularly *Hegel,* showed him in command of both the Anglo-American and Continental traditions—among academic philosophers, Taylor is considered a "bridge" figure. In the two volumes of *Philosophical Papers* and the first hundred pages of *Sources of the Self* he draws on the work of Merleau-Ponty, Heidegger, and Wittgenstein to construct a critique of, and alternative to, naturalism.

What is, or is supposed to be, the "scientific" attitude toward morality? Most fundamentally, perhaps, that values are not "real," that judgments about good and bad are not "objective"; they are preferences, which can be explained or interpreted, adjusted if one was mistaken about relevant facts, or modified in response to new feelings and experiences, but not justified, not proved true or false. From this follows a conception of moral philosophy as neutral and procedural: its purpose is not to expound the nature of the Good or of virtue but to work out social and interpersonal rules, institutions, decision-procedures that will seem fair and just to most people, whatever their values or their vision of the good life. Both utilitarianism and rights-based liberalism, probably the most common varieties of political philosophy in the English-speaking world, presuppose this value neutrality.

In the social sciences, naturalism prescribes striving for intersubjective validity. Data that only the subject can testify to, that can't be recorded by and read off some instrument, and theories that require informal, unspecifiable qualities of imagination or judgment to apply—these don't count.

Taylor objects that naturalism's methodological restrictions have impoverished philosophy and social theory, and thereby public life. Neutralism about values inevitably slides over into subjectivism, the glib dismissal of all values as "fictitious," or relativism, the equally mindless acceptance of all values as equally valid and beyond rational adjudication. Individualism slides into atomism, the denial that some common good, over and above the goals of individuals or aggregates, may rightly command a person's loyalty, even obedience.

Against all these modern views, Taylor argues that moral theory can't be neutral, because a person's identity cannot be specified without reference to her or his commitments, stance, values. His proof of this gets a little technical, but is roughly: We are what we say about ourselves to our language community, what we answer to the question "Who am I?" This always involves saying what we most deeply care about or aspire to. What matters most to us is what matters most about us.

Politically, too, the individual is constituted in and through a community. The rights and desires of liberalism and utilitarian theory are only intelligible, can only be exercised, in communities of a certain sort. Since the survival and flourishing of such communities is a precondition of our fulfilling (or even having) those rights and desires, a commitment to the former takes precedence over asserting the latter.

This is, of course, a highly compressed rendering of an enormously complex argument. At this point, however, instead of adding qualifications, I'd like to get subjective. Something about Taylor's tremendously impressive effort rubs me the wrong way.

It's not Taylor himself; his authorial voice is dignified but friendly, on the whole quite likable. And while others may find fault with his treatment of Platonism, Puritanism, Romanticism, or modernism, I cannot. Perhaps it's just impossible not to resent a forceful challenge to some of one's most cherished beliefs. Taylor manages to shake my faith without quite converting me—yes, I admit it: I'm a naturalist.

Not, of course, a fundamentalist one. I don't believe that science will ever explain all human behavior, or that all values are illusory. I'm comfortable with entities and explanations above the molecular level. I'm not, that is, a flaming positivist or a roaring reductionist. But I do think that where a naturalistic (neurochemical, sociobiological, psychoanalytic, economic) explanation for someone's belief or behavior seems adequate, it may well *be* adequate; and that although "community" is an indispensable political metaphor, it is, in the end, only a metaphor. I'm a pragmatic naturalist. Usually, in fact, I just say "pragmatist," but Taylor's harsh strictures elicited a stubborn residual allegiance to the old creed.

For one thing, there is his too-sweeping disparagement of naturalistic social science. Not that I have much use for present-day quantitative academic social science: on the contrary. Still, I feel Taylor ought, just by virtue of being so astute and influential a critic, to disavow the sentimental tosh frequently talked about the uniqueness and ineffability of human beings and the preposterousness, even perversity, of behaviorism. Behaviorism works, after all: in prisons, police states, marketing strategies, and electoral campaigns, just to name some of the main institutions and modes of social control in modern societies. True, it did not work in *Walden Two*, because there Skinner proposed a subtler, nobler goal than eliciting or suppressing discrete, overt behaviors over a limited span. But if this latter aim is all you want a "science of behavior" for, then a perfectly adequate one is available to you, notwithstanding the ineffable depth and complexity of human beings when they are treated like human beings. As always, what counts as truth depends on one's purpose.

I suppose this is a quibble, however, compared with the issues raised by Taylor's moral critique. One of Taylor's central claims in *Sources of the Self*—it is almost a leitmotif—is that a naturalistic ethic like utilitarianism or Marxism is "confused" and "deeply incoherent" (the deadliest of philosophical epithets) in one crucial respect: all such theories presuppose in practice some moral value or ideal, like universal and impartial benevolence in the case of the *philosophes* and Benthamites, social justice in the case of Marxists, or simply, in the most general case, to reduce suffering, while in principle denying that any such value is other than an arbitrary, subjective preference. Pressed repeatedly, this claim made me first uncomfortable, then defiant. For suppose it is true? It may be that my moral heroes—Godwin and Bentham, Mill and Marx, Morris, Luxemburg, Orwell, and Russell—would have been somehow better off for having a proper metaphysical foundation for their aspirations. On the other hand, maybe the fact that they scraped along awfully well without one means that the question "Why care about others?" and the larger question "Why act rightly?"—which Taylor thinks can be answered definitively only by invoking some "constitutive good"—can't be answered definitively at all. And needn't be.

Taylor is continually saying things like:

> To see the standard Enlightenment view as one-dimensional is to see no place in it for what makes life significant. Human life seems a matter merely of desire-fulfillment, but the very basis for strong evaluation, for there being desires or goals which are intrinsically worth fulfilling, seems missing.

It's clear that Taylor the man and citizen admires the ultranaturalist *philosophes,* by and large, and considers their lives not just significant but exemplary. But for Taylor the philosopher, some "transcendental conditions" are apparently required to make a life "significant"; likewise to make desires and goals "intrinsically" worth fulfilling. It's not that the *philosophes* didn't have the right sort of desires and goals, just that they lacked an adequate "moral ontology," hence access to the "moral sources" and "constitutive goods" that would have allowed them to articulate the significance of their lives. They denied (or ought, on their own principles, to have denied) the reality of the virtues they practiced and the values they lived for.

Well, maybe so, but this contradiction doesn't seem to have slowed them down much. Taylor suggests this is because the *philosophes,* and altruistic unbelievers ever since, have drawn spiritual sustenance from religious traditions, still potent in the eighteenth century though dwindling in influence today. But, he warns, this can't go on forever. No culture can permanently endure so basic a tension between its morality and its metaphysics (or antimetaphysics). "High standards need strong sources," he writes in the final pages of *Sources of the Self.*

> The question which arises from all this is whether or not we are living beyond our moral means in continuing allegiance to our standards of justice and benevolence. Do we have ways of seeing-good which are still credible to us, which are powerful enough to sustain these standards? If not, it would be both more honest and more prudent to moderate them. . . . Is the naturalist seeing-good, which turns on the rejection of the calumny of religion against nature, fundamentally parasitic? This it might be in two senses: not only that it derives its affirmation through rejecting an alleged negation, but also that the original model for its universal benevolence is agape. How well could it survive the demise of the religion it strives to abolish? With the "calumny" gone, could the affirmation continue?

That is: perseverance in virtue will sometimes require self-sacrifice; and self-sacrifice seems to require some transcendental justification or motivation, of which the most common, and perhaps the most logical, is belief in the existence of God. Or so Taylor argues, circumspectly. Since modern freedom entails the rejection of transcendence, modern virtue is wholly contingent. Can we be good for long without God? Taylor's doubts are daunting.

And there lies the nerve of my discomfort: the suspicion, powerfully and plausibly albeit tactfully and tentatively expressed, that the ideals I most prize are at bottom inadequate. I confess I see no alternative to living with this suspicion, perhaps permanently.

But if it's not clear what, in the long run, best sustains commitments to justice and compassion, it's less difficult to see what, in the short run, precludes them (and most other fine and fruitful qualities as well): deprivation, insecurity, ideological manipulation. Is it too light-minded to suggest that even if altruism gives out, curiosity—a very keen appetite, after all—may continue to motivate efforts to eliminate these evils? Just to see what humankind turns out to be like: just to see who was right, Taylor or Nietzsche or Condorcet?

5

SOLIDARITY EVER?

Robert Bellah and Barbara Ehrenreich

One of the keywords in the modern vocabulary is "emancipation." It has several meanings: politically, from arbitrary authority; economically, from privilege and inherited status; intellectually, from received wisdom; morally, from custom—in all cases, of individuals or discrete groups from restraints imposed by, or in the name of, some community. These installments of emancipation are chapters in an integral narrative that we might call "The Growth of Freedom in the West."

In this multivolume epic, the history of the United States is often perceived as an especially glorious episode. Here, in the first (the only?) society born free, authority is suspect and the moral sovereignty of the individual is unchallenged. "Mind your own business" and "It's a free country": these two quintessential Americanisms are generally assumed to stand in a causal relation. And indeed, American individualism in its nobler manifestations—Shays' Rebellion, Whitman's *Democratic Vistas*, the Wobbly bards, the freewheeling critics Randolph Bourne and Dwight Macdonald, jazz, feminism—has been one of the wonders of the world, one of the genuine achievements of civilization.

But progress is dialectical: Every historic advance exacts a price. Modernity—which means, among other things, the rise of a national labor market and of mass consumption—requires emancipation from the constraints on individual mobility and development entailed by premodern structures and values: family, locality, ethnic group, church, religious doctrine, and patriotic myth. But that which constrains may also support. Shared beliefs, loyalties, membership create attachments among believers, loyalists, members. These attachments are a promise of mutual aid and comfort, of a sort that money cannot buy and without which life is, for all but the most fortunate, painfully insecure. Even more important, perhaps, these structures and values frame our lives, give them coherence, relieve us of the sometimes vertiginous sense of fragility and contingency to which the unaffiliated and unbelieving are vulnerable.

When insecurity and anomie are widespread, social stability is at risk. The United States has largely evaded this risk, in part because religious and civic allegiances have persisted alongside, and accommodated to, modernization. In recent decades, that accommodation is under strain, with consequences brilliantly depicted in *Habits of the Heart: Individualism and Commitment in American Life* (1985) by Robert N. Bellah, Richard Madsen, William M. Sullivan, Ann Swidler, and Steven M. Tipton.

Bellah et al.'s portrait of the contemporary American character descends from a tradition of sociological fretting about the costs of modernity. Tocqueville, Durkheim, Weber, Tönnies, the Lynds, David Riesman, Christopher Lasch, and many if not most other important modern social theorists have sounded similar themes. But what was for sociology's founders only a disturbing possibility is now a mass phenomenon. For most Americans (especially middle-class Americans, the chief subjects of *Habits*), the binding force of extended and even nuclear families, neighborhoods and regions, religious organizations, ethnic societies, and other small-to-medium-scale bodies has greatly diminished. These ties could not survive the enormous increase in residential and occupational mobility required for success within an economy and society dominated by large-scale organizations, corporate, governmental, and academic. As a result, individuals now matter far less to those they live and work among, and vice versa.

Since we must all feel that we matter to someone, we have begun to matter more to ourselves. There being fewer competing claims on us, and more resources at hand, we have taken to cultivating those selves, translating our resources into experiences and, to the extent we can afford, it, into lifestyles. This is pretty much the prevailing ethos among the educated middle class. Bellah et al. call it "expressive individualism" and describe its genesis, forms, and psychological effects with much subtlety and nuance.

Because expressive individualism is now so much the norm, the evocation in *Habits of the Heart* of older ideals of work and citizenship is a great part of the book's value. Before work became a means of making a living and (at least for some) self-expression, it was a "calling": "a practical ideal of activity and character that . . . subsumes the self into a community of disciplined practice and sound judgment [and] links a person to the larger community, in which the calling of each is a contribution to the good of all."

Similarly, citizenship was not merely a matter of advancing individual or group self-interest, as in liberal political theory, but of pursuing the common good "in a society organized through public dialogue," which "can be sustained only by communities of memory, whether religious or civic." It is clear why work and citizenship so conceived would produce a very different character structure from the anxious, acquisitive, manipulative, self-protective type current in our world of bureaucracies, commodities, and universal competition.

This contrast between modern individualism and an archaic, or at least submerged, communitarianism is the organizing principle of *Habits of the Heart.* But though the authors expound the contrast forcefully and lay bare its historical roots, they go no further. Having identified the separation of public and private life and the "ontological individualism" of Locke as the original sins of modernity, they cannot imagine an alternative. Instead, eloquently but a little vaguely, they hope that "the older civic and biblical traditions have the capacity to reformulate themselves while simultaneously remaining faithful to their own deepest insights" and call for "reducing the inordinate rewards of ambition and our inordinate fears of ending up as losers." I assume this means a more progressive tax structure and more generous social-welfare programs, in which case, amen. But will these fine sentiments vanquish the modernist Moloch?

The academic response to *Habits of the Heart* has been multifarious. Perhaps the most substantial sequel so far is *Community in America: The Challenge of "Habits of the Heart,"* edited by Charles H. Reynolds and Ralph V. Norman. Contributions are diverse. Roland Delattre links addictive consumption to the dependence and anxiety generated by the "corporate culture of professionals, experts, and managers," taking military weapons procurement as an example of this dynamic. Ernest Wallwork argues the shallowness of the "therapeutic ethos" and reminds us that Freud's thought remains our best guide to the scope and limits of individual autonomy. Stanley Hauerwas admonishes communitarians that Christianity can only judge or instruct, not enter into dialogue with, the earthly city. Frederic Jameson offers a sophisticated postmodern-Marxist alternative reading of the situation *Habits* surveys—so sophisticated, Bellah protests in his afterword to *Community in America,* that it can scarcely have much resonance beyond a thin stratum of left-wing academic intellectuals. Bernard Yack argues that liberal societies have their own traditions, virtues, practices, and forms of community, which *Habits* overlooks, and that the values associated with individualism—"self-reliance, individual responsibility, and respect for constitutional authority and legal agreements"—morally integrate American society today, just as the more visibly other-directed values of the religious and republican traditions did formerly.

So ambitious a book as *Habits* is bound to leave many questions unanswered, but two seem especially urgent. The first is: What if the religious and republican traditions went into eclipse for good reasons—what if they depend upon beliefs that are not true? The references in *Habits of the Heart* to the actual content of these traditions are vague to the point of vacuousness. At one point, the authors remind the reader that "we did not create ourselves"; at another, they allude to a "covenant" between God and His people. But surely a great many even of their most sympathetic readers cannot believe in any sort of creation, or covenant, or God? And a second question: According to *Habits,* the essence of republican virtue is recognition of and devotion to the "common good." But what if there is no common good—what if the history of all hitherto existing societies is the history of class struggles? And what if the average modern individualist understands all this, however dimly and inarticulately, and can see no other reason—no other philosophical reason—not to eat, screw, and be mellow?

Jeffrey Stout's contribution to *Community in America* is the only one to acknowledge that the cognitive content of the traditions *Habits* invokes somehow matters—that *Habits* may be less rather than more persuasive because of its dependence on a particular "public philosophy." There is no reason, he observes, why the authors should have sought to derive their valuable critique of American individualism from dubious philosophical first principles rather than from their splendidly thick descriptions. Not philosophical foundations but reliable reports and modest proposals are what a society in trouble needs. We should gratefully accept *Habits*'s ethnography and politely ignore its theology.

More questions arise. The separation of public and private life is a necessary consequence of mass production and the spread of market relations. What economic changes would allow that separation to be healed, would allow work once again to be a "calling"? *Habits* is little help here. Christopher Lasch's brief but illuminating essay in *Community in America* does address the question.

Lasch takes up the Aristotelian idea (recently revived by Alasdair MacIntyre in *After Virtue*) of "practices." Practices are activities like poetry, medicine, and sport that are ends in themselves, with internal standards of excellence and characteristic virtues. Lasch points out that although "practices have to be sustained by institutions"—medicine by hospitals, scholarship by universities, and so on—the latter "in the very nature of things tend to corrupt the practices they sustain" by rewarding practitioners with external goods like money and social status and by "subjecting [them] to standards of productivity derived from the marketplace." The purpose of liberal politics is to regulate the pursuit of self-interest; the purpose of communitarian politics, Lasch concludes, is to protect the integrity of practices.

So far, so good; but can the production of necessities be organized into practices? If so, how? If not, then a good deal of the industrial system will have to go, or else some people will work at mass production and others at practices. In the former case, how much? And in the latter, how can such an arrangement be made equitable? In either case, decisions about investment and credit allocation must be made. By whom and by what criteria? In short, what social relations of production do Lasch and the authors of *Habits* have in mind? And why does one come away from both the book and the essay with a suspicion that the phrasing of that last question would provoke a certain impatience—as though it missed the point? There are two scant references to "class" in the index of *Habits of the Heart.* "Power" does not appear at all.

The best and most useful response to *Habits* that I've encountered is a symposium comment in *The Nation* by Barbara Ehrenreich. Though appreciative of the book's humane intentions and "fine dissection of the therapeutic mentality," she takes issue with its diagnosis—

> The problem is not just the emptiness of middle-class life, even for the emptiest among us. The problem includes all the pain and dread that have been pressed back into the margins and final, wistful pages of "Habits of the Heart": the hunger of the world's majority, the draining misery of most people's daily labor, torture and repression, the threat of nuclear annihilation. If we who are currently comfortable and affluent need a moral reference point, we will not find it in the mirror tricks of therapy or religion, but in other people's pain.

—and with its prescription:

> [Socialism] is still the only word we have that attempts to bridge the gap between our private notions of decency and morality and the public sphere of the political economy. And it is still the only vision—the only modernist vision, that is—of a world in which individual desire might be reconciled with collective need. To neglect the socialist tradition as much as Bellah and his colleagues do is to contribute to the impoverishment of the political imagination they have so ably documented.

Ehrenreich is the author of *The Hearts of Men: American Dreams and the Flight from Commitment,* which traced an evolution within American society away from "a moral climate that honored . . . responsibility, self-discipline, and a protective commitment to women and children" toward "a moral climate that endorsed irresponsibility, self-indulgence, and an isolationist detachment from the claims of others." In *The Hearts of Men* and her follow-up, *Fear of Falling,* Ehrenreich, like the authors of *Habits,* has charted "the inner life of the middle class." There is important common ground here, though in method (social history rather than interpretive sociology), provenance (Marx rather than Tocqueville), and style (witty and direct rather than earnest and edifying), her account is quite different.

For Bellah and his colleagues, middle-class American life represents the triumph of liberalism's emancipatory program. Their story emphasizes the individual's liberation, for better or worse, from traditional obligations and allegiances. For Ehrenreich, modern life represents the defeat of liberalism's universalist, egalitarian aspirations. Her story is about the middle class's growing awareness—and uneasy acceptance—of itself as an elite.

Near the end of the nineteenth century the older middle class, or gentry, of independent farmers, small businessmen, self-employed lawyers, doctors, and ministers found itself squeezed between an insurgent lower class and a powerful new capitalist class. Its response was to transform itself into a "professional middle class." Professionalism created a new form of capital: "expertise," which was acquired by training and certification rather than by economic activity in the marketplace. The professions were self-regulating, which allowed them to restrict their numbers and so avoid significant competition. Also, professionals marketed themselves to business as part of a "rational" response to labor conflict. The social sciences, social work, public health, engineering, and the new professional schools of "management" all gained funding and respectability by cooperating to inculcate proper attitudes in, and construct the proper environment around, an unruly working class.

This history is familiar enough. What's original in *Fear of Falling* is Ehrenreich's narrative of middle-class consciousness since the 1960s. At the beginning of that decade, the middle class chiefly inhabited suburbia, from which vantage point affluence looked so universal and secure as to seem potentially enervating. Of any "other America" they had no inkling until Michael Harrington's book of that name came to President Kennedy's attention. The resulting War on Poverty aimed not at redistributing wealth but at combating the "culture of poverty," a collection of pathologies that had supposedly kept the poor from achieving "normal" middle-class careers and living standards.

In those innocent days, the poor were perceived to be passive and unthreatening, while Blacks mobilized by the civil rights movement seemed to be demanding inclusion rather than fundamental social change. Middle-class liberals might feel considerable guilt, but they had no reason to feel that their societal prerogatives, their very self-definition, was being challenged.

It was the student movement, especially in its countercultural aspect, that set off their alarms. Central to the ethos of professionalism are the ideals of objectivity and rigor and the virtues of perseverance and self-denial. It was just these qualities that the poor were said to lack, evoking middle-class condescension, and that the counterculture rejected, arousing middle-class horror. For the rebellious students were largely the professional middle class's own children, and their revolt seemed to signify the older generation's failure to reproduce itself in anything like its own image. The blame for this failure was laid to "permissiveness," an insidious and ubiquitous disease of modern civilization transmitted by a New Class of secular liberal intellectuals, who administered and continually enlarged the welfare state.

Ehrenreich links this preoccupation with permissiveness among neoconservatives and the New Right to the middle class's chronic "fear of falling": a fear of "inner weakness, of growing soft, of failing to strive, of losing discipline and will"—and, in consequence, losing status. There is, of course, a powerful tendency toward just this sort of narcissistic character structure in contemporary society. But its source is nothing so nebulous as "modern civilization" or so nefarious as a self-aggrandizing New Class. Its source is the culture of consumption, promoted by advertising and essential to the health of developed capitalism. The hedonism, such as it was, of the counterculture only mirrored what Daniel Bell once described as "the hedonism stimulated by mass consumption, [without which] the very structure of business enterprises would collapse."

The New Right was unwilling, however, to blame capitalism for permissiveness (or anything else). So it evolved a largely mythical ideology that counterposed the New Class, or "liberal elite," along with its underclass, minority, and "deviant" constituencies, to the virtuous and productive upholders of traditional values: business and the white working class. Since the 1980s, when it was invented, this right-wing populism has swept all before it, a half-truth whose time has come. Unsparingly but tactfully, Ehrenreich sets out the confusions besetting this worldview as it has sought desperately to reconcile the cultural contradictions of capitalism. And with equal astuteness she locates the origins of neoconservatism in the dilemma of the professional middle class, caught between its ideals of intellectual independence and public service and its need to market itself in an era of declining public expenditure and increasing corporate hegemony.

Obviously, populism can be manipulated and professionalism can rationalize privilege. But both contain nobler possibilities: populism's instinct for justice and equality; professionalism's encouragement of curiosity and altruism. As Ehrenreich points out, there is a way to combine these qualities through a currently unheard-of political program: interesting work for everyone. It's a demand that implies a number of others—above all, a more equal distribution of wealth, but also subsidized child care, job training and relocation, flexible technology and job design, worker self-management. It connects up, too, with the idea of "practices." The biblical or republican concept of a "calling" and the expressive-individualist notion of "fulfilling work" may not be identical, but they have enough in common—enough political-economic prerequisites, at any rate—to sustain a stable alliance of communitarians and democratic socialists.

Of course, most people are neither communitarians nor democratic socialists. By and large, America's elites do not believe they are morally obliged to sacrifice substantially for the sake of ordinary people. By and large, ordinary people do not believe in their own right and ability to force elites to do so. Perhaps, then, those who are communitarians and socialists should refurbish our usual answers to some fundamental questions of political morality. Why care about others? Why pay extra taxes, spend extra time, put our status, security, children's prospects, or whatever else we cherish, even slightly at risk? Why not remain radical individualists, each of us trusting to our own strength and ingenuity and to the rough justice of the marketplace?

"Because we are one Body," reply the authors of *Habits of the Heart,* "and our happiness lies in realizing our common good." "Because we are two classes," replies Ehrenreich, "and we must all suffer separately until we abolish exploitation together." These are different visions, or at least different rhetorics, of human fulfillment: on the one hand, full membership in a beloved community; on the other, equal rights in a rational collectivity. One is libertarian, egalitarian, secular; the other is . . . well, all those things, too, but ambivalently.

Both visions are plausible; both are honorable. Both may be irrelevant. As a species, we may simply not be up to either. The indefinite persistence of possessive individualism and bureaucratic authoritarianism seems equally likely. Four decades of brutally callous and mindlessly improvident leadership in the world's foremost democracy compels the attenuation, if not the abandonment, of radical hopes. "Socialism or barbarism" is the battle cry of Ehrenreich's tradition; "You cannot serve God and mammon" is that of Bellah's. The victory—not final, perhaps, but decisive for our lifetime—of mammon and barbarism is a prospect that must haunt anyone who has lived through the long Republican ascendancy.

Habits of the Heart is a slight enough blow against modern anomie, as *Fear of Falling* is against class divisions. But their convergence, however accidental and partial, is encouraging. Because probably, if there is to be any ground for hope, the first requirement is solidarity among the partisans of solidarity: communitarian and individualist, republican and socialist, religious and secular.

6

THE CONTRADICTIONS OF CONSERVATISM

William F. Buckley Jr.

A specter has always haunted conservatism. "All we can do," wrote Burke, "and that human wisdom can do, is to provide that change shall proceed by insensible degrees." In *The Conservative Mind,* Russell Kirk expounded Burke's deepest fear: "Men's appetites are voracious and sanguinary, Burke knew; they are restrained by this collective and immemorial wisdom we call prejudice, tradition, customary morality. . . . Whenever the crust of prejudice and prescription is perforated at any point, flames shoot up from beneath, and terrible danger impends that the crack may widen, even to the annihilation of civilization. If men are discharged of reverence for ancient usage, they will treat this world, almost certainly, as if it were their private property, to be consumed for their sensual gratification; and thus they will destroy in their lust for enjoyment the property of future generations, of their own contemporaries, and indeed their very own."

In the generation after Burke's, the "crust of prejudice" was shattered, a process described in *The Communist Manifesto* in language whose rhetorical power equals—and whose tropes strikingly parallel—Burke's own. That capitalism is subversive of "prejudice, tradition, customary morality" is something thoughtful conservatives have generally understood and honest conservatives generally admitted. William F. Buckley Jr. has not, a failure that is the center of gravity of his career and of a new biography, *William F. Buckley, Jr.: Patron Saint of the Conservatives,* by John B. Judis.

Judis does ample justice to Buckley's full and fascinating life. His unusual childhood is fully, amusingly rendered, and the sources of his ferocious argumentativeness are shrewdly suggested (among other things, he was sixth among ten children and so had to compete for the attention of his adored parents). The internal life of *National Review* over the decades, including continual skirmishing, principled and merely personal, among Willmoore Kendall, James Burnham, Whittaker Chambers, Brent Bozell, Garry Wills, George Will, and William Rusher, is a dependably interesting motif. And Buckley's gradual transformation from voice in the wilderness to celebrity generates many piquant quotes and anecdotes.

From the mid-1950s through the early 1970s, Buckley was not only the most visible conservative public intellectual in America, he was also the founder and editor of our only halfway respectable conservative journal of opinion and the creator of television's most successful political talk show. He has had nearly unlimited access to, and in some cases longstanding friendships with, Goldwater, Nixon, Kissinger, Reagan, and Bush. His brother was a United States senator, and his brother's successor, Daniel Patrick Moynihan, is a friend. He launched the Young Americans for Freedom and the American Conservative Union. He ran for mayor of New York in 1965 and got more than 13 percent of the vote. He is a member of the Council on Foreign Relations and the ultra-élite Bohemian Grove. He served briefly in the CIA and became friendly with Howard Hunt, who told him the full truth about Watergate before it was known to anyone except the co-conspirators and their lawyers. He has carried on public friendships with Norman Mailer and John Kenneth Galbraith and public feuds with Gore Vidal and Arthur Schlesinger Jr. He's written several best-selling novels whose hero (a CIA agent) seems to be modeled on himself; and his sailing memoirs are frequently excerpted in the *New Yorker.* Even a minimally competent biography could hardly be dull, and *Patron Saint* is more than competent.

Judis devotes a chapter and several passages to the "big book" that Buckley long projected but never finished, a theoretical work that would reformulate and extend the insights of his intellectual heroes: Oakeshott, Ortega, Voegelin. This crucial failure was surely overdetermined—by Buckley's temperament and by the contradictions of contemporary conservatism. Although Judis mentions both, only his discussion of the former is satisfactory. It was by no means merely the pleasures of celebrity that distracted Buckley; it was also, and chiefly, the demands of an extraordinarily full and fruitful life, "a life, as he saw it," Judis writes, "of steady, unremitting good works": three columns a week, seventy speeches and a novel each year, much occasional writing, *National Review* and *Firing Line,* fund-raising, an enormous correspondence, and a fair amount of private charity. It would beg the question to suppose that all this activity served mainly to insulate Buckley from a devastating recognition of his own philosophical inadequacy. That recognition came, and was acknowledged with admirable, even affecting, grace:

> the theoretical depth is *there,* and if I have not myself dug deep the foundations of American conservativism, at least I have advertised their profundity. How can I hope to do

> better against positivism than Voegelin has done? Improve on Oakeshott's analysis of rationalism? . . . What does it take to *satisfy*, to satisfy *truly, wholly*? . . . A sense of social usefulness . . . How will I satisfy those who listen to me today, *tomorrow*? Hell, how will I satisfy *myself* tomorrow, satisfying . . . myself so imperfectly, which is not to say insufficiently, today; at cruising speed?

He appears to have had (to coin a Buckleyesque phrase) a vocation for the quotidian. And, in all humility, to have accepted it.

But the larger project was futile, anyway. In its "theoretical depths," modern conservatism affirms values that cannot be reconciled: on the one hand, social stability, sustained by an immutable moral order and religious orthodoxy; on the other, a minimal state and an unregulated market. Competition creates new needs, which undermine old solidarities and deferences. For all his noisy devotion to capitalism, he had not understood the most essential thing about it, identified by both Marx ("All that is solid melts into air") and Schumpeter ("creative destruction"). There's no knowing whether Buckley ever, alone in his study, glimpsed this ineluctable conflict, which made nonsense of his life. Probably not: he was so busy, and we're all very gifted at escaping contradictions.

Curiously, the *National Review* colleague whom Buckley loved and admired most came very near to rubbing his nose in this contradiction. In December 1958, Whittaker Chambers wrote in a letter to Buckley: "I claim that capitalism is not, and by its essential nature cannot conceivably be, conservative. . . . Conservatism is alien to the very nature of capitalism whose love of life and growth is perpetual change. . . . Capitalism, whenever it seeks to become conservative in any quarter, at once settles into mere reaction." Chambers again, quoted in Buckley's affectionate memoir *Odyssey of a Friend:*

> As I have said ad nauseam, I hold capitalism to be profoundly anticonservative. I have met capitalists who thought otherwise; would, in fact, be outraged by such a statement. I have concluded that they knew their craft extremely well, but not its implications; and that what they supposed to be a Conservative Position was chiefly a rationalization rooted in worry. The result is the oddest contradiction in terms. But then, the world is full of august contradictions.

Unlike Buckley's writings, which, for all their wit and rigor, are, as Chambers gently hinted in another letter, utterly undialectical.

Buckley might have learned a similar lesson from his own excellent anthology of twentieth-century conservatism, *Did You Ever See a Dream Walking?* One of the lead essays in this collection is Michael Oakeshott's "The Masses in Representative Democracy." (Buckley's "big book" had been tentatively titled *The Revolt Against the Masses.*) Introducing this essay, Buckley praised Oakeshott's writings as "trenchant . . . exhilarating . . . sublime . . . the finest distillate I know of traditional conservatism" and endorsed Oakeshott's thesis that "the discovery of the individual was the pre-eminent fact of modern European history" and "conservatism is the politics of the individual."

It's remarkable that Buckley failed to notice the implications of Oakeshotts's argument. According to Oakeshott, European individuality began to emerge in the fourteenth century "as a consequence of the collapse of a closely integrated manner of living." For the first time, "men examined themselves and were not dismayed by their own lack of perfection." Gradually but inexorably, "the old certainties of belief, of occupation and of status were being dissolved." By the middle of the sixteenth century, "not all the severity of the Calvinist *régime* in Geneva was sufficient to quell the impulse to think and behave as an independent individual. The disposition to regard a high degree of individuality in conduct and belief as the condition proper to mankind and as the main ingredient of human happiness" had established itself: a "moral revolution" that appears in retrospect as "the event of supreme and seminal importance in modern European history."

Buckley's fervent and wholly orthodox Catholicism was his deepest commitment, his essential identity, as he has often made clear. Did he really not understand that Oakeshott is describing the decline of religious orthodoxy as a precondition for the emergence of individuality? In its terms and stages, Oakeshott's account virtually *is* the classical liberal account of modernity: emancipation from communal faith and customary morality, defiance of temporal and spiritual authority, the desacralization or "disenchantment" of the world. What could Buckley have supposed was meant by "the old certainties of belief" that were being "dissolved," or by Oakeshott's reference to the new individualism's "conflict with [sixteenth-century] moral sentiment, still fixed in its loyalty to the morality of communal ties"? Individualism and secularism are inseparable, are aspects of the same historical development, as orthodox churchmen from the sixteenth century to the present have recognized (and deplored), even if Buckley did not. "The Church did well to mistrust Roger Bacon," Chambers once reminded him. What did Buckley make of *that?*

Another former *National Review* colleague—Buckley's college debating partner and brother-in-law, Brent Bozell—once argued forcefully, in the theologically conservative but politically radical Catholic journal *New Oxford Review,* that "unmitigated capitalism" means "war against the development of virtue as the goal of public life," that is, against the Catholic ideal of society. (There's currently a lively debate in conservative Catholic circles on this question, of interest even to unbelievers. Soon after Bozell's article, an editor of *New Oxford Review* chimed in: "How can the [conservative] defend tradition while ignoring one of its prime destroyers? Industrial capitalism simply cannot be squared with the values he cherishes.") The relationship between Buckley and Bozell was apparently a complicated and poignant one, as Bozell's emotional instability drove him from conservatism to monarchism to theocracy to mental illness. Although they started out as acknowledged intellectual equals, and from virtually identical premises, Buckley's temperament and his opportunities—to perform all those "steady, unremitting good works"—have kept him clear of the various personal hells into which Bozell's unchecked dogmatism has led him. But Bozell has evidently not returned from Hell with empty hands.

Commenting in 1970 on his ambivalence toward then-president Nixon, Buckley admitted: "It's always more difficult to be rhetorically ruthless with somebody with whom you spend time." The same goes for the subject of a biography. It is difficult to loathe someone whose press conferences, during his campaign for mayor of New York, contained exchanges like this:

> Q.: Do you want to be Mayor, sir?
> A.: I have never considered it.
>
> Q.: Do you think you have any chance of winning?
> A.: No.
>
> Q.: How many votes do you expect to get, conservatively speaking?
> A.: Conservatively speaking, one.

Or whose column on Election Day 1970 was a good-natured but quite persuasive defense of the early Beethoven against an intemperate critique in the previous issue of *National Review.*

Or who can unexpectedly end a lengthy and bitter account of his feud with Gore Vidal with a qualified but genuine apology.

On the other hand, it is difficult not to loathe someone who can write, in *Up from Liberalism,* his most substantial philosophical defense of conservatism:

> It is a part of the conservative intuition that economic freedom is the most precious temporal freedom, for the reason that it alone gives to each one of us, in our comings and goings in our complex society, sovereignty

—this in bland disregard of the familiar and extensive literature on the economic hardships, in both the United States and Europe, of industrialization under capitalist auspices, hardships mitigated only (apart from the prosperity induced by the self-destruction of America's international competitors in two world wars) by the social-welfare legislation that Buckley has devoted his career to disparaging.

Or who can remark, in an interview with *Playboy* in May 1970:

> I can't think of any country that we've "dominated" or "imperialized" . . . that is worse off as a result of its experience with America than it would have been had we not entered into a temporary relationship with [that is, invaded or subverted] it.

When this was written, the United States bore substantial responsibility for large-scale massacres in Indonesia, Guatemala, and El Salvador; for intense repression, often accompanied by torture, in Iran, Paraguay, Nicaragua, and Brazil; and for horrifying poverty in Honduras, the Dominican Republic, Haiti, and the Philippines. Buckley's apparent assumption is that preventing a government not hospitable to American economic penetration (the operative definition of Third World "communism") justifies any quantity of suffering inflicted on a country's population. This is a common enough assumption among American intellectuals, but usually implicit. It's the explicitness, the relentlessness, the enthusiasm with which Buckley has enforced this assumption that is hard to forgive.

Patron Saint, for all its historical and psychological acuity, is not a critical biography; it does not explore the question "What, ultimately, do conservatives like Buckley seek to conserve?" If one disbelieves their own answer—"traditional morality and individual freedoms"—the only plausible remaining answer is "privilege." There is something to be said for privilege: it has bequeathed us much great art and many good works, not to mention aristocratic individuals of high polish and charm, like Buckley. But in its enshrinement of irrationality, of blind chance, it is undeniably part of humanity's moral childhood. Buckley, for all his aspiration to sound "theoretical depths," never penetrated to this.

7

CLOSING TIME

Allan Bloom

Allan Bloom's *The Closing of the American Mind* struck a nerve among American intellectuals. One or another of them suggested that Bloom's understanding of classical thought is deficient, his account of modern intellectual history implausible, and his willingness or ability to argue his opinions, rather than merely pronounce them, no better than intermittent. One of them, David Rieff, lost patience altogether: *Closing,* he wrote, is "a book decent people would be ashamed of having written." But since half a million Americans were not ashamed to read it, or at any rate buy it, it seems worth considering why *Closing* has spoken so compellingly to so many. Even a bad book may raise interesting questions.

Closing has two strains: first, contemporary culture criticism, based largely on Bloom's observations of college students and including a long denunciation of the 1960s; and second, a disjointed meditation on the history of political philosophy. The culture criticism is often shrewd but just as often glib, even mean-spirited. Occasionally Bloom sounds like Christopher Lasch (who is, surprisingly, not mentioned in *Closing*). But Lasch is a vastly more discriminating critic, incapable of provocative oversimplifications like Bloom's "*All* literature up to today is sexist" (his italics). Bloom evidently does not grasp that works in which sexual inequality is not at issue may not be feminist but are not sexist either; you actually have to endorse sexual inequality to be sexist. "Most of the great European novelists and poets of the last two hundred years were men of the Right," Bloom informs us. Really? Keats? Dickens? George Eliot? Pushkin? Tolstoy? Turgenev? Chekhov? Flaubert? Proust? Rilke? Kafka? Musil? Most irritating are Bloom's references to "the Nietzscheanization of the American left" during the 1960s, meaning that a new existentialist discourse of "commitment" and "will" and "values" allegedly displaced the traditional radical language of rights, justice, and equality, with destructive consequences. To anyone familiar—as Bloom clearly is not—with the theory and practice of participatory democracy within the New Left, or who has read its founding document, the Port Huron Statement, Bloom's notion is a badly limping half-truth.

Still, there is much insight and even pathos in Bloom's characterization of students at elite universities, who often arrive jaded at adolescence, for whom "survivalism has taken the place of heroism as the admired quality" and who display the early, poignant effects of what Lasch called "the narcissistic personality of our time." In particular, *Closing* contains a fine evocation of naïveté as a desirable educational disposition. Bloom points out that the capacity to be transformed by new knowledge is not a constant capacity, automatically triggered by encounters with great books, but is a fleeting and easily aborted developmental stage. Premature exposure to advanced ideas, like too-early exposure to sexual or emotional complexities, may generate defenses against hyperstimulation. The typical form of this defense is a flattening of affect, manifested at present, according to Bloom, in a too-easy tolerance, an unreflective cultural relativism—what he calls "openness" and describes ironically as "our virtue."

It is not, he acknowledges, that such openness is not valuable, but only when earned by living down one's prejudices. And prejudices presuppose myths, which enlightened educational theory proscribes. Bloom's argument about education is parallel—though he seems unaware of it—to a now-familiar psychoanalytic one: just as emotional maturity requires the gradual mastery of illusions about an internalized omnipotent father, so intellectual maturity requires gradual emancipation from inherited political and religious myths. In both cases, eliminating these painful struggles also eliminates the possibility of depth, emotional or imaginative. Bloom's extrapolation of his observations about education to marriage and family life, contemporary literature, attitudes toward death, and practically every other aspect of present-day American culture yields mostly polysyllabic peeves. But here, too, *Closing* has its moments. For example, concluding a paragraph of otherwise simplistic anti-feminist blather, Bloom asks: "What substitute is there for the forms of relatedness that are dismantled in the name of the new justice?" What I think he means is: The structures of authority and obligation entailed by marriage and the family serve some benign purposes as well as some oppressive ones. So do those of universities, police forces, and governments. Shouldn't anyone demanding that those institutions be abolished or replaced first show how their positive goods can be achieved in whatever you want to replace them with? It is clear that Bloom himself will be no help in answering this question; yet it is an urgent question, and he formulates it well.

The root of all contemporary troubles, Bloom contends, is our neglect or misunderstanding of the wisdom of the Greeks. Only they rightly understood "the relationship of the philosopher to the political community"; and this relationship is the really important thing, the alpha and the omega of political theory. For Plato in *The Republic*, the ideal form of this relationship is straightforward enough: "Unless philosophers rule as kings, or those now called kings and chiefs genuinely and adequately philosophize . . . there is no rest from ills for the cities . . . nor, I think, for human kind." Since this fortunate condition never has been and never will be realized, the responsibility of intellectuals, Bloom writes (following his mentor Leo Strauss), is to look out for themselves:

> The toleration of philosophy requires its being thought to serve powerful elements in society without actually becoming their servant. The philosopher must come to terms with the deepest prejudices of men always, and of the men of his time. The one thing he cannot change and will not try to change is their fear of death and the whole superstructure of beliefs and institutions that make death bearable, ward it off or deny it. . . . Changing the character of his relationship to [other men] is impossible because the disproportion between him and them is firmly rooted in nature. . . . In antiquity all philosophers had the same practical politics, inasmuch as none believed it feasible *or salutary* [my italics] to change the relations between the rich and poor in a fundamental or permanently progressive way.

Neither, it appears, does Bloom.

To dismiss Bloom out of hand as elitist, authoritarian, antidemocratic, regressive, and a crank would be, in a way, to repeat the error of our noble democratic forebears, the Athenian citizens who condemned Socrates to death. Bloom is indeed all those unpleasant things. But by making a clever and influential, though specious, case against popular sovereignty, Bloom and Socrates offer its defenders an opportunity to refine and deepen the case for equality.

It is clear that such refinements are necessary. For modernity has not turned out altogether well. To the pioneers of the Enlightenment, it appeared that false certainties and artificial hierarchies were the chief obstacles to general happiness. To many the suspicion has by now occurred that there are no true certainties and no natural hierarchies, yet also that individual and social well-being require *some* certainties, some hierarchies. The rapid increase in mobility and choice, in sheer volume of stimuli that followed the erosion of traditional ways of life and thought, has taxed, and occasionally overwhelmed, nearly every modern man or woman. This no longer seems, even to the most optimistic partisans of modernity, merely a phenomenon of transition. It may be that just as in any generation there are broad limits to physical and intellectual development, so also there are psychological limits, which likewise alter slowly. "Human nature," in short, though in an empirical rather than a metaphysical sense: not eternal and immutable, but with enough continuity—or inertia—to generate illusions of essence and a need for roots.

Bloom repeatedly invokes Nietzsche, whose lifework was a supremely effective demonstration that humankind—most of us, at any rate—cannot bear very much reality. Like Socrates, Nietzsche believed that only those who could endure complete disillusionment ought to rule. But since, like virtually every other modern thinker, he could not take Socratic/Platonic metaphysics seriously, he assumed that Socrates was motivated by spite, by resentment of aristocratic exuberance, which could dispense both with democratic solidarity and with metaphysical mysticism. To this perennial exuberance of the few, incarnated henceforth in the warrior/artist/statesman/seer, Nietzsche ascribed political sovereignty, warning that self-rule by the unheroic, uninspired many must result in universal mediocrity. "The happiness of the last man" (a prosaic contemporary translation might be "the welfare of the average citizen") was Nietzsche's name for the goal of democratic regimes, including social tolerance, rough material equality, and other policies designed to minimize suffering and risk. But though suffering and risk may crush ordinary natures, they stimulate great natures; and the latter alone produce culture, which makes life worth living.

But suppose Socrates, Nietzsche, and Bloom are right, and the truth about our moral psychology is less benign? Suppose that solidarity does inhibit sublimity? Democrats must face this possibility. Fortunately, one of the greatest already has. Around the time Nietzsche was writing *Thus Spake Zarathustra,* throwing down the gauntlet to democratic humanism, Walt Whitman wrote *Democratic Vistas,* which met the challenge:

> America . . . must, for her purposes, cease to recognize a theory of character grown of feudal aristocracies, or form'd by merely literary standards, or from any ultramarine, full-dress formulas of culture, polish, caste, &c., and must sternly promulgate her own new standard, yet old enough, and accepting the old, the perennial elements, and combining them into groups, unities, appropriate to the modern, the democratic, the west, and to the practical occasions and needs of our own cities, and of the agricultural regions. Ever the most precious in the common.

The genius or splendor of the few may afford the rest of their society a sense of participation in infinity and immortality. But if the maturation of a people requires the sacrifice of this vicarious experience for the direct experience by the many of their own more limited individuality, then such an exchange should—with a proper sense of the genuine loss that maturation always involves—be accepted. Growing up has its compensations. Whitman describes those of democratic society with incomparable verve:

> I can conceive a community, to-day and here, in which, on a sufficient scale, the perfect personalities, without noise, meet; say in some pleasant western settlement or town,

> where a couple of hundred best men and women, of ordinary worldly status, have by luck been drawn together, with nothing extra of genius or wealth, but virtuous, chaste, industrious, cheerful, resolute, friendly and devout. I can conceive such a community organized in running order, powers judiciously delegated—farming, building, trade, courts, mails, schools, elections, all attended to; and then the rest of life, the main thing, freely branching and blossoming in each individual, and bearing golden fruit. I can see there, in every young and old man, after his kind, and in every woman after hers, a true personality, develop'd, exercised proportionately in body, mind, and spirit. I can imagine this case as one not necessarily rare or difficult, but in buoyant accordance with the municipal and general requirements of our times. And I can realize in it the culmination of something better than any stereotyped *éclat* of history or poems. Perhaps, unsung, undramatized, unput in essays or biographies—perhaps even some such community already exists, in Ohio, Illinois, Missouri, or somewhere, practically fulfilling itself, and thus outvying, in cheapest vulgar life, all that has been hitherto shown in best ideal pictures.

Plato is a peerless philosopher-poet. But Whitman intuited a truth truer than Plato's. Bloom the Nietzschean-Straussian would "open" a few American minds by chilling a great many American hearts. Unfortunately, a great many Americans appear to be tempted by that proposition.

8

REASONS AND PASSIONS

Jonathan Haidt

The last few decades have been bitter medicine for the left. In the late 1970s, the achievements of the New Deal seemed secure, embraced even by Richard Nixon, the most conservative president since Herbert Hoover. Labor unions were an accepted feature of economic and political life. In the wake of Medicare and Medicaid, inaugurated in the 1960s, the path to universal health care seemed open. Nixon himself had created the Environmental Protection Agency, an important victory for the cause of governmental regulation. Jimmy Carter acknowledged that the corporate-loophole-ridden tax code was a "disgrace" and promised to make human rights the "soul" of American foreign policy. Despite much unhappiness over busing and *Roe v. Wade,* the feminist and civil rights movements appeared triumphant. But in the intervening decades, the country's political center of gravity shifted far to the right. How has it happened?

Jonathan Haidt's fascinating, important, and exasperating new book offers one set of answers. A social psychologist at the University of Virginia and a professed liberal Democrat, Haidt was dismayed by liberalism's eclipse. Seeking to understand it, he proposed a new theory of our moral and political judgments, called Moral Foundations Theory.

As we all know and often forget, humans are not purely rational. We have a long, complex evolutionary history, which has left us with a tangled, multilayered psyche and many more motives than we are usually conscious of. Making use of research by a couple of generations of psychologists, anthropologists, and behavioral economists, Haidt claims to have excavated these psychic structures, beginning with the First Principle of any adequate moral psychology: "Intuitions come first, strategic reasoning second."

Experiments repeatedly show that—to oversimplify only a little—we all believe what we want to, regardless of reasons. Changing one's views in response to an opponent's arguments is rare indeed. Arguments are largely instrumental; they are meant for attack or defense. Most of the time, we argue like lawyers rather than philosophers, like Alan Dershowitz rather than John Rawls. As Hume said: "Reason is and ought only to be the slave of the passions and can never pretend to any other office than to serve and obey them."

Where, then, do our moral judgments come from? According to Moral Foundations Theory, morality begins as a set of evolution-derived intuitions, which each child then learns to apply within his or her culture. There are six dimensions or categories or "foundations," into which nearly all our intuitions fall: 1) Help those in need and minimize suffering everywhere (the Care/Harm foundation); 2) Reward people according to what they contribute (Fairness/Cheating); 3) Advance the fortunes of your group (Loyalty/Betrayal); 4) Defer to legitimate superiors and protect subordinates (Authority/Subversion); 5) Resist domination by illegitimate authority (Liberty/Oppression); 6) Respect your group's totems and taboos (Sanctity/Degradation).

By Haidt's reckoning, liberals focus too narrowly on the first and a special version of the second foundation. Compassion is the supreme liberal virtue, supplemented by egalitarianism, which relies on a view of contributing that emphasizes effort rather than output. Because it is individuals who suffer and need, liberalism is individualistic.

Conservatives, by contrast, have a more balanced moral matrix, resting more equally on all six foundations. Compared with liberals, conservatives are less attuned to individual freedom and fulfillment, more concerned about the cohesion and stability of groups. They are instinctive Durkheimians, agreeing with the great French sociologist that every society is unified by sacred, unchallengeable beliefs, and that "to free man from all social pressures is to abandon and demoralize him." Even before "social capital" became a social-scientific buzzword, conservatives understood that communities are fragile and require continual shoring up, sometimes at the expense of individual welfare. "If you are trying to change an organization or a society and you do not consider the effects of your changes on moral capital," Haidt affirms, "you're asking for trouble. This is the fundamental blind spot of the left." Where liberals see individuals in need, conservatives see social structures at risk.

Some of this has been said before (by George Lakoff among others), though not so systematically or with so large a background of experimental data. What should we make of it? What is true and valuable, in the first place, is the reminder that every utterance is the tip of an iceberg, merely the surface layer of a deep linguistic (Wittgenstein) or psychic (Freud) substrate. To understand someone, even for conversational purposes—much less to persuade—takes a lot of patient, skillful work. So, for example, an opinion about immigration or the Affordable Care Act may have little to do with that issue or law and much more to do with one party's feeling about the other, or about which group or tribe the opinion is associated with. In that case, facts and reasoning about policy will not get the discussants far. Unless they go deeper, baring their fundamental commitments and identifications to each other, they should save their breath.

How, then, do minds ever change? They rarely do, Haidt claims. "Whether you end up on the right or the left of the political spectrum turns out to be just as heritable as most other traits: genetics explains between a third and a half of the variability among people on their political attitudes. Being raised in a liberal or conservative household accounts for much less." Presumably political campaigns, discussions with friends and co-workers, television programs, books and articles, and even one's education count for still less.

Are society-wide misunderstanding and mistrust inevitable, then? Haidt's practical recommendations for avoiding them are not much help. "I believe that psychologists must work with political scientists to identify changes that will undermine Manichaeism." More research is necessary, as always. Beyond that, he can only suggest that perhaps if congressional families all lived in Washington, D.C., and their children played sports together, congressional Republicans and Democrats might be less polarized.

For secular rationalists, all this is discouraging. But we get no sympathy from Haidt, who scourges the "rationalist delusion": the idea that "reasoning is our most noble attribute," which usually goes along with "a claim that the rational caste (philosophers or scientists) should have more power" as well as "a utopian program for raising more rational children." We had better reconcile ourselves to religion, Haidt advises, and if possible even adopt one. Lack of belief is no problem: "it is religious belonging that matters for [social capital] . . . not religious belief."

Truth or falsity is beside the point for Haidt; the social benefits of religion are too great to allow for such quibbles. Religions "help groups to cohere, solve free rider problems, and win the competition for group-level survival"; and they make individuals "less selfish and more loving." Gods and religions are "tools that let people bind themselves together" or, in the language of evolutionary psychology, "group-level adaptations for producing cohesiveness and trust." The data suggest, Haidt claims, that religious people are happier, more generous, more productive, and better behaved than the non-religious.

At the very least, unbelievers should keep their skepticism to themselves. "Asking people to give up all forms of sacralized belonging and live in a world of purely 'rational' beliefs might be like asking people to give up the Earth and live in colonies orbiting the moon." Like the serpent in Eden, reason promises a brave new world but can only bring homelessness and exile.

The Righteous Mind is an easy book for a liberal (or even a genuinely religious person) to dislike. The habit of believing things because they are true, rather than for the sake of social cohesiveness, is extremely hard to break. And then, minds do sometimes change; the voice of reason, though small and soft, as Freud pointed out, does eventually get a hearing. Mightn't it be fruitful to ask how this can happen rather than assuming, as Haidt does, that it hardly ever will? Mightn't there be some material conditions in which rationality is not invincibly more difficult than unthinking allegiance, and in which cooperative inquiry seems as natural as strategic reasoning?

Strategic reasoning is a mechanism of intergroup competition, and competition is premised on insecurity. Universal radical insecurity—the inevitable and intended result of "flexible labor markets" and "minimal government"; that is, of contemporary capitalism—is not conducive to imaginative receptivity or disinterested reflection. A liberal politician famously observed that it is all but impossible to get a man to understand something when his salary depends on his not understanding it. The same goes for his tax breaks, his regulatory exemptions, his government contracts, and other matters on which a man's survival, or his accustomed lifestyle, may depend. When the middle class is shrinking and one person in four or five is below, at, or not far from poverty level, most people will hunker down, not open up. Some degree of competition, insecurity, and inequality will probably always be with us. But the price of our present extreme degree of those things is a lessened ability to reason together about difficult matters.

Moreover, we are all increasingly hyperstimulated. The sheer volume of commercial messages, entertainment, and social media makes inner compensation necessary, so we double down on our inner stabilizers, otherwise known as prejudices. Deep experiences of any kind—grappling with art or philosophy, having one's mind changed about politics, or simply possessing one's soul—require a modicum of silence, slowness, and solitude. For most Americans, that modicum is vanishing.

For secular liberals, the message of Haidt's book is a sobering one: achieving large-scale trust, comity, and mutual aid will be very hard. Though it has sometimes been done in the past, secular liberals are barred from using the old methods. We want social bonds, we want limits, we want authority; but we don't want illusions. The will of God, the infallibility of Scripture, and the divine right of husbands and fathers seem to us illusions. Even "My country right or wrong" is an illusion if it means, as it frequently does in the mouths of false patriots, "My country can do no wrong." We can't accept these illusions, and we can't ask others to accept them—even if it will make them better behaved.

But we also owe it to conservatives—and to ourselves—to devise ways of promoting stability and solidarity that don't rely on illusions. Here liberals have indeed failed—like everyone else—to resolve the immemorial tensions between reason and instinct or individual and group. Perhaps the best we can do for now is to point out, patiently, persistently, and with as much love for our equally stubborn fellow citizens as we can muster, that some social arrangements might make it easier to hear one another than others do.

PART II

POLITICS AND CULTURE

9

DEMOCRATIC VISTAS, 2025

The crash of 2007–8 hit Harvard University especially hard. Thanks to the overweeningly brilliant, unflappably self-confident financial guidance of its then president Lawrence Summers ("As a former Secretary of the Treasury, I assure you that interest rates will not fall below X," he is rumored to have told the governing board, who were anxious about a particularly daring credit-default swap he was proposing), Harvard lost nearly a third of its $36 billion endowment in one year. Every department's belt was tightened several notches, and widespread layoffs were anticipated (though eventually averted by offering early retirement to older employees, hundreds of whom accepted).

The talk was grim around my office, the building services center of a large research complex at Harvard. Contractors came by frequently for keys and instructions, and the more gregarious ones often stayed to schmooze. Sports and celebrities, our usual topics, were replaced that year by political griping. As the details of the bank bailout emerged, imprecations were fervently heaped on both bankers and politicians; a respectful hearing was even accorded the office radical (me), usually humored or ignored. But these conversations always ended the same way.

One or another of those tough, no-bullshit, can-do guys would shrug and say: "Hey, what can *we* do about it? Nothin'." And the rest would chorus: "Yeah, what can ya do?" It was an epitome of twenty-first-century American democracy: people used to coping with dauntingly complex mechanical systems simply took their political impotence for granted.

Their fatalism was entirely appropriate. As we sat around the office grumbling, Congress began responding to nationwide calls for financial reform. The two-year process that resulted in the Wall Street Reform and Consumer Protection Act of 2010, known as Dodd-Frank, bestowed on the still-battered nation what the (as ever) smilingly earnest President Obama called "the strongest consumer financial protections in history." He paused for emphasis and repeated to his enthusiastic audience, "in *history*."

Another two years on, *Rolling Stone*'s invaluable investigative reporter Matt Taibbi wrote a lengthy obsequy for Dodd-Frank.

> The fate of Dodd-Frank over the past two years is an object lesson in the government's inability to institute even the simplest and most obvious reforms. . . . From the moment it was signed into law, lobbyists and lawyers have fought regulators over every line in the rulemaking process. Congressmen and presidents may be able to get a law passed once in a while—but they can no longer make sure it *stays* passed. You win the modern financial-regulation game by filing the most motions, attending the most hearings, giving the most money to the most politicians, and above all, by keeping at it, day after day, year after fiscal year, until stealing is legal again. "It's like a scorched-earth policy," says a former regulator who was heavily involved with the drafting of Dodd-Frank. "It requires constant combat. And it never ends."

The final words of Taibbi's article toll the death knell of contemporary American democracy:

> You can't buy votes in a democracy, at least not directly. But our democracy is run through a bureaucracy. Human beings can cast a vote, or rally together during protests and elections, but real people—even committed professionals—get tired of running through mazes of motions and countermotions, or reading thousands of pages about swaps-execution facilities and NRSROs. They will fight through it for five days, or maybe even six, but on the seventh they will watch a baseball game, or *Tanked,* instead of diving into that morass of hellish acronyms one more time.
>
> But money never gets tired.

It goes without saying that, in this regard, the financial industry is no worse than the energy, defense, chemical, pharmaceutical, insurance, entertainment, food-processing, or any other large industry. America is a plutocracy. Freedom House has long published a comprehensive international index of formal democracy, which the U.S. State Department found extremely convenient during the Cold War. If anyone today published a similarly careful and thorough index of effective democracy—a measure of the degree to which governments solicit and respond to public sentiment rather than money in the formation of law and policy—the United States would surely rank as low as many Communist tyrannies ranked on the Freedom House index.

In truth, American democracy has been a long time dying. *Equality* (1897), Edward Bellamy's sequel to the fabulously popular *Looking Backward* (1888), opens with a conversation between the reawakened nineteenth-century hero Julian West and his generously indignant, increasingly incredulous twentieth-going-on-twenty-first-century fiancée Edith Leete.

Edith asks: "If these people all had an equal voice in the government . . . why did they not without a moment's delay put an end to the inequalities from which they suffered?"

Julian replies: "The capitalists advanced the money necessary to procure the election of the office-seekers on the understanding that when elected the latter should do what the capitalists wanted. But I ought not to give you the impression that the bulk of the votes were bought outright. That would have been too open a confession of the sham of popular government as well as too expensive. The money contributed by the capitalists to procure the election of the office-seekers was mainly expended to influence the people by indirect means. Immense sums under the name of campaign funds were raised for this purpose and used in innumerable devices . . . the object of which was to galvanize the people to a sufficient degree of interest in the election to go through the motion of voting."

Edith persists: "But why did not the people elect officials and representatives of their own class, who would look out for the interests of the masses?" She can scarcely credit Julian's explanation:

"The people who voted had little choice for whom they should vote. That question was determined by the political party organizations, which were beggars to the capitalists for pecuniary support. No man who was opposed to capitalist interests was permitted the opportunity as a candidate to appeal to the people. For a public official to support the people's interest as against that of the capitalists would be a sure way of sacrificing his career. . . . His public position he held only from election to election, and rarely long. His permanent, lifelong, and all-controlling interest, like that of us all, was his livelihood, and that was dependent, not on the applause of the people, but on the favor and patronage of capital, and this he could not afford to imperil in the pursuit of the bubbles of popularity. These circumstances, even if there had been no instances of direct bribery, sufficiently explained why our politicians and officeholders with few exceptions were vassals and tools of the capitalists."

This dismal situation did not originate in the Gilded Age. Thirty years earlier, in *Democratic Vistas* (1867), before canvassing the magnificent possibilities of American democracy, Walt Whitman paused to acknowledge the ghastly actuality:

> An acute and candid person, in the revenue department in Washington, who is led by the course of his employment to regularly visit the cities, north, south and west, to investigate frauds, has talk'd much with me about his discoveries. The depravity of the business classes of our country is not less than has been supposed, but infinitely greater. The official services of America, national, state, and municipal, in all their branches and departments, except the judiciary, are saturated in corruption, bribery, falsehood, mal-administration; and the judiciary is tainted. The great cities reek with respectable as much as non-respectable robbery and scoundrelism. . . . The magician's serpent in the fable ate up all the other serpents; and money-making is our magician's serpent, remaining to-day sole master of the field.

Ten years before that, Emerson growled in his journal:

> Is there no check to this class of privileged thieves that infest our politics? We mark & lock up the petty thief or we raise the hue & cry in the street, and do not hesitate to draw our revolvers out of the box, when one is in the house. But here are certain well-dressed well-bred fellows, infinitely more mischievous, who get into the government & rob without stint, & without disgrace. They do it with a high hand, & by the device of having a

> party to whitewash them, to abet the act, & lie, & vote for them. And often each of the larger rogues has his newspaper, called "his organ," to say that it was not stealing, this which he did; that if there was stealing, it was you who stole, & not he.

It should be noted that there are two sides to this question. Tocqueville, with his usual quasi-Martian apriorism, confidently declared that plutocracy in America was an impossibility:

> As the great majority of those who create the laws have no taxable property, all the money that is spent for the community appears to be spent to their advantage, at no cost of their own, and those who have some little property readily find means of so regulating the taxes that they weigh upon the wealthy and profit the poor, although the rich cannot take the same advantage when they are in possession of the government. . . .
>
> Again, it may be objected that the poor never have the sole power of making the laws; but I reply that wherever universal suffrage has been established, the majority unquestionably exercises the legislative authority; and if it be proved that the poor always constitute the majority, may it not be added with perfect truth that in the countries in which they possess the elective franchise they possess the sole power of making the laws? It is certain that in all the nations of the world the greater number has always consisted of those persons who hold no property, or of those whose property is insufficient to exempt them from the necessity of working in order to procure a comfortable subsistence. Universal suffrage, therefore, in point of fact does invest the poor with the government of society.

Justice Anthony Kennedy, speaking for the Supreme Court majority in *Citizens United,* displayed a similarly breezy indifference to fact, though with two centuries' less excuse than Tocqueville: "We now conclude that independent expenditures, including those made by corporations, do not give rise to corruption or the appearance of corruption."

Is it otiose, in the absence of democracy, to reflect on what democracy might and should be, or at any rate might have been? The money power may be overthrown someday—Marx's theory, never yet put to the test, may well be true. Marx predicted that globalization, financialization, the concentration of ownership, and the proletarianization of nearly everyone would result in either socialism or barbarism. Stable barbarism—the unsleeping plutocracy Taibbi describes—seems more likely in the near and medium term. But the world revolves; all things change. The citizens of a post-capitalist world, if it ever arrives, will need to maintain a society-wide conversation, consisting of millions of smaller local ones, about how to govern themselves. Perhaps we can help by keeping the subject alive even in the dark times.

The first illusion to kill on the way to self-government is professionalism. Currently, the profession of legislators is getting reelected. Estimates I have seen of the amount of time legislators spend raising money seem to average around 50 percent. I don't know what percentage of time they spend traveling to and from the district, giving boilerplate speeches, and frequenting prostitutes or otherwise cavorting, but it can hardly be less than 10 or 20 percent. The time they spend studying legislative questions—reading through policy proposals and discussing them with colleagues, staff, and constituents, and acquiring sufficient background knowledge to make those discussions fruitful—must be minimal. (Though plenty of time doubtless goes to taking instructions from lobbyists.) Even an intelligent and conscientious legislator—not likely, in any case, to have survived either major party's candidate-selection process—would scarcely be able to acquire anything resembling expertise, much less wisdom, under these conditions, which may well be inescapable in any system of electoral competition.

Shouldn't I have said "in any system of *privately financed* electoral competition"? Wouldn't public financing of campaigns change everything? No, it would not. Thanks to the ingenuity of the public-relations industry and the complaisance of the Supreme Court's conservative majority, most of the expenses of political competition are or soon will be incurred not by candidates but by supporters—usually very rich—operating, often anonymously, through ad hoc committees. Political money, it has been often and wisely observed, is a hydraulic system; if you stop a leak in one place, it breaks out somewhere else.

Perhaps we should replace competition with sortition, the drawing of lots. What is the purpose of political competition, anyway? According to the founders of the republic, it is to produce a legislative body that represents—that is, speaks with the same mind as—the populace. According to Madison: "The government ought to possess not only, first, the force, but secondly, the mind or sense of the people at large. The legislature ought to be the most exact transcript of the whole society." John Adams seconded this: the legislature "should be an exact portrait, in miniature, of the people at large, as it should think, feel, reason, and act like them." Even that arch-plutocrat William F. Buckley Jr., posing as a democrat, famously proclaimed that he would rather be governed by the first two thousand people in any big-city telephone directory than by the Harvard faculty. (Though his antipathy to Harvard was undoubtedly genuine, it is highly doubtful that he would have countenanced the rule of ordinary citizens who had not bent the knee to wealthy donors. After all, he strongly supported his brother's baneful lawsuit, *Buckley v. Valeo,* aimed at preventing precisely that.)

Is the present American national legislature an "exact transcript of the whole society"? The question invites ridicule. Racially, sexually, economically, and ideologically, the members of Congress more closely resemble the executive ranks of most large corporations, or the membership of most large country clubs, than they do the society as a whole. Polls consistently reveal a sharp variance between the views of the citizenry and those of the political class, which it is the job of political consultants and communications specialists to finesse during election season. Popular approval of Congress, never robust in recent years, has lately been plunging toward the single digits—one of the few hopeful signs in contemporary American political culture.

We can scarcely do worse than what we have; on this the country seems agreed. How would sortition work? Fortunately, there is a blueprint to hand: a short book called *A Citizen Legislature* by Ernest Callenbach (author of *Ecotopia,* one of the finest utopian novels ever written) and Michael Phillips. The process is not complicated. Every county in America maintains a list of prospective jurors. Combine these lists in one national master list, and a computer may easily be programmed to choose a random sample of 435 (the size of the present House of Representatives). The same categories of people would be excluded from the selection pool: felons, noncitizens, the institutionalized. The resulting Representative House would (unlike the House of Representatives) be an exact, or near-exact, transcript of the society: roughly the same proportion of women, minorities, academics, professionals, blue- and white-collar workers, homemakers, millionaires, and unemployed persons as in the general population. The representatives would train intensively for three months, would serve for three years, and would then return to their communities (or stay in Washington as lobbyists, though perhaps less as a matter of course than at present). One-third of the House would be replaced each year. The Senate and the Executive Branch would, for the time being, remain unchanged. (Though in a rational world, the undemocratic Senate's days would be numbered.)

Would sortition rule out government by the "best"? This question, too, can scarcely be considered with a straight face. We all know what Mark Twain said about congressmen, and matters have not notably improved since. Besides, as Callenbach and Phillips write, "pure intelligence—if there is such a thing—is certainly not directly related to political wisdom. The only reasonable assumption is that both are broadly distributed through the population."

This was apparently the Athenians' assumption as well. The Assembly, the city's governing body, was chosen by lot. And Athens was not, as the popular conception has it, a "democracy of orators," of citizens speaking and listening by turns and then, having said their piece, voting. It was much more like Callenbach and Phillips's Representative House of ordinary shlubs. Political theorist Daniela Cammack has carefully analyzed virtually all uses of the three Greek terms for "to deliberate." Two of them involve speaking; the other—the only one nearly always applied to the membership of the Assembly as a whole—means "reflection" and has an exclusively internal reference. There were orators and advocates, of course, but their function was advisory. There was, Cammack writes,

> a greater cleavage between speakers and listeners in the assembly than is usually imagined. . . . The [language] suggests that a small number of citizens were conceived as "advisors" to the group, who by the very act of speaking cast themselves outside of the deliberating unit. . . . Speak-

> ers did not cease to be voters, of course, when they came forward to speak; in that sense, they remained part of the decision-making unit. . . . [But] the key tasks of ordinary citizens did not include speaking. Listening, thinking, judging, voting, and finally holding speakers to account were all far more important.*

The Athenians, that is, entrusted their civic destiny not to experts or professionals (though they made use of them) but to ordinary citizens, selected at random in order to produce a faithful representation of the society as a whole. There is no reason why the United States should not do the same. The only alternative is elections, and the American electoral process is fundamentally, irredeemably corrupt. Elections cost money, vast and increasing amounts. As long as economic resources are distributed as unequally as they are at present, elections cannot be fair.

Would random selection of legislators produce a less lively political culture? This is yet another question that answers itself. Contemporary American political culture is comatose, kept alive only by such artificial life supports as televised debates between candidates, radio and TV talk shows, and the protracted electoral news cycle, reporting on polls, trends, gaffes, and gossip for eighteen to twenty-four months before each presidential election and nine to twelve months before each congressional election. The degree to which this panoply of triviality is initiated or controlled by ordinary Americans is zero. Political messaging in our society is, like commercial messaging, wholly unidirectional. Voters, like consumers, exercise only an unavoidable

* That last phrase refers to an aspect of Athenian democracy perhaps worth reviving: speakers who were later judged to have given foolish or dishonest advice could be impeached and fined. President Obama has shown no interest in calling to account those who lied their country into war, but the Athenians did.

and irreducible minimum of choice at the very end of a process from which their self-organized and unmanipulated input is entirely absent.

What might a lively political culture look like? It would no doubt feature some version of the "committees of correspondence" that flourished in the American colonial period, only more permanent and less ad hoc. There would be continuous discussion, in small groups, in living rooms, church halls, school buildings, workplace lounges, libraries, municipal buildings, and other venues about political issues, organized by ordinary citizens, employees, neighbors, and so on. These groups would make use of information about these issues collected by public agencies and made available on the Web, information equal in quality and depth to the information available to policymakers and industry lobbyists. The meetings of these groups would be regularly attended by public officials, who would have plenty to time to do so once they were released from the time-consuming obligations of fund-raising and electioneering.

The local discussion groups would communicate regularly with one another, sharing information and conclusions, and would join in formulating questions and instructions for local officials and legislators. They would also send delegates to state and regional citizens' groups, which would conduct discussions with one another and then, jointly or separately, with state and national legislators and policymakers. (Unions would have a parallel structure of member involvement, unlike today.) These delegates would be in continual contact with the smaller bodies that sent them, and would be readily recallable.

Such groups at all levels, particularly the higher-level ones, would also monitor and criticize media coverage of issues that interest them, exactly as industry and other (for example, religious) interest groups do today. They would commission, and in some cases write, articles for the media—articles that, unlike the continuous stream of corporate propaganda that largely constitutes present-day "reporting" in many local and regional newspapers, would be openly acknowledged—and would propose guests on radio and television discussions of contentious issues. And just as advertisers boycott publications or media programs considered ideologically unsound, the citizen and worker groups would orchestrate pressure, including boycotts, of chronically biased outlets. This is not a complete remedy for the extreme concentration of ownership in newspapers, radio, and television at present, with all the possibilities for censorship and ideological homogenization that implies. But it's a step.

Something like this scheme might help restore some substance to this society's hollow democratic pretensions. Of course, genuine democracy in any form depends on broad economic equality. The preconditions of democracy are that: 1) minimum economic security is universal, so that individuals' economic welfare cannot be jeopardized by political activism that may be anathema to their economic or political superiors; 2) gross inequality of resources does not give some political opinions vastly greater possibilities of publicity or promotion (lobbying) than others, as at present; and 3) the material prerequisites of political activity—leisure, education, at least modest disposable income—are universally available. Even this bare preliminary statement suggests how many light-years the United States is from anything worthy to be called democracy, and also makes clear how rapidly we're traveling away from, rather than toward, the ideal.

Granted, no one can be forced to be free or self-governing. Those who are addicted to television, or allergic to meetings, or simply don't give a damn about other people, are perfectly free to blow the whole democracy thing off, though their neighbors will be equally free to call them what the Greeks did: *idiotes*.

Will all—or any—of the above happen? Over Money's dead body. Far more likely is a continued bread-and-circuses electoral oligarchy, with increased surveillance and repression as the allotment of grub and gadgets to the lower orders has to be parceled out among a growing global army of proletarians. Technology without democracy: a *Blade Runner* world.

The American empire has already found its Gibbon, at least in rough draft. The medieval intellectual historian turned social critic Morris Berman has produced a trilogy of works—*The Twilight of American Culture* (2000); *Dark Ages America* (2006); *Why America Failed* (2011)—that diagnose and forecast the country's decline in real time with an imaginative freedom and an unyielding pessimism that no conventional academic historian would permit him- or herself. He has naturally been ignored when not (as, for example, by that bellwether of the middlebrow, Michiko Kakutani, in the *New York Times*) ridiculed.

Unfortunately for his trilogy's commercial and critical prospects, Berman has no last-minute proposals to save us from the long descent he foresees into soft authoritarianism and cultural debasement. Possessive individualism has thoroughly routed civic republicanism; hucksterism has vanquished virtue; a mindless commitment to economic growth has rendered the ideals of simplicity, balance, and voluntary renunciation all but unintelligible as guides to public policy rather than merely to individual salvation. It is too late for a happy ending.

It is indeed late. And yet, all things change. The Dark Ages, if they arrive, may eventually be followed by another Enlightenment, which our present efforts may assist, even if we've gone under. We may as well give Money a good fight. Hey, what else can ya do?

10

WHERE HAS OUR VIRTUE GONE?

David Bosworth and Steve Fraser

Economists use a suggestive word to describe a developing country's increasing involvement with international finance: they speak of the "deepening" of its capital market. As more transactions take place between borrowers and lenders, as more mediating institutions are formed, more financial instruments introduced, and more laws and regulations devised, something intricate and integrated emerges across national borders: the mighty "financial markets" that dictate government policies and decide the fate of populations. With innumerable connecting threads forming a complex, near-organic unity, this spectral entity is at once extraordinarily sensitive and extraordinarily stable. The slightest external stimulus registers, its effects transmitted rapidly throughout the system; but as with all complex organisms, a homeostatic process swiftly restores equilibrium. Deep enough markets are impossible for individuals to dominate or disrupt: there are simply too many controls, shock absorbers, balancing mechanisms. By the same token, non-market-based purposes and motives—such as equality or the general welfare—can get no traction. The constraints are structural: no one is visibly oppressed or discriminated against in the financial markets. Everyone's money is equally green, and procedural fairness is rigorously enforced. The same rules apply to the 99.9 percent as to the 0.1 percent; as the great capitalist philosopher Thomas Friedman sagely observed, the rules put everyone, rich and poor, in the same "golden straitjacket." What could be fairer?

Steve Fraser's *The Age of Acquiescence* (2015) and David Bosworth's *The Demise of Virtue in Virtual America* (2014) brilliantly document a parallel form of "deepening": the long-term undermining of popular sovereignty and its replacement by the sovereignty of organized money over an atomized, impotent populace. Like the market, the American political system (though not those who actually staff it) commands considerable public legitimacy, even while generating inequality, cynicism, and apathy. In both cases, an elaborate legal structure produces an appearance of fairness, while the vastness and intricacy of each system seems to suggest that there is no alternative, that elite dominance is inevitable and popular resistance futile, even irrational. In market democracies, Amartya Sen writes, "discontent is replaced by acceptance, hopeless rebellion by conformist quiet and . . . suffering by cheerful endurance."

This sense of frustrated and bewildered acquiescence is something new in American history, argues Fraser, an accomplished journalist and historian. In previous eras, "the sinews of resistance were tougher and more resilient . . . the popular imagination audaciously leapt beyond the boundaries of business as usual. Great waves of social upheaval regularly rolled across the landscape of American life. Their reverberations lent public affairs a frisson we no longer sense." Comparisons between post-Reagan America and the first Gilded Age in the late nineteenth and the early twentieth century are now commonplace: levels of inequality, corruption, and financial buccaneering are strikingly similar. What's starkly different, however, is the temper of politics today: the absence of organized resistance and the "frailty and passivity" of the left.

To point up the contrast, *The Age of Acquiescence* offers a short but vivid history of class warfare in America's first industrial age. Capitalism always begins with primitive accumulation, the large-scale expropriation of labor and natural resources. Freed slaves and prisoners (very often, in the South, the same persons) formed a large part of this new proletariat, but the majority were dispossessed farmers, artisans, and shopkeepers, whipsawed by mortgage and other interest payments on the one hand and volatile commodity prices on the other. By the end of the nineteenth century, the indomitable American yeomanry celebrated by Tocqueville and Lincoln had largely vanished, absorbed into a mass of industrial wage laborers alongside streams of immigrants, welcomed then as now by employers for the downward pressure they exerted on wages.

Early industrial America was wracked by financial crises, occasioning great pain among workers, which they did not take lying down. *The Age of Acquiescence* opens with a description of the Great Uprising of 1877, a countrywide railroad strike that many ruling-class voices warned would incite a new civil war. Sabotage, arson, and occupation by workers were met with murderous violence by police, militias, and private armies. Though the uprising was defeated, many novelists, clergymen, professors, and journalists—along with millions of workers and farmers—questioned the viability and legitimacy of capitalism. In subsequent decades, large agrarian and working-class organizations flourished: the Knights of Labor, the People's Party, and the Socialist Party, for example, sometimes wielding considerable economic and electoral power.

Their challenge to capitalism failed. Historians have usually attributed this to the dampening effect of American prosperity—socialism here foundered on "reefs of roast beef and apple pie," wrote one foreign observer. That judgment surely understates the ferocity of official repression. Nearly every time in those decades that a strike or a factory occupation had to be broken or a demonstration quashed, municipal, state, and federal authorities placed themselves at the service of employers, while judges reliably issued injunctions and punished agitators harshly. Finally, using World War I and the Russian Revolution as pretexts, the Wilson administration decimated the anticapitalist left.

That ideological and institutional bloodletting ensured that the next great crisis of capitalism, in 1929, produced no fundamental transformation but only top-down reforms. The economy languished until another global war made another cycle of primitive accumulation possible. The New Deal reforms, and the Keynesian ideas on which they were based, "civilized" capitalism. For a few golden (in retrospect) post–World War II decades, unionized white workers did unprecedentedly well. "Pensions and medical insurance, vacations, cost-of-living and productivity escalators, credit unions, and sick days—all that and more became the norm for a sizable segment of the American working class," Fraser observes.

The Indochina war, the OPEC oil embargo, and other costs of empire, along with the increasing competitiveness of Western Europe and Japan, put an end to this civilized interlude. American capitalism began to cannibalize itself in the 1980s, morphing from a manufacturing economy to a finance-based one. Individual plants and whole companies were sold off or drastically downsized, the proceeds going to hedge funds or private equity firms, or else directed overseas to regions with cheap labor and few regulations. Unionized jobs (and unions) disappeared, government revenues plummeted, public services starved, and infrastructure decayed. Levels of median income, home ownership, public health, and educational performance all tanked. In nearly every measure of general welfare, the United States fell below nearly every other developed country. *The Age of Acquiescence* does a stellar job portraying this protracted devastation of a way of life.

Fraser's purpose, however, is not to point out how bad things are, which every newspaper reader already knows. It's to ask how the authors of this catastrophe have gotten away with it—why there is so little organized resistance to plutocracy in the second Gilded Age. Occupy Wall Street was an inspiring outburst but left little institutional residue. Minority-rights and gender-equality struggles scored great successes but have not carried over into opposition to economic inequality and corporate dominance. Why, compared with the tempests of a century ago, are there only scattered showers of resistance now?

The most obvious reason is the decline of organized labor. This was not a spontaneous development; it was the primary element in business's strategy of rolling back the New Deal. In the wake of the civil rights movement of the 1960s, the Republican Party played the "race card," inflaming resentment among Southern whites, which was a major obstacle to labor organizing there. A large-scale odyssey of manufacturing industry to the non-union Sun Belt followed. The Reagan administration began the now decades-long practice of stacking the National Labor Relations Board with anti-labor appointees determined not to enforce the Fair Labor Practices Act. And then came globalization.

During the Cold War, "the Free World" meant that part of the world in which American business could operate free of unruly unions or excessively welfare-minded governments. Democracy was unimportant to U.S. policymakers, except for public relations purposes; and "communism" simply meant unwillingness to provide a sufficiently favorable investment climate. When the Cold War ended, business rejoiced, not because people were liberated but because capital was. A century after it was launched, the Open Door Policy triumphed on a global scale. One "free trade" agreement after another has extended a common regime of "investor rights" worldwide, empowering creditors and sharply limiting the ability of workers or consumers to organize and of states to tax, regulate, or provide essential services.

In addition to attaining this stranglehold on economic life, business has undertaken a long march through the political landscape. Concentrating media ownership in a few giant corporations; slashing public funding for education at all levels; creating a cottage industry of junk science and dubious policy research; placing industry flacks at the head of regulatory agencies; packing the appellate judiciary with young and inexperienced but rabidly partisan conservative judges; and, most important, spending huge sums to elect friendly legislators and providing them with lucrative employment when they leave office: these are the mechanisms of business hegemony in twenty-first-century America. The resulting political system is as dense and intricate a web as the financial markets; and, like the latter, it wonderfully facilitates certain kinds of initiative—money-driven ones—while efficiently frustrating citizen-driven ones. It has been skillfully engineered to make fundamental change extremely difficult—not that there is much demand for such change beyond a tiny, marginalized left.

Why isn't there? What makes "flexible" capitalism tolerable to its victims? Like all societies, ours has its legitimating myths. "Three fables of freedom in particular," Fraser writes, "have marked the last half century: emancipation through consumption; freedom through the 'free agency' of work; and freedom through the heroism of risk, a fable in which the businessman emerges as plebeian liberator."

Advertising is the primary motor of consumption, of course. About the average American, an authoritative observer wrote: "Nearly everything he sees, hears, touches, tastes, and smells is an attempt to sell him something. To break through his protective shell the advertisers must continuously shock, tease, tickle or irritate him, or wear him down by the drip-drip-drip Chinese water torture method of endless repetition. Advertising is the handwriting on the wall, sign in the sky, the bush that burns regularly every night." No, this is not Vance Packard or some other left-wing social critic; it is *Fortune* magazine in the innocent 1950s.

And as Fraser shrewdly notes, consumerism has an even deeper source. Some minimum of pleasure and autonomy is a necessity in every life, and contemporary capitalism has managed to render work, for most people, both stultifying and insecure. (A recent book by journalist Simon Head, *Mindless: Why Smarter Machines Are Making Dumber Humans,* is an eye-opening tour around the new world of Computerized Business Systems, designed to eliminate initiative, skill, or judgment in the workplace.) Consumption is a haven in this heartless, boring world. "Leveraged by debt, consumer culture has helped make the state of permanent wage labor—even a declining, downwardly mobile one—tolerable."

Another thing that made it tolerable was the overthrow of the old ruling elite—the WASP, Ivy League, Social Register elite. Not, alas, by a popular movement but by a new cadre of swashbuckling financial entrepreneurs like Gordon Gekko, determined to "rip their fucking throats out." This manhandling of the genteel Establishment didn't do the rest of us any good—on the contrary—but it vicariously released some of our aggression. Michael Milken, Carl Icahn, and their ilk became heroes. Even though they were no less rapacious than the aristocrats they replaced, at least they hadn't inherited their money. They were *our* sons-of-bitches.

And if they did it through sheer greed and grit, why shouldn't we? If they thrived on risk, mobility, freedom of action, on breaking ties and burning bridges, scorning institutional support and civic obligations, why shouldn't we? So much for solidarity. The difference between a nation of individuals and a nation of individualists is the difference between a republic and a barely sublimated war of all against all.

Critiques of capitalism's false promises are not exactly a novelty, of course. If Fraser's nevertheless packs a punch, it is not only because, unlike most of his academic and Marxist predecessors, he writes lively prose and furnishes much colorful detail. It is, even more important, because he insistently contrasts the typical character structures of America then and now, two countries "geographically the same, separated by a century, one on the rise, a developing country, one in decay, becoming an underdeveloped country":

> During the first Gilded Age the work ethic constituted the nuclear core of American cultural belief and practice. That era's emphasis on capital accumulation presumed frugality, saving, and delayed gratification as well as disciplined, methodical labor. That ethos frowned on self-indulgence, was wary of debt, denounced wealth not transparently connected to useful, tangible outputs, and feared libidinal excess whether that took the form of gambling, sumptuary display, leisured indolence, or uninhibited sexuality.
>
> How at odds that all is with the moral and psychic economy of our own second Gilded Age. An economy kept aloft by finance and mass consumption has for a long time rested on an ethos of immediate gratification, enjoyed a love affair with debt, speculation, and risk, erased the distinction between productive labor and pursuits once upon a time judged parasitic, and became endlessly inventive about ways to supercharge with libido even the homeliest of household wares.

> Can these two diverging political economies—one resting on industry, the other on finance—and these two polarized sensibilities—one fearing God, the other living in an impromptu moment to moment—explain the Great Noise of the first Gilded Age and the Great Silence of the second? So too, is it possible that people still attached by custom and belief to ways of subsisting that had originated outside the orbit of capital accumulation were for that very reason both psychologically and politically more existentially desperate, more capable, and more audacious in envisioning a noncapitalist future than those who had come of age knowing nothing else?

To readers of the late Christopher Lasch, the above reasoning will sound familiar. Throughout his career, and especially in his masterpiece *The True and Only Heaven,* Lasch argued that the advent of mass production and the new relations of authority it introduced in every sphere of social life wrought a fateful change in the prevailing American character structure. Psychological maturation depended crucially on a rhythm and scale that industrialism disrupted. The result was a weakened self, more easily regimented than its preindustrial forebear and less able to resist illegitimate authority. Unfortunately Lasch, following Freud, called this new self a "narcissistic personality," which practically guaranteed that he would be misunderstood as merely scolding the rest of us for our triviality and self-absorption.

Lasch died prematurely, and his complex, wide-ranging argument has not found many echoes among social critics since. It seems to have found one now in novelist (*The Death of Descartes*) David Bosworth's powerful polemic *The Demise of Virtue in Virtual America.* Bosworth aims to tell "the story of a profound transformation in the national character," through which "an American ethos initially geared toward prudence, pragmatism, and plain speaking came to generate instead the greatest con game in human history." Fraser frames exactly this history in the categories of political economy, Bosworth in those of moral psychology. Fraser's narrative is fast-paced and broad-gauged; Bosworth's is granular, with frequent parables and case studies.

The "American ethos" whose decline Bosworth chronicles had three main sources: Protestant Christianity, local self-government, and agrarian/artisanal producerism. The virtues these practices fostered were self-control, self-reliance, integrity, diligence, and neighborliness, among others. What has made these virtues superfluous, even a little ridiculous, is the triumph of Evangelical Mammonism—the pseudo-religion of the "free market," uniting blind faith in progress with fervent worship of profits. "Through a relentless campaign of architectural enclosure and psychological saturation over the last sixty years, our consumer economy has managed to gain effective control over both our physical and virtual homes."

> An intensely cynical entertainment industry imagineered a "mythic America" oozing with sentimentality, its highly rationalized engines of narrative production formulaically projecting the romantic fantasies of feel-good triumph.
>
> A Protestantism once rooted in a sober recognition of sinfulness, and whose savior threw the money-lenders out of the temple, began to sell instead the promissory notes of a prosperity theology: spiritual deal-making for material and psychological profit-taking in the here-and-now.
>
> A whole host of cultural liberators proclaimed their righteous freedom from this or that oppressive system only to commit to alternative regimens that proved more punitive than the ones they rejected: from a heady pursuit of bacchanalian bliss or therapeutic mood enhancement

> into the deadening trap of chemical dependency; from a giddy promotion of "consumer choice" into the grim schedules of compulsive shopping and credit-card indebtedness; from a libertarian rejection of governmental regulation into the draconian regimes of corporate efficiency and the rigged markets of global monopolies and Ponzi schemes; from a celebration of the "sovereign self" into a passive submission to the robotic schedules of self-esteem and self-help.

Bosworth sees Evangelical Mammonism everywhere: in the disappearance, for example, from his hometown (and thousands of others) of nearby woods, where little epiphanies of stillness sometimes visited children pausing from play; in the airport lounge where his request to turn off one or two of the ubiquitous blaring televisions was met with incomprehension; in the mall, where security cameras suss out any civic activity or other distraction that might momentarily disrupt the flow of happy shopping; in the prettifying by Disney and others of fairy tales like "Pinocchio" and "Three Little Pigs," which in their original form sometimes exposed children to nasty or frightening emotions and so helped them grow up. With these and dozens of other examples, from antidepressants to Prosperity Gospel preachers to the hucksterism of Wayne Dyer and Tom Peters, and with excursions into the psychic roots of recent mass delusions like the Iraq War and the housing bubble, Bosworth probes the decay of American culture as skillfully and as clinically as a dentist. (An exceptionally literate and eloquent dentist, that is.) For the reader/patient/citizen, the accompanying pain is acute but necessary.

Decay can sometimes be reversed, but not always. Can the collective solidarities and individual virtues whose decline Fraser and Bosworth lament be preserved or, if they're already too far gone, reconstituted? It's not clear: in the economy, polity, and culture alike, the rot is very deep. The worst are not only full of passionate intensity, they are also damnably ingenious. Still, "decline is no more predestined than Progress was once thought to be," Fraser helpfully reminds us. And Bosworth promises a sequel, programmatic where this one was diagnostic.

Discouragement is, in any case, out of the question. "We are never permitted to despair of the commonwealth," Thomas Jefferson wrote. The people united may be defeated again and again, maybe forever. But maybe not.

11

PREMATURE ANTI-UTOPIANS

Partisan Review

The first two *Partisan Review* anthologies, published in 1946 and 1953 and now out of print, were of an almost unbelievable richness. The contributors whose names began with *A* were Lionel Abel, James Agee, Conrad Aiken, Sherwood Anderson, Hannah Arendt, W. H. Auden, and Erich Auerbach. Those whose names began with *B* included Isaac Babel, James Baldwin, Saul Bellow, John Berryman, Elizabeth Bishop, R. P. Blackmur, Louise Bogan, Paul Bowles, and James Burnham . . . you get the idea. *Writers and Partisans: A Partisan Review Reader*, published in 1983 and also out of print, was slenderer but still distinguished, with essays by Arendt, Daniel Bell, Albert Camus, Nicola Chiaromonte, Irving Howe, Arthur Koestler, Dwight Macdonald, Czeslaw Milosz, Susan Sontag, Stephen Spender, and Leon Trotsky, among others. The book-length fiftieth-anniversary edition (1984) was a grand family reunion, with contributions from eminent members of every *Partisan* generation.

A hard act to follow, but here is *A Partisan Century: Political Writings from Partisan Review*, edited by Edith Kurzweil (1996). *A Partisan Century* isn't really meant to be definitive, or even representative. There is no poetry, fiction, or literary criticism, and except for Sontag's "Notes on Camp" and two or three other pieces, no cultural commentary of the kind whose breadth, verve, and authority made the magazine famous. The new anthology is designed, rather, to answer the question "What have *Partisan Review*'s politics been during its sixty years?"

The short answer is: liberal anticommunism. True, the magazine started out well to the left of liberalism. (An "Editorial Statement" in the inaugural issue announced, a trifle solemnly: "*Partisan Review* is aware of its responsibility to the revolutionary movement.") And on the other hand, in recent years its liberalism has largely consisted of infrequent digs at neoconservatism, whose proponents nonetheless seem very much at home in *Partisan*'s pages. For the most part, though, "liberal anticommunism" will do. Politically, the magazine has majored in criticizing America's critics, with a minor in criticizing America.

It was not an unreasonable choice—someone had to keep left-wing intellectuals honest (or try). And *Partisan* was, after all, primarily a literary magazine, not a policy review or a newsmagazine or even a journal of political opinion. Investigative journalism, programmatic advocacy, and scholarly research were not its bailiwick. Its specialty was generality: its purpose was to make overall sense of facts and judge the quality of arguments; to penetrate ambiguities, disclose incongruities, and highlight ironies; to leaven political debate with that famous sense of variousness, possibility, complexity, and difficulty. Culturally, they were players; politically, they were kibitzers. That was why Dwight Macdonald left in 1943 to start *Politics,* which (like *Dissent* a decade later) was everything *Partisan Review* ought to have been—if it had been a political magazine.

The kibitzing was, however, abundant and, at least as represented in *A Partisan Century,* generally of high quality. André Gide's "Second Thoughts on the USSR" (1937) is still inspiring and Trotsky's "Art and Politics" (1938) still provoking. George Orwell's "London Letter" and Chiaromonte's "Paris Letters" evoke the cosmopolitan though beleaguered intellectual camaraderie of the 1940s. The celebrated polemics can still get one's juices flowing: for example, Macdonald and Clement Greenberg's "Ten Propositions on the War" (1941), urging nonsupport for Roosevelt and Churchill, with Philip Rahv's caustic reply; and William Barrett's "The Liberal Fifth Column" (1946), a slashing attack on the pro-Soviet apologetics of that era's *Nation* and *New Republic.* Diana Trilling's "The Oppenheimer Case" (1954), a close reading of the transcript of Oppenheimer's loyalty hearings, shows that the interpretive subtleties of lawyers are child's play compared with those of a skilled literary critic. James Baldwin's "A Letter from the South" (1959) shows that the same relation holds between the descriptive powers of journalists and those of novelists. And among the anthology's unexpected pleasures are these still eloquent avowals by the young Norman Podhoretz from a symposium, "The Cold War and the West" (1962). Protesting against the *realpolitik* then dominant among intellectuals, he praised utopian thinking in terms that would surprise his later admirers:

> To me, the most hopeful development in years is the recent appearance of a body of utopian social criticism based on a very clear vision of what a decent life on this planet might look like and full of concrete ideas which, if they have little chance of being put into immediate effect, at least serve to refresh and nourish our fading sense of what the liberal-radical tradition has always stood for and how far short we still are of achieving it. The priests are forever distorting the prophets. . . . And the only remedy is for the prophets to say them nay and remind them of what the Lord really demands of man.

Podhoretz may have been gently chiding his editors; "utopian social criticism" was never *Partisan Review*'s long suit. And now that the Cold War is over, the journal's fierce anticommunism has been succeeded by a slightly mellower anti-utopianism, represented in *A Partisan Century* by Ralf Dahrendorf's "No Third Way" (1990) and Jeffrey Herf's "The Polish Spring" (1990). Both, interestingly, are addressed to Central European student audiences, Herf's an address, Dahrendorf's an open letter. Herf, earnest and fraternal, speaks for "deradicalized" American New Leftists; Dahrendorf, wry and avuncular, for disillusioned West European social democrats. Both essays counsel patience, moderation, pragmatism, avoidance of rancor, eschewal of "system thinking," and recognition of the political-economic law of gravity: Capitalism is associated with freedom, socialism with unfreedom. Both essays are well worth reading and arguing with.

One might begin by arguing with this observation by Herf: "Why [are] some nations richer than others? The short and simple answer is that where governments allow markets, encourage entrepreneurship, and foster private investment decisions and the free movement of labor, economic growth takes place. Where, on the other hand, government bureaucrats have tried to plan economies, discourage entrepreneurship, concentrate investment decisions in the state, and prevent the free movement of labor, economic growth does not take place. The phenomenal economic successes of South Korea, Taiwan, Singapore, and Hong Kong have been a huge embarrassment for [radical critics of capitalism]." But government bureaucrats in South Korea, Taiwan, Singapore, Hong Kong, Japan, and now China have done plenty of planning, discouraging, concentrating, and preventing. And when American economic policy in 1929 (and 1893 and 1873) corresponded pretty closely to Herf's recommendations, economic growth did not take place—on the contrary. Perhaps Herf's "short and simple answer" needs some leftist qualifications, after all. Likewise Dahrendorf's dictum "Whoever sets out to implement Utopian plans will in the first instance have to wipe clean the canvas on which the real world is painted. This is a brutal process of destruction." Cold War liberals were unable to imagine a society not ruled by either businessmen or apparatchiks. This defect of imagination ruled out the possibility that utopian plans might be implemented, or at any rate pursued, democratically. Of course—as the young Podhoretz might have pointed out—a democratic utopian movement will have to be preceded by decades or even generations of "utopian social criticism." But that is no reason to allow Dahrendorf to wipe the horizon clean of utopian hopes.

According to the memoirists, William Phillips did most of the work around the magazine and held together the *Partisan* circle. But Philip Rahv seems to have been its presiding spirit, at least during its first two decades, and Rahv's "The Sense and Nonsense of Whittaker Chambers" (1952) is a quintessential *Partisan Review* essay. Chambers's monumental *Witness* activated all Rahv's critical powers: literary, philosophical, historical, and political. In authoritative accents he confirms Chambers's indictment of the Popular Front mind, corrects his account of the New Deal, dismisses his antipolitical mysticism and antirationalist metaphysics, and portrays Chambers's curious sensibility as "Dostoevskyean in essence," exhibiting "that peculiar note of personal intensity and spiritual truculence, of commitment to the 'Idea' so absolute as to suggest that life has no meaning apart from it, all oddly combined with a flair for mystification and melodrama." The employment, in this fashion, of literary resources to interpret historical and political experience was the characteristic move of the New York intellectuals. (Likewise, of course, of European intellectuals such as Silone, Chiaromonte, Camus, and Orwell.) The resulting critical gravity, nuance, and flair are uncommon nowadays. Also uncommon are ideologically discriminating judgments like the following, which make one regret that Rahv did not live long enough to turn his polemical scorn on contemporary neoconservative superficialities:

> [Chambers] reproaches Western civilization for its "three centuries of rationalism." Now rationalism has its fallacies, to be sure, but is it fair to hold it to account for the horrors of the Russian police state, which has behind it not even one, much less three, centuries of rationalism? Soviet society bears the indelible stamp of the long Russian past of feudal-bureaucratic rule, an absolutist rule of the mind as of the body. Of course, the Marxist teaching is not exempt from censure for the consequences of the Revolution. It should be added, however, that this teaching, Western in its main origins and holding a heavy charge of Judaeo-Christian ethics, has suffered a strange metamorphosis in its Muscovite captivity. And now, in its movement deeper into the East, it is seized upon, with all the fervor of native absolutism, by the backward, semi-mendicant intelligentsia of the Asian countries. This intelligentsia, untrained in habits of social responsibility and unformed in the traditions of humanist and rationalist thought, has converted Marxism into a dogma of nothing less than incendiary content. Its detachment from the West is virtually complete.

Rahv is (along with Delmore Schwartz) the protagonist of William Barrett's *The Truants,* the best of the many books about the *Partisan* circle. It may not be the most accurate or complete account, but it's the most literate, and its verdict on the whole enterprise—conveyed by the book's title—cuts deepest. With none of the rancor that commonly disfigures such criticism, with affection even, Barrett rebukes his younger self and his former comrades for intellectual irresponsibility and bad faith. Infatuated by seemingly "original and sweeping ideas," he writes, the contemporary American radical is prone to "conveniently forget the humbling conditions of his own existence"; in particular, that "his own continued existence as a dissenter depends on the survival of the United States as a free nation in a world going increasingly totalitarian." Like the makers of the French Revolution—those prototypical modern truants—the *Partisan* crowd were "literary intellectuals" who "loved large and sweeping abstractions," which blur ineradicable differences and intractable conflicts, thus making possible "the first step toward Gulag." Their radical skepticism led them—most poignantly the tough-minded Rahv, Barrett claims—into a terrifying nihilism, which they could only escape through unquestioning faith in a socialist utopia. Willfully, desperately, they blinded themselves to the most humbling and fundamental of moral facts, that "the truth about human nature . . . is very bad news for socialism."

No one should reject this diagnosis out of hand, at least when made as urbanely and charitably as it is in *The Truants*. But as Rahv would surely have pointed out, Barrett, like nearly all other religious critics of modernity, offers only warnings about skepticism, never reasons for belief. And as for Barrett's suggestion that totalitarianism in other countries renders searching criticism of one's own country frivolous, or that dissent somehow implies indifference to "the survival of the United States as free nation"—that is itself frivolous.

If the *Partisan Review* intellectuals are to be faulted, it must be for something homelier than nihilism or unpatriotism. It seems to me their moral imagination was simply a little stunted by their self-importance. "A generation of anticommunists wasted its talents in obsessive polemics," William Phillips lamented in *A Partisan View* (his own memoir, written partly in response to Barrett's). Not really wasted, of course; anticommunist polemics were necessary work. But there is a grain of truth in Phillips's remark, and it betokens a moral failing as much as a strategic misjudgment.

For it does appear, in hindsight, that liberal anticommunists might perhaps have spared just a little of the time they spent denouncing Stalinism and even Nazism—to which, after all, most American citizens and policymakers were already strongly opposed—in order to decry some equally catastrophic but more mundane evils, about which their compatriots were almost wholly ignorant or unconcerned. I mean the miseries of backwardness—the absence of clean water and clean air, of vaccines and mosquito netting, of disinfectants and nourishing food—which have killed more human beings in modern history than even the Holocaust and the Gulag. Unfortunately, these boring and pedestrian problems, however deadly, do not offer equally rich opportunities for the ideological virtuosity and polemical display that filled the pages of *Partisan Review.* Occasional editorials on this subject would not, of course, have had much effect on the perennial suffering of the invisible poor. But they would have placed the magazine's reputation for intellectual and moral seriousness on an even firmer footing than *A Partisan Century.*

12

THE DANDY

Dwight Macdonald

Why do we still care about the New York intellectuals? Partly, perhaps, because they embodied, conceivably for the last time in American history, a venerable modern ideal, practiced also by the *philosophes* and praised by Goethe and Marx: *vielseitigkeit,* or many-sidedness. Their versatility was astonishing. Their apparent mastery (or at any rate their tone of authority) in pronouncing on both culture and politics, and in relating one set of judgments to the other, now seems as attractive as it does unattainable. In the Age of Information, mastery even of a single field is an implausible aspiration, and casual authority over a whole range of them an anachronistic one.

Then, too, their pronouncements seemed to matter. To a sensitive moral imagination, all times are dark times, but the late 1930s and early 1940s have a special pathos. Rarely can so many catastrophes—global economic depression, world war, the Gulag, the Holocaust—have thronged a single decade. The need to make sense of these traumas was widely felt; and with so many people listening, even those tough-minded erstwhile historical materialists may be forgiven for forgetting about the irrelevance of radical ideas in a capitalist democracy—or, to put it another way, for taking themselves so seriously. One of them, Dwight Macdonald, took himself remarkably unseriously, even while taking radical ideas seriously long after most of his contemporaries had ceased to.

Macdonald was one of the few Ivy League, non-Jewish New York intellectuals. He went to Exeter, where he and two other students proclaimed themselves "dandies" and founded the Hedonists Club. There, and later at Yale, he annoyed his teachers by correcting their reasoning and grammar. After graduating, he went to work for another Yale man, Henry Luce, at *Fortune.* The college tie could not save Macdonald after he wrote a long piece harshly criticizing U.S. Steel for various misdeeds. This was not the magazine's mission, Luce informed him. Eventually he married and was supported (not at all lavishly) by his wife.

The New York intellectuals led fairly public lives, and in any case could be relied on to reveal one another's secrets, especially discreditable ones. So there are few surprises in Michael Wrezsin's *A Rebel in Defense of Tradition,* the first biography of Macdonald. He drank a lot, had a squeaky laugh, and drove recklessly; he was not the best of fathers; he occasionally—as when exercised by Rahv's or Phillips's subtleties—tossed off an anti-Semitic crack; and his late-life writer's block makes painful reading. But for the most part he was what he reads like: decency itself, universally liked even if not always (by truly serious people, that is) respected.

There are no major historical or interpretive novelties in Wrezsin's biography, either, though there are a few nuggets. His versions of the 1949 Waldorf-Astoria Conference—an international gathering to promote "world peace," organized by Communists and loudly denounced by anticommunists, including most of the New York intellectuals—as well as Macdonald's stint at *Encounter,* where his articles critical of America displeased the magazine's CIA funder, are full and entertaining. There are generous selections from Dwight's correspondence, most notably with Nicola Chiaromonte; and the New York intellectuals' summer frolics on Cape Cod are high comedy. But for all Wrezsin's thoroughness and judiciousness, Stephen Whitfield's much shorter *A Critical American* (1984) is still the best introduction (apart from Macdonald) to Macdonald.

Whatever they may have disagreed about (practically everything), the New York intellectuals seem to have been virtually unanimous in regarding Macdonald with exasperated condescension. He was "Yogi Macdonald" (Rahv and Phillips), a "sentimental dilettante" (James Burnham), "Bohemian . . . irresponsible" (Sidney Hook), "the 13th disciple" (Howe), a "kibitzer . . . thinks with his typewriter" (Paul Goodman), "has made a fetish of confusion and drift" (C. Wright Mills), a "truant" (William Barrett), a "dandy" (Hilton Kramer), a "boyish innocent . . . singularly lacking in self-consciousness" (Diana Trilling, 1957); "It was difficult to stay angry at him; he was too childlike, too seemingly innocent" (Diana Trilling, 1994). Even Trotsky chimed in: "Everyone has the right to be stupid on occasion, but Comrade Macdonald abuses the privilege."

Can so many and diverse eminences have been wrong? Yes, I think so. Turgenev once observed that "in politics, the honorable man will end by not knowing where to live." He might have added that such a man's less brave and imaginative contemporaries will mock his homelessness. The 1930s and 1940s confronted political critics with dilemmas to which one, perhaps the only, honest response was confusion and despair. Macdonald initially opposed American participation in World War II, believing that capitalist governments could not effectively prosecute the war without themselves veering toward fascism. His more dramatic predictions, at least, were mistaken and occasioned much sarcasm. But they proceeded from a sound intuition—that war is the health of the state—which his polemical opponents gave no evidence of sharing. This inchoate, global skepticism allowed Macdonald to perceive the Allies' criminal misconduct: the mass bombings of civilians, the insistence on unconditional surrender, the refusal of asylum to the Jews, and "the annihilation of all European underground movements against fascism and Nazism, which succeeded because it was the one of the very few items on which the Allied powers wholeheartedly agreed . . . [and] for which only now are we beginning to pay the full price" (this from Hannah Arendt's introduction to Macdonald's *Politics Past*). It was Macdonald and his fellow contributors to *Politics* who documented and denounced all these things and so in a small way redeemed the honor of American intellectuals, not the *Partisan Review* "realists." NSC 68, the existence of high-level State Department and Council on Foreign Relations planning groups that in effect designed the Pax Americana, and the evolution of huge, uncontrollable national security bureaucracies originating in this period also seem, in retrospect, to validate Macdonald's confused intuitions about the untrustworthiness of capitalist governments.

Macdonald's "negativism" also earned him a good deal of superior admonition. In "The Root Is Man" (1946) and elsewhere, he confessed his disenchantment with all the available forms of organized political action. (That essay prompted a young wise guy named Irving Howe to send *Politics* a six-thousand-word critique, which Macdonald published in full.) "What seems necessary," Macdonald wrote, after surveying in the preceding pages (and embracing in the previous decade) virtually every form of radical ideology, "is to encourage attitudes of disrespect, skepticism, ridicule towards the State and all authority, rather than to build up a competing authority." The only hope he could see, modest enough, "seems to be through symbolic individual actions, based on one person's insistence on his own values, and through the creation of small fraternal groups which will support such actions, keep alive a sense of our ultimate goals, and both act as a leavening in the dough of mass society and attract more and more of the alienated and frustrated members of that society."

It is difficult to understand why, except to the terminally tough-minded, any of this should have sounded frivolous, irresponsible, quietist, or defeatist. It's not as though there were practical alternatives, then or now. "Negativism" did not mean abandoning radical politics, just pruning it of empty pretensions and bad faith. It meant resisting the simplifying urgencies of war and Cold War, admitting one's impotence and uncertainty, sitting tight, listening. It required moral poise, a kind of ideological negative capability. It required genuine intellectual humility—rather than the mere profession of it, which is a very common article. Although his fellow New York intellectuals thought him wacky, others saw his floundering differently. Czeslaw Milosz, for one, paid tribute to Macdonald as a successor to "Thoreau, Whitman, and Melville . . . a specific American type—the completely free man, capable of making decisions at all times and about all things strictly according to his personal moral judgments."

But even at his most confused, discouraged, or doctrinaire, Macdonald criticized. He quotes Alexander Herzen on "two Russian liberals who made their peace with Czar Nicholas I: 'I shall be told that under the aegis of devotion to the Imperial power, the truth can be spoken more boldly. Why, then, did they not speak it?' So, too, with the critical supporters of the war—why, then, do they not criticize?" The same question might be asked of the New York intellectuals who teed off on Macdonald. *Politics* was read fervently in army camps and union halls across the country; and frivolous, irresponsible Yogi Macdonald more or less single-handedly launched the War on Poverty with "Our

Invisible Poor," his *New Yorker* essay on Michael Harrington' s *The Other America*. Altogether, Hook-Burnham-Rahv-Phillips-Kramer-Trilling disparaging Macdonald politically strikes me as no less implausible than, say, James Gould Cozzens ridiculing D. H. Lawrence or Mortimer J. Adler lecturing Wittgenstein.

From the 1950s on, Macdonald mainly occupied himself with what he called (borrowing T. S. Eliot's definition of the function of criticism) "the correction of taste." He became, as Stephen Whitfield put it, mid-century America's Mencken as well as its Bourne, slaying various middlebrow dragons such as the pseudo-populist third edition of Webster's dictionary, the vulgarized Revised Standard Version of the Bible, and the ineffably pompous University of Chicago Great Books project. He justified this flight from politics with an eloquent 1950 anti-manifesto:

> The scale of things is too big, the levers of power too far removed from people like us (and perhaps from people like Stalin and Truman), the mood of the general population, after generations of Pavlovian conditioning by industrialism, world wars, and state bureaucracies, too demoralized and apathetic to respond to our appeals. Even if we could make them with the old fervor and rationality. Which we can't. For fervor we now have routine moralizing; for reason, the old stock of antiquated abstractions. . . . The pacifist and socialist writings of today are to those of two generations ago as hay is to grass. Which is why I am no longer a pacifist, a socialist, or any kind of -ist.

But of course it was not really a flight from politics; it was a continuation of politics by other means. In the decades since Macdonald resigned as a revolutionist, systematic social theory, both liberal and radical, has lumbered around to an understanding of the strategic importance of mass culture and moral psychology; has begun to appreciate the ideological functions of cant and kitsch, among other mass-cultural phenomena. Though Macdonald theorized a bit himself (his 1953 essay "A Theory of Mass Culture" was fairly widely reprinted), he mostly went in for practical criticism, with significant effects on American intellectual hygiene.

Eventually he took to calling himself a "conservative radical"—partly, one suspects, to pull everyone's leg, but also because the standards he sought to apply to our culture, the strict standards of honest intellectual craftsmanship, are at once deeply conservative and deeply subversive. "To think clearly is a necessary first step towards political regeneration," Orwell wrote in "Politics and the English Language" (1946), "so that the fight against bad English is not frivolous and is not the exclusive concern of professional writers." Macdonald's career is an almost unimprovable gloss on Orwell's essay.

13

DEMOCRACY-PROOF

Robert Dahl

In *The Frozen Republic: How the Constitution Is Paralyzing Democracy* (1996), Daniel Lazare points out that the U.S. Constitution was adopted unconstitutionally. The Articles of Confederation, our first governing compact, contained a provision that any amendment would require the consent of all thirteen states. Yet the Articles were supplanted without unanimous consent of the states. That's because Article VII of the new Constitution provided that it would take effect if ratified by only nine of the thirteen states. Wasn't Article VII therefore in violation of the original governing document?

In *Federalist* 40, Madison dismissed this objection. It would be "absurd," he declared, to "subject the fate of twelve States to the perverseness or corruption of a thirteenth." Surely this was obvious to "every citizen who has felt for the wounded honor and prosperity of his country." End of discussion. So much for the original intention of those who framed the Articles of Confederation.

The new Constitution contained an equally "absurd" provision. According to Article V, "no State, without its Consent, shall be deprived of its equal Suffrage in the Senate." Each state, regardless of population, was to have two senators. As a result, two centuries later half the U.S. population sends eighteen senators to Washington while the other half sends eighty-two. Twenty senators represent 54 percent of the population; another twenty represent less than 3 percent. California gets two senators; the twenty least populous states, which combined have roughly the same number of people as California, get forty senators. Senators elected by 11 percent of the population can kill proposed legislation with a filibuster; senators elected by as little as 5 percent of the population can block a constitutional amendment. For two centuries this blatantly undemocratic institution—"perhaps the most unrepresentative legislative body in the world," Lazare observes—has survived without serious challenge, thanks partly to elite (especially slaveholder) self-interest and partly to popular Constitution-worship. But by the logic of *Federalist* 40, a people in earnest about equal representation for all, and therefore determined to reform the Senate, should not be obstructed.

The composition of the Senate is not the only undemocratic feature of the Constitution, as Robert Dahl reminds us in *How Democratic Is the American Constitution?* Of the others, the most flagrant is the Electoral College. There is nothing to be said for this institution. It has no other purpose or result than to frustrate equal representation for all citizens, and its effect on our political history has been calamitous. It was rejected several times at the Constitutional Convention until it slipped by on a last-minute vote. It has never functioned as intended, as a deliberative body. Within a dozen years it had caused a constitutional crisis (the deadlocked election of 1800). Several decades later, after another deadlocked election in 1876, Electoral College horse-trading resulted in the abandonment of federal efforts to enforce civil rights in the South. In five presidential elections, the candidate with the greatest number of popular votes was not chosen as president. Overwhelming majorities regularly tell pollsters that the Electoral College should be abolished. Seven hundred proposals to reform or abolish it have been introduced in the House, the most recent of which in 1989 passed with an 83 percent majority. As always, the Senate blocked any action.

How Democratic Is the American Constitution? is a short book, not only because Dahl is a masterly expositor but also because the case against Constitution-worship is not very difficult to make. To begin with, the early republic did not worship it. The Framers were a gifted and experienced group—though some, like Alexander Hamilton and Gouverneur Morris, were not particularly well disposed toward democracy. But divisions among them were sharp. Even Hamilton, for example, said that giving each state the same number of senators "shocks too much the ideas of justice and every human feeling." And some of the most eminent among them, such as Elbridge Gerry and Edmund Randolph, refused to sign or signed only with grave reservations. The debate in the country over ratification was extremely vigorous (see the two splendid Library of America volumes on the subject). The decision was not made by popular vote but by elected delegates, more than a third of whom voted against ratification. In short, our forebears did not in the least regard the Constitution as an inspired deliverance from heaven.

Moreover, there were some distinguished second thoughts. Conservatives endlessly cite Madison's *Federalist* 10 on the dangers of faction and the need to curb popular majorities. But as Dahl points out, Madison soon reconsidered. Within a few years he was writing in an anti-Federalist journal that "in every political society, parties are unavoidable" (a "natural offspring of Freedom," as he put it still later), and that political competition could be made fairer "by withholding unnecessary opportunities from a few to increase the inequality of property by an immoderate, and especially an unmerited, accumulation of riches," and "by the silent operation of the laws, which, without violating the rights of property, reduce extreme wealth towards a state of mediocrity and raise extreme indigence towards a state of comfort." Madison the radical!

Other democracies do not particularly admire our Constitution, at least to the extent of imitating it. In a chapter titled "The Constitution as a Model: An American Illusion," Dahl notes that "among the countries most comparable to the United States"—he lists twenty-two—"and where democratic institutions have long existed without breakdown, not one has adopted our American constitutional system." Our combination of an executive branch independent of the legislature, a "first-past-the-post" electoral system that practically rules out third parties and coalition governments, extensive judicial review of federal legislative enactments, and strong bicameralism with highly unequal representation in the upper chamber is unique.

So ours is an inefficient and undemocratic system. The Senate and the Electoral College merit no further discussion. First-past-the-post, or strictly majoritarian, elections are also plainly unfair. In theory, at least, a party that gained a one-vote plurality in every election district would win 100 percent of the seats in the legislature—an obvious absurdity. In practice, voters know that a vote for any except the two major parties is likely to be "wasted," producing no representation. This is, of course, convenient for the two major parties, but it leaves some (possibly many) voters unrepresented. A proportional system in which each party's legislative membership corresponds to its percentage of votes received would reflect the popular will more accurately without, Dahl contends, any loss of effectiveness. All the established democracies except Canada and (for the time being) the United Kingdom have a proportional, or "consensus," system rather than a majoritarian one.

The steady growth of presidential powers is also an American exception, Dahl contends. Actually, the U.S. government was not designed to have such a powerful chief executive. For all the talk then and now about the separation of powers, Dahl writes, those who framed and ratified the Constitution believed that "the only legitimate representative of the popular will was the Congress, not the president." The "myth of the presidential mandate" is a subsequent creation. Policy—including foreign policy—was (is) supposed to issue from the deliberations of a body of elected lawmakers, not from one elected chief administrator in consultation with his appointees. No other mature democracy, Dahl points out, has a "single popularly elected chief executive with important constitutional powers."

Regardless, the main question remains: Does our constitutional system at least work well for us? Dahl is skeptical, though he has to acknowledge the uncertain relevance of political arrangements to social and economic indicators, as well as the difficulty of comparing countries that differ in size and homogeneity. There's not much data in the book, although its references are helpful on this score. From the work of Arend Lijphart (former president of the American Political Science Association, as is Dahl) and other social scientists, it is clear, at any rate, that majoritarian democracies such as ours do not generally outperform consensus democracies on such measures as voter satisfaction, accountability, macroeconomic management, or the control of violence.

In any case, Dahl has not come to bury the Constitution, only to undermine complacency about it. Besides, as he acknowledges in the book's sobering conclusion, there's not much we can do. The Constitution is virtually democracy-proof. A Supreme Court that promulgates and upholds a *Buckley v. Valeo* (not to mention a *Bush v. Gore*) is all too likely to find constitutional problems with any serious move in the direction of popular sovereignty.

It is hard to imagine a Congress unified and determined enough to reassert its primacy over the Executive Branch. And however indefensible, the Senate in its present form is here to stay.

For all these reasons, Dahl avowed a "measured pessimism" about the prospects for a more democratic political system anytime soon. The only hope—a long-term one—is to help along the evolution of a more democratic political culture. How? By trying to "reduce the vast inequalities in the existing distribution of political resources." I presume that by "resources" he means information, experience, and money. Unfortunately, this intriguing suggestion comes in the book's penultimate paragraph and receives no elaboration. That is disappointing; but then Dahl spent much of his career elaborating it in other books, many of them as valuable as this one.

During that long career, Dahl received nearly every accolade for which a political scientist is eligible. I can't forbear adding my mite of praise to the heap. Dahl's work seems to me an admirable, even inspiring blend of normative and analytical, citizenly and scholarly, generous and disinterested. *How Democratic Is the American Constitution?*, along with his other books, such as *Democracy and Its Critics* and *A Preface to Economic Democracy,* will continue for quite a while to remind the rest of us, gently but persistently, that our professed ideal of democratic equality is a good deal more demanding than we seem to have noticed.

14

THE LOGIC OF MASS DESTRUCTION

John Dower

In 1937, as part of its assault on China, the Japanese Imperial Army began bombing Chinese cities. The world erupted in protest, led by the United States. In September of that year, the State Department declared that "any general bombing of an extensive area wherein there resides a large population engaged in peaceful pursuits is unwarranted and contrary to principles of law and humanity." The next month, in his well-known "Quarantine Speech," Franklin Roosevelt also condemned the Japanese assault, charging that "civilians, including vast numbers of women and children, are being ruthlessly murdered with bombs from the air." In June of the following year, referring to both the Japanese in China and the Germans in Spain, the State Department denounced the "inhuman bombing of civilian populations."

When war broke out in Europe in September 1939, Roosevelt immediately dispatched an impassioned public letter to the belligerents, calling on them to refrain from "inhuman barbarism" of this kind. "The ruthless bombing from the air of civilians in unfortified centers of population . . . during the past few years, which has resulted in the maiming and death of thousands of defenseless men, women, and children, has sickened the hearts of every civilized man and woman, and has profoundly shaken the conscience of humanity."

Britain joined in. In 1939, after the Germans bombed Warsaw, the Foreign Office denounced "these inhuman methods" and promised never to indulge in them: "His Majesty's Government have made it clear that it is no part of their policy to bomb nonmilitary objectives, no matter what the policy of the German Government may be." Even Churchill claimed to agree, calling the bombing of cities "a new and odious form of attack." Roosevelt returned to the subject in 1940, recalling with pride that "the United States has consistently taken the lead in urging that this inhuman practice be prohibited."

As John Dower observed in *War Without Mercy* (1986), his magnificent study of World War II in the Pacific, these eloquent words and earnest promises counted for very little:

> By 1942 . . . the Royal Air Force and U.S. Army Air Forces became the apostles of strategic bombing and proceeded to perfect the techniques of massive urban destruction with incendiary bombs. . . . British and American planners had, in fact, secretly agreed on the desirability of bombing enemy cities many months before Pearl Harbor.

By summer 1942, the RAF began using incendiaries in dense "area" bombings of German cities "to destroy civilian morale." Even before Pearl Harbor, General George Marshall, the U.S. Army's chief of staff, demanded plans for "general incendiary attacks to burn up the wood and paper structures of the densely populated Japanese cities." Churchill, the eloquent brute, frequently called for grinding the Japanese to powder and reducing their cities to ash.

The toll of British and American "strategic" bombing (as this form of warfare was antiseptically called) was indeed gruesome. A half-million German civilians were killed and 7.5 million rendered homeless. At least 400,000 Japanese civilians were killed (counting the victims of Hiroshima and Nagasaki), and 66 Japanese cities were completely destroyed. Most of the bombing was not strictly necessary—it occurred after the military tide had turned and Allied victory was no longer in doubt. Nor was there any pretense, at least internally, that the primary targets of the bombing were military: soldiers, war materiel, or weapons factories. The acknowledged purpose was to hasten the end of the war by "breaking the morale" of the civilian population. In a word, terror.

Naturally, officials disliked that word. When the Associated Press reported that the Allies had decided "to adopt deliberate terror bombing of German cities as a ruthless expedient to hasten Hitler's doom," British officials objected and the report was suppressed. Churchill sent a memo to his generals asking whether the "bombing of German cities simply for the sake of increasing the terror, though under other pretexts, should be reviewed"—not for humanitarian reasons, of course, but because "we may not, for instance, be able to get housing materials out of Germany for our own needs"—and meekly proposed "more precise concentration upon military objectives . . . rather than on mere acts of terror and wanton destruction, however impressive." The generals were annoyed by this momentary lapse into candor, however secret, so Churchill obligingly withdrew his memo. If a mid-twentieth-century Wikileaks had published this memo, posterity might have been spared a great deal of misplaced reverence for Churchill, as well as a great deal of Western self-righteousness about "terrorism."

Why did Allied decision-makers disregard their frequently and (for the most part) sincerely professed beliefs about terror bombing? And why, sixty years after Japan launched its disastrous war of choice against the United States with a surprise attack, did the United States respond to another surprise attack by launching its own disastrous war of choice in Iraq? As a historian of the Pacific War and the postwar occupation (his book about the latter, *Embracing Defeat*, won the Pulitzer and Bancroft Prizes and the National Book Award) and an appalled citizen during the Iraq War, Dower could not help thinking comparatively about the two episodes. The result is *Cultures of War: Pearl Harbor/Hiroshima/9-11/Iraq* (2011), an extraordinarily rich and insightful study of "some of the broader themes and morbidities of our times and our modern and contemporary wars."

Perhaps the most salient feature of the culture of war is chauvinism, or irrational belief in the superiority of one's own group. *War Without Mercy* was a stark, graphically illustrated, often stomach-turning record of both American and Japanese race hatred during World War II. Apparently something was learned from that ugly history, and Muslim-hatred in the United States after 9/11 was far more muted. But Dower finds correspondences nonetheless. The savage air assault on Japanese cities and the catastrophic U.N. (essentially U.S.) sanctions against Iraq in the 1990s would not, Dower suggests, have been perpetrated against whites. (The British bombing of German civilians may count somewhat against this suggestion.)

Race prejudice had more subtle effects as well. The United States had a great deal of evidence that the Japanese were planning to open hostilities with a surprise attack, and many indications pointed to Pearl Harbor. Postwar congressional inquiries unearthed the usual interdepartmental turf battles and unwillingness to share information. But there was something else. Despite a clear warning from Washington ten days before Pearl

Harbor that an attack somewhere in the Pacific was imminent, virtually the entire U.S. fleet was left in port, riding peacefully at anchor. Pressed afterwards about this, the commanding admiral admitted: "All right . . . I'll give you your answer—I never thought those little yellow sons-of-bitches could pull off such an attack, so far from Japan."

What Dower calls "the 'little yellow men' mindset" operated before 9/11 as well. Despite nearly forty warnings that an attack by al-Qaeda somewhere in the United States was being planned, policymakers could not believe, according to the CIA's chief Bin-Laden watcher, that "a polyglot bunch of Arabs wearing robes, sporting scraggly beards, and squatting around campfires in Afghan deserts and mountains could pose a mortal threat to the United States." Dower says comparatively little about the Vietnam War, but it too would seem to exemplify the "little yellow men" mindset, with the accompanying "psychological unpreparedness, prejudices and preconceptions, gross underestimation of intentions and capabilities," as well as horrendous violence against nonwhite populations, of a kind that one cannot imagine being loosed on people more like us.

Three generations; three humiliating and costly miscalculations; three waves of mass death inflicted in retribution on non-Western civilians, including—perhaps even mostly—women and children. There is evidently something distinctive about the American culture of war.

Inability to imagine the sufferings of others is not a uniquely American failing, however; and anyway, there was another dynamic at work in these cases. Dower calls it "the irresistible logic of mass destruction." In a riveting analysis of the decision to drop the atomic bomb, he shows how, whether militarily necessary or not (the official justification, that fanatical Japanese resistance would have forced an even more costly invasion, is widely contested), use of the bomb was bureaucratically inevitable. The arguments against—simple decency, and setting an example of restraint for the postwar world—hardly counted against the powerful incentives in favor: reluctance to resort to patient diplomacy rather than overwhelming force; unwillingness to give up the demand for Japan's unconditional surrender; intimidating the Soviet Union; fear that unless the bomb was used, Republicans would attack the Truman administration for being "soft" and for wasting taxpayers' money; and, most illogically, that the effects of the bomb would be so horrible that future wars would be unthinkable.

Similar pathologies of crackpot realism, partisan politics, bureaucratic inertia, technological fantasy, and rank greed appeared during the Bush administration's headlong war and stumbling occupation in Iraq. The resort to force was overdetermined. For one thing, to have complied with international law would have meant acknowledging and reinforcing the authority of international law, with its constraints on national sovereignty. No American administration or Congress would do this. Conservatives simply do not believe in the legitimacy of international law when its application would be inconvenient. Liberals are invariably paralyzed by fear of being portrayed as weak. And both sides agree on the necessity of preserving American "credibility," the belief of others in America's willingness to use force, which might be undermined by our betraying any scruples about legality.

For another thing, people with fancy gadgets like to play with them. As Madeleine Albright complained to Colin Powell: "What's the point of having this superb military you're always talking about, if we can't use it?" They need to know whether the gadgets work; they need to justify having spent so much of other people's money on the gadgets; and the people who make the gadgets (and profit hugely from them) want to sell new gadgets and so offer enormous inducements in the form of campaign contributions and lucrative jobs and consultancies to military and civilian decision-makers who make the decisions that make those profits possible.

A universal feature of war culture is the pressure to conform, the drive toward unity of purpose and belief. In emergencies, all governments suppress dissent among their citizens and all bureaucracies discourage independent thinking among their members. This tendency toward groupthink is a leitmotif of *Cultures of War*. Japan's decision to make war on the richer, more populous United States appears, in retrospect, suicidal. But once the decision was made, the emperor and the senior militarists relentlessly promoted an almost mystical cult of national unity. In the run-up toward invading Iraq, the factitious doctrine of the "unitary executive" was employed to cloak what was essentially, according to Secretary of State Powell's chief of staff, "a cabal between the vice president of the United States, Richard Cheney, and the secretary of defense, Donald Rumsfeld." The unconvinced were marginalized (like Powell) or forced out (like the chairman of the Joint Chiefs).

The Japanese military could not, or at any rate did not, think realistically about the prospect of protracted war with the more powerful United States. The Cheney-Rumsfeld "cabal" did not, and perhaps could not, think realistically about the aftermath of defeating Saddam. With a dazzling show of historical incomprehension, they invoked the democratization of Japan under the post–World War II occupation as a precedent for "liberated" Iraq, while at the same time emphatically disavowing the methods used in the earlier occupation: "nation-building." As Dower shows in a detailed comparison of the two episodes, the occupation of Iraq was a disaster not merely because, as nearly everyone outside the cabal recognized, Japan was a far more integrated society than Iraq, but also because the complex interagency coordination during the former occupation was hardly possible for an administration that distrusted government agencies in principle and outsourced basic functions to unaccountable private contractors.

On the last page of *Cultures of War,* having brought before us a long, disheartening parade of arrogance, prejudice, and misjudgment and vividly portrayed their lethal consequences for millions of innocent people over the last eighty years or so, Dower quotes a sentence that sounds like an epitaph for this sorry history: "The system filters out the thoughtful and replaces them with the faithful." In fact, that judgment, though it exactly fits the cultures of war Dower has analyzed so painstakingly, was uttered in and about a different culture. Unexpectedly, the last few pages of the book are devoted to the culture of the financial system that collapsed late in the last decade, and the quoted sentence comes from an anonymous financial analyst explaining in the *Economist* what made that catastrophe inevitable.

It is a fine narrative stroke: to show in a few pages how the two apparently unrelated calamities that have brought this seemingly invincible superpower low were produced by the same dysfunction, and to have found a sentence that describes that dysfunction perfectly: *The system filters out the thoughtful and replaces them with the faithful.* It has to: in war and business, whenever conflict and competition are fierce, dissent is costly and inefficient.

And this, finally, allows for a tragic perspective on what had seemed only moral and intellectual disgrace. For it is virtually the nature of a "system" to isolate and disable challenges to its fundamental assumptions. When the machine is racing furiously, doubts are just so much sand in the gears. Faith and thought; fervor and detachment; loyalty and criticism; united hearts and independent minds: can any system accommodate both? And yet, wars must be won; and wars, like all other vast undertakings, require vast systems to carry them out.

It is, Dower concludes stoically, "highly uncertain" whether this paradox can be resolved, whether humankind can ever "truly control and transcend" its "deeper psychological and institutional pathologies." The truth will make us free, Jesus said. But what if, as Jack Nicholson's character informed the rest of us at the end of *A Few Good Men,* we can't handle the truth?

15

FAREWELL, HITCH

Christopher Hitchens

If a Hall of Fame were established for contemporary book reviewers (and why not?—there's one for ad executives, real estate salesmen, and probably porn stars), Christopher Hitchens would very likely be its second inductee. (James Wood, of course, would be the first.) About an amazing range of literary and political figures—Proust, Joyce, Borges, Byron, Bellow, Orhan Pamuk, Tom Paine, Trotsky, Churchill, Conor Cruise O'Brien, Israel Shahak, and a hundred others—he has supplied the basic information, limned the relevant controversies, hazarded an original perception or two, and bestowed half a dozen fine phrases, causing between fifteen and forty-five minutes of reading time to pass entirely unnoticed. His very frequent political columns have occasionally seemed tossed off, it's true; but his books about Cyprus, the Palestinians, the British monarchy, and the Elgin marbles are seriously argued. He lives in Washington and is said to be very fond of fancy parties, but he has famously insulted and called for the incarceration of a sitting president and a ubiquitously befriended diplomat and Nobel laureate. And he gets to appear on all those fatuously self-important TV talk shows without wearing a tie. How can you not admire someone like that?

Actually, it's not so hard. All the someone in question has to do is begin thinking differently from me about a few important matters, and in no time I find that his qualities have subtly metamorphosed. His abundance of colorful anecdotes now looks like incessant and ingenious self-promotion. His marvelous copiousness and fluency sound like mere mellifluous facility and mechanical prolixity. A prose style I thought deliciously suave and sinuous I now find preening and over-elaborate. His fearless cheekiness has become truculent bravado; his name-dropping has gone from endearing foible to excruciating tic; his extraordinary dialectical agility seems like resourceful and unscrupulous sophistry; his entertaining literary asides like garrulousness and vulgar display; his bracing contrariness, tiresome perversity. Strange, this alteration of perspective; and even stranger, I sometimes think that if he changed his opinions again and agreed with me, all his qualities would once more reverse polarity and appear in their original splendor. A very instructive experience, epistemologically speaking.

Then again, it's not just his changing his mind that's got my goat. His hero and mine, Dwight Macdonald, did that often enough. But one may do it gracefully or gracelessly. Even when all the provocations Hitchens has recently endured are acknowledged (especially the not-infrequent hint that booze has befogged his brain), they don't excuse his zeal not merely to correct his former comrades but to bait, ridicule, and occasionally slander them, caricaturing their arguments and questioning their good faith. Not having formerly recognized a truth ought to make you more patient, not less, with people who do not recognize it yet; and less certain, not more, that whoever you currently disagree with is contemptibly benighted. Besides, if you must discharge such large quantities of remonstrance and sarcasm, shouldn't you consider saving a bit more of them for your disagreements (he must still have some, though they're less and less frequently voiced these days) with those who control the three branches of government and own the media and other means of production?

Hitchens might want to insist, contrarily, that although he has changed his allies, he has not changed his opinions. Unlike, say, David Horowitz, he still believes that the Cold War was an inter-imperial rivalry, that the Vietnam War was immoral, that the overthrow of Allende was infamous, and that American support for Mobutu, Suharto, the Greek colonels, the Guatemalan and Salvadoran generals, the Shah of Iran, and the Israeli dispossession of Palestinians was and is indefensible. He still believes in progressive taxation, the New Deal, vigilant environmental, occupational-safety, and consumer-protection regulation, unions (or some form of worker self-organization), and in general, firm and constant opposition to the very frequent efforts of the rich and their agents to grind the faces of the poor. It's just that he now cordially despises most of the other people who actively proclaim or advocate these things. Why?

It began with the Balkan wars. Hitchens supported NATO intervention, in particular the bombing of Serbia in March 1999. Some of his opponents on the left argued that NATO gave up too easily on (or indeed sabotaged) diplomacy, was wrong not to seek UN authorization to use force, and may have precipitated a humanitarian catastrophe (the flight and deportation of hundreds of thousands of Kosovar Albanians after the bombing began) that might not otherwise have occurred. Hitchens replied furiously—though not, by and large, to these arguments; rather, to other ones, either nonexistent or easier to refute, such as opposition "in principle in any case to any intervention," or insistence that in view of its imperialist past the United States could never in any circumstances be a force for good. His most reflective comments did seem to take his opponents' point: "Skeptical though one ought to be about things like the reliance of NATO on air power and the domination of the UN by the nuclear states, the 'double standard' may still be made to operate against itself." But such moments were few.

After 9/11, reflectiveness and skepticism went on holiday from his political writing. Logic and good manners also frequently called in sick. "Embattled" is too mild a description of his state of mind; it's been inflamed. Those who returned different answers than he did to the questions "Why did 9/11 happen?" and "What should we do about it?" were not to be taken seriously. They were Osama's useful idiots, "soft on crime and soft on fascism," their thinking "utterly rotten to its very core."

What provoked that last epithet was a suggestion that "Bin Laden could not get volunteers to stuff envelopes if Israel had withdrawn from Jerusalem . . . and the US stopped the sanctions and bombing of Iraq." Hitchens went ballistic. The hapless fool who wrote this, he thundered, either "knows what was in the minds of the murderers," in which case "it is his solemn responsibility to inform us of the source of his information, and also to share it with the authorities," or else he doesn't know, in which case it is "rash" and "indecent" to speculate.

Hitchens proceeded to speculate. Al-Qaeda, like their allies the Taliban, aim first "to bring their own societies under the reign of the most pitiless and inflexible declension of shari'a law," and then, since they regard all unbelievers as "fit only for slaughter and contempt," they will seek to "spread the contagion and visit hell upon the unrighteous." Talk of "Muslim grievances" is rubbish; al-Qaeda's only grievance is that they have not yet enslaved the whole world. Jihad means, simply, the obligatory conquest or destruction of everything outside Islam.

Hitchens has asserted this insistently: for him, to talk about "grievances expressed by the people of the Middle East" in connection with 9/11 is obscene. Bin-Laden and al-Qaeda are "medieval fanatics"; they "wish us ill"; no more need be said. To presume to "lend an ear to the suppressed and distorted cry for help that comes, not from the victims, but from the perpetrators" just amounts to "rationalizing" terror. Denouncing one's opponents as soft on terror has been the first or last resort of many scoundrels in the political debates of the last few decades in America. (Actually, it's such a dubious tactic that even the scoundrels don't usually get further than broad hints.) One is surprised to see Hitchens doing it. But even more important: Is he right about al-Qaeda? Does he know "what was in the minds of the murderers"?

In *Imperial Hubris* veteran CIA analyst Michael Scheuer, former head of the Agency's al-Qaeda task force, writes:

> Bin Laden and most militant Islamists [are] motivated by . . . their hatred for a few, specific US policies and actions they believe are damaging—and threatening to destroy—the things they love. Theirs is a war against a specific target and for specific, limited purposes. While they will use whatever weapon comes to hand—including weapons of mass destruction—their goal is not to wipe out our secular democracy, but to deter us by military means from attacking the things they love. Bin Laden et al are not eternal warriors; there is no evidence that they are fighting for fighting's sake, or that they would be lost for things to do without a war to wage. . . .
>
> To understand the perspective of the [myriad] supporters of Bin Laden, we must accept that there are many Muslims in the world who believe that US foreign policy is irretrievably biased in favor of Israel, trigger happy in attacking the poor and ill-defended Muslim countries, Sudan, Iraq, Afghanistan, Somalia, and so forth; rapacious in controlling and consuming the Islamic

> world's energy resources; blasphemous in allowing Israel to occupy Jerusalem and US troops to be based in Saudi Arabia; and hypocritical and cruel in its denial of Palestinian rights, use of economic sanctions against the Muslim people of Iraq, and support for the Muslim world's absolutist kings and dictators.

For holding essentially these views about al-Qaeda's motives, Hitchens's leftist opponents were labeled apologists, rationalizers, and eager excusers of terror. A few moments' reflection and/or a few grains of knowledge would have saved Hitchens from indulging in these slurs, so damaging to his reputation for fairness and urbanity (insofar, that is, as anyone cares about slanders against leftists). But although his prose has (mostly) retained its poise since 9/11, his thinking has not.

On and on Hitchens's polemics against the left have raged, a tempest of inaccuracy, illogic, and malice. Naomi Klein opines that since most Iraqis agree with the insurgents at least in wanting an end to the occupation, the United States should end it. Without disputing her premise, Hitchens condemns her "nasty, stupid" conclusion as an "endorsement of jihad" and "applause for the holy warriors" and "swooning support for theocratic fascism." He jeers repeatedly at the antiwar left for having predicted that Saddam would use WMD against a U.S. invasion, conveniently forgetting that what the left actually predicted was that if, as the administration insisted (without evidence), Saddam had WMD, then the most likely scenario for their use was against a U.S. invasion. And that was true. He fiercely ridicules the antiwar argument that there was no contact and no sympathy between Saddam and al-Qaeda—only that wasn't the argument. The argument was that it was so unlikely Saddam would entrust weapons of mass destruction to al-Qaeda or any other uncontrollable agent that the United States was not justified in invading Iraq in order to prevent it. And that was true too. He continually deplores left-wing "isolationism," even though his opponents are, on the contrary, trying to remind Americans that the U.N. Charter is the most solemn international agreement ever made ("the first universal social contract," Hitchens's friend Erskine Childers once observed), embodying the deep, desperate hope of the weaker nations that the stronger ones will someday submit themselves consistently to the rule of law, while the Bush administration is—not reluctantly but purposefully—undermining it. "The antiwar left," Hitchens scoffs, "used to demand the lifting of sanctions without conditions, which would only have gratified Saddam Hussein and his sons and allowed them to re-arm." Not quite true—all leftists agreed that import restrictions on military materials were justified. But more important, a gratified Saddam would not have been the "only" result of ending sanctions. Besides killing hundreds of thousands, the sanctions left Iraqi society helpless, disorganized, and dependent on the state, thus blocking the most likely and legitimate path to regime change—the path followed in Romania, Haiti, Indonesia, South Korea, the Philippines, and other dictatorships, all of them more broadly based, and all (except South Korea) ruling poorer and less-educated societies, than pre-sanctions Iraq. Hitchens seems to have gotten the idea somewhere that the antiwar left doesn't care every damned bit as much as he and the neocons do about the sufferings of Iraqis.

About any sufferings that cannot serve as a pretext for American military intervention, moreover, Hitchens appears to have stopped caring. He is "a single-issue person at present," he wrote in endorsing President Bush for reelection. This issue, compared with which everything else is "not even in second or third place," is "the tenacious and unapologetic defense of civilized societies against the intensifying menace of clerical barbarism." The invasion of Iraq is a justified act of self-defense against clerical barbarism, and the Bush administration is to be praised and supported for undertaking it.

A lot of suffering people would disagree, I think—and not just the perennial ones, betrayed by every U.S. administration: the tens of millions who die annually for lack of clean water, cheap vaccines, mosquito nets, or another thousand daily calories while the United States devotes 0.2 percent of its GDP to international aid (one-thirtieth of its military budget and less than one-tenth the cost so far of invading Iraq). These unfortunates are not part of "civilized society under attack from clerical barbarism," so they're out of luck. No, I mean a new class of suffering people, specifically attributable to the new tenacious and unapologetic compassionate conservatism. From its first days in office the Bush administration has made clear its determination to reverse as much as possible of the modest progress made in the twentieth century toward public provision for the unfortunate, public encouragement of worker, consumer, and neighborhood self-organization, public influence on the daily operation of government and access to the record of its activities, public protection of the commons, and public restraint of concentrated financial and corporate power. And from the first weeks after 9/11, as Paul Krugman and many others have documented, the administration has found ways to take advantage of that atrocity to achieve its fundamental goals. The results, now and in the future, of this return to unfettered, predatory capitalism have been and will be a truly vast amount of suffering. Enough, one would think, to be worth Hitchens's mentioning in the second or third place, after the dangers of clerical barbarism. Not a word, however. But perhaps he is whispering a few words about these matters in the ear of the "bleeding heart" (Hitchens's description) Paul Wolfowitz and his other newly adopted neoconservative allies.

From Hitchens, this silence about Republican depredations is very peculiar. So is another silence. The South African critic and historian R. W. Johnson once alluded to George Orwell's "simple detestation of untruth." Hitchens was once thought (and not only by me) to feel the same way. *No One Left to Lie To,* his indignant critique of Bill Clinton's "contemptible evasions" about his sexual predations and even more contemptible efforts to intimidate potential accusers, convinced many of us that Clinton should have resigned and faced criminal prosecution or at least been served with a sealed indictment at the end of his second term. It's a short book, though, with only 103 pages of text. You would need more than that just for a preface to an adequate critique of the lies of the Bush administration. As the journalist Paul Waldman has remarked: "Bush tells more lies about policy in a week than Bill Clinton did in eight years." He has lied about taxes, budgets, and deficits; about employment statistics; about veterans' benefits; about the Social Security trust fund and the costs of privatization; about climate change; about environmental policy; about oil drilling in the Arctic; about the California electricity crisis; about stem-cell research; about Enron and Harken; about the Florida recount process in November 2000; about his National Guard service and his record as governor of Texas; and about most of his political opponents. And then there are his lies about Iraq. The Bush administration is the most ambitiously and skillfully dishonest pack of liars as American history has seen. And since 9/11, Hitchens has never said a mumbling world about it.

Why? What accounts for Hitchens's astonishing loss of moral and intellectual balance? I can only guess. Anyone intelligent enough to understand that there are deep institutional and structural constraints on the behavior of states will also understand how difficult it is to budge those constraints and produce a fundamental change in policy. To make the United States an effective democracy—to shift control over the state from the centers of financial and industrial power, now global in reach, to broadly based, self-financed and self-governing groups of active citizens with only average resources—will take several generations, at least. This is a daunting prospect for just about anyone.

For someone of Hitchens's generous and romantic temperament, it is potentially demoralizing. The temptation to believe that this long, slow process could be speeded up if only he could find and ally himself with a faction of sympathetic souls close to the seat of executive power who really understood—the neoconservatives, the only ones, Hitchens has written, willing to take "the radical risk of regime change"—must have been overpowering.

And why not? It is hardly dishonorable to try to influence even arbitrary, undemocratic power in a more humane direction. Hitchens has rebuked the American left for its supposedly intransigent refusal to consider supporting the American government in any military undertaking "unless it had done everything right, and done it for everybody." He is mistaken. Here is Noam Chomsky, at the end of a lengthy essay on humanitarian intervention:

> The conclusions that a rational observer will draw about [the probable motives of] US-led "humanitarian intervention" do not answer the question whether such intervention should nevertheless be undertaken. That is a separate matter, to be faced without illusions about our unique nobility. We can, in short, ask whether the pursuit of self-interest might happen to benefit others in particular cases, or whether unremitting public pressure might overcome the demands of the principal architects of policy and the interests they serve.

I think this is exactly right. It was as plain as day to me that the Bush administration's chief purposes in invading Iraq were: to establish a commanding military presence in the region where the most important natural resource in the world is located; to turn a large and potentially rich country into a virtually unregulated investors' paradise; to impress the rest of the world once again with America's insuperable lead in military technology; to exploit the near-universal hatred of Saddam to legitimize (by establishing a precedent for) the doctrine of unilateral American military intervention expounded in the National Security Strategy Document of September 2002; and to unify the electorate behind an administration that was making a hash of the economy and the environment in order to reward its campaign contributors. Still, this is not why I opposed the war. If I had not also believed that the invasion would strike a sledgehammer blow at most of the world's fragile hopes for international order and the rule of law, I might have calculated that, whatever the government's motives, the potentially huge expenditure of lives and money it contemplated would be better employed in removing Saddam than in, say, providing clean water, cheap vaccines, mosquito nets, et cetera to the world's wretched invisibles, and so saving tens of millions of lives. Not likely, but it would have been a decision based on calculation rather than principle.

Even at their easiest, such calculations are excruciating. Weighing immediate costs and benefits is hard enough; figuring in the effects of setting a good or bad precedent, though often just as important, is devilishly hard. The conscientious have always struggled with these difficulties, and sometimes lost patience with them. Randolph Bourne, criticizing the *New Republic* liberals of his era for supporting America's entry into World War I, wondered in his great essay "War and the Intellectuals"

> whether realism is always a stern and intelligent grappling with realities. May it not sometimes be a mere surrender to the actual, an abdication of the ideal through a sheer fatigue from intellectual suspense? . . .

> With how many of the acceptors of war has it been mostly a dread of intellectual suspense? It is a mistake to suppose that intellectuality makes for suspended judgments. The intellect craves certitude. It takes effort to keep it supple and pliable. In a time of danger and disaster we jump desperately for some dogma to cling to. The time comes, if we try to hold out, when our nerves are sick with fatigue, and we seize in a great healing wave of release some doctrine that can be immediately translated into action.

Compare Hitchens's widely quoted response to 9/11: "I felt a kind of exhilaration . . . at last, a war of everything I loved against everything I hated." More recently, in a *Nation* article last November, "Why I'm (Slightly) for Bush," he testified again to the therapeutic value of his new commitment: "Myself, I have made my own escape from your self-imposed quandary. Believe me when I say . . . the relief is unbelievable." I believe him.

Will Hitchens ever regain his moral and intellectual balance? Near the end of his Bush endorsement, Hitchens defiantly assures his former *Nation* readers that "once you have done it"—abandoned cowardly and equivocating left-wing "isolationism" and made common cause with neoconservatives in their "willingness to risk a dangerous confrontation with an untenable and indefensible status quo"—there is "no going back." Well, going back wouldn't be easy. After heavy-handedly insulting so many former friends, misrepresenting their positions and motives, and generally making an egregious ass of himself, it would require immense, almost inconceivable courage for Hitchens to acknowledge that he went too far; that his appreciation of the sources and dangers of Islamic terrorism was neither wholly accurate nor, to the extent it was accurate, exceptional; that he was mistaken about the purposes and likely effects of the strategy he associated himself with and preached so sulfurously; and that there is no honorable alternative to—no "relief" to be had from—the frustrations of always keeping the conventional wisdom at arm's length and speaking up instead for principles that have as yet no powerful constituents. But it would be right.

16

CORRUPTION, CRUELTY, CANT

Seymour Hersh on Henry Kissinger

In *Lives of the Emperors* Suetonius records Nero's obsession with artistic pre-eminence:

> His jealousy of rivals, and his dread of those who were to sit in judgment on his performance, could scarcely be believed. Though outwardly gracious and charming to his colleagues, he abused them behind their backs and sometimes even insulted them to their faces. . . . He divided his attendants into claques to learn various methods of applause and provide it liberally whenever he sang; [and] whether he offered people his friendship or showed them his displeasure depended on how vigorously or how feebly they had applauded him. . . . After every performance he would address his auditors politely, saying that he had done his best and the decision was now up to them and to Fortune. But they, being sensible people, knew better than to let Fortune have anything to do with it.

That was in AD 68. Mutatis mutandis, it sounds remarkably like the meeting room of the National Security Council circa AD

1969, if one may believe Seymour Hersh's *The Price of Power: Kissinger in the Nixon White House* (1983).

Like his patrician predecessor, ace investigative reporter Hersh has fashioned, from the palace intrigues of a mighty empire, an epic of personal squalor. The theme of this epic—the price of Kissinger's vast bureaucratic power—is subservience: our hero's utter, abject subservience to the foul-mouthed, mean-spirited, paranoid megalomaniac who was the 37th president of the United States; and the demeaning subservience that Kissinger in turn required of his own subordinates. The payoff for all his subservience was Kissinger's unprecedented dominance of the foreign-policy bureaucracy. To rule, says an ancient maxim, one must know how to obey. In the Nixon White House, this apparently became: To bully, one must know how to fawn.

The Price of Power is a sprawling, hybrid book, not precisely a history or a biography or a work of social criticism. It is not primarily concerned with analyzing or evaluating American foreign policy, whose roots and goals were fundamentally the same during the Nixon era as before and since. Nor is the book solely an attempt at demythologizing Kissinger, welcome and necessary though that effort may be. It is a study of the shaping—and corruption—of policy by personality.

According to Hersh, Nixon entered the White House determined to centralize foreign-policy decision-making in his own hands. He found a willing tool in Kissinger, whose position as National Security Adviser was only as powerful as the president allowed. Together they rigged the decision-making process: cutting out the State and Defense Departments from the normal flow of information and debate; setting up committees chaired by Nixon or Kissinger that excluded or downgraded input from State and Defense; creating secret communications "backchannels" to bypass their bureaucratic enemies. To some extent, what motivated this pernicious partnership was a shared worldview:

aggressive anticommunism—the waging of what Nixon would later call "the real war" and what Kissinger constantly referred to as "the geopolitical struggle." But to a far larger extent, it was mere opportunism. By Hersh's account, Nixon's personal insecurity was very nearly a clinical phenomenon: he was morbidly fearful of criticism, confrontation, or loss of control. And Kissinger, wholly dependent on the president's favor for bureaucratic advancement, needed to make himself indispensable. It was an effective symbiosis. But their radical centralization of power necessitated inordinate secrecy and duplicity, which became (to appropriate a phrase) "a cancer on the presidency."

Hersh charts this pathology in a series of case studies: Vietnam, Chile, Cuba, Berlin, Biafra, the Mideast, SALT, the opening to China. It is hard to know which of these episodes is the most appalling. Certainly the costliest—potentially, at least—was Kissinger's mishandling of the SALT negotiations, and especially his failure to press for a ban on MIRVs (Multiple Independently Targeted Reentry Vehicles). Nearly everyone now agrees that MIRVs were the most fateful and disastrous innovation in the history of the arms race. The Pentagon, protecting its turf, wanted MIRVs. Nixon did not understand arms-control issues and did not much care about them, except for their domestic political impact. Kissinger later claimed that he hadn't given the matter sufficient attention. But as Hersh makes clear, Kissinger well understood the implications of MIRVing, and he so dominated the SALT negotiations that his firm support for a ban (which Congress and the arms-control agencies also favored) would probably have made a crucial difference. The chance to ban MIRVs was lost because Kissinger was, as always, unwilling to be outflanked on the right by a bureaucratic rival (in this case, Defense Secretary Laird).

Hersh also makes clear that much of the value of SALT I was lost because of Kissinger's insistence on conducting the negotiations single-handedly and in secret. He offended the State Department and the Arms Control and Disarmament Agency by ignoring the SALT delegation in Geneva. He offended the Pentagon by making technical blunders (confusing silo "size" with "volume," and confusing one class of Soviet submarine with another). He offended the CIA by requesting it to falsify intelligence estimates in order to justify his negotiating positions. He offended Congress by denying it information. And he offended everyone by his frequent, self-serving leaks to the press. As a result, no one but Kissinger had a bureaucratic vested interest in the SALT agreement (except Nixon, who got to sign it at the Moscow summit of May 1972, thereby boosting his reelection prospects). And the ill will aroused by Kissinger's pointless razzle-dazzle soured many in the government, according to Hersh, on arms control altogether.

The opening to China was another of Kissinger's vaunted achievements. It, too, was accomplished in secret, using China's ally, Pakistan, as an intermediary. Pakistan was rewarded with American support (the infamous "tilt") at a time when it was carrying out near-genocidal massacres of the Bengali secessionists of East Pakistan (later Bangladesh). What was already known about this tilt was scandalous enough, but Hersh adds further damning details. For one thing, maintaining secrecy—the rationale for the tilt—was unnecessary: the Chinese were puzzled and even annoyed by it, and there were other secret channels available anyway, like Romania. But secrecy allowed Kissinger to cut the State Department out of the action; and his clandestine trip to Peking in 1971—his supreme personal triumph—required Pakistan's cooperation. So much for the Bengalis, more than a million of whom were slaughtered by Pakistani dictator Agha Muhammad Yahya Khan, whom Nixon praised in the midst of the massacres for his "great delicacy and tact."

Even worse, if that's possible, was Nixon's and Kissinger's willingness to provoke a nuclear confrontation with the Soviets over India's attempt to prevent further carnage. Hersh reveals secret testimony by Nixon to the Watergate prosecutors that "we had threatened to go to nuclear war with the Russians" over the India-Pakistan conflict. Why? Because of his and Kissinger's characteristic insistence on interpreting local conflicts in global terms. The Russians (who seem to have taken Nixon's "madman theory" more seriously than anyone else) were urging caution and restraint on their ally India. But Kissinger would not be moved. As he summed up the situation at the time, in one of his more elegant geopolitical formulations (reported in Nixon's memoirs): "We don't really have any choice. We can't allow a friend of ours and China's to get screwed in a conflict with a friend of Russia's."

Kissinger's indifference to elementary humanitarian considerations embraced Africans as well as Asians. In 1967 the province of Biafra attempted to secede from Nigeria. The rebellion was doomed, and by 1969 the province was sealed off. Mass starvation ensued. The State Department opposed pressuring Nigeria to allow extensive relief efforts. In early 1970, after Biafra surrendered, Nixon and Kissinger were presented with authoritative evidence that hundreds of thousands would starve over the next few weeks. They did nothing. Roger Morris, a disenchanted Kissinger aide who pressed unsuccessfully for massive aid to Biafra, told Hersh:

> After one meeting with Elliott Richardson and other State Department officials, all of whom downplayed the estimates of Biafran starvation, Nixon telephoned Kissinger and, Morris recalls, said simply of his State Department: "They're going to let them starve, aren't they, Henry?" Kissinger's answer, according to Morris, was "Yes." He and Nixon then began discussing some of the foreign pol-

> icy passages in the State of the Union speech. Morris concluded, "Henry understood the issues perfectly. . . . He had no rational reason for letting those kids starve; he was just afraid to alienate Richardson [his only State Department ally] because he and Richardson had other fish to fry. And with the President, Henry just didn't want to bother him. He'd look soft.

So much for the Biafrans.

Kissinger's "shuttle diplomacy" after the 1973 Arab-Israeli war is legendary. Nearly everyone was impressed; even Anthony Lewis (who once wrote of Kissinger, "His jokes have about them the air of the grave. That we honor a person who has done such things is a comment on us") consistently praised Kissinger's Mideast efforts and even urged sending him to the region as a special U.S. envoy. Hersh shows that such admiration is unfounded. As soon as Anwar Sadat took office in 1970, he made it clear that he wanted Egypt to leave the Soviet orbit and enter the American one. He pressed for disengagement in the Sinai, promised to open the Suez Canal, and offered Israel a peace settlement on more generous terms than were eventually agreed to at Camp David. But Kissinger was having none of it. Nixon had assigned responsibility for the Middle East to the State Department, partly to mollify his otherwise ignored secretary of state, William Rogers. The prospect of Rogers's receiving credit for diplomatic progress in the region alarmed Kissinger. Moreover, his geopolitical fantasies intruded once again. Israel reacted to Sadat's overtures by escalating the constant border tensions between the two countries, launching deep-penetration bombing raids on Egyptian cities. Kissinger supported these raids enthusiastically: for an American client to humiliate a Soviet client—that, presumably, was real progress. Sadat, rebuffed, sent numerous public and private signals during the next few years that if he could not get a peace settlement any other way, he would go to war; and in October 1973, he did. Whereupon Kissinger's brilliant shuttle diplomacy helped bring to a close a war that he, as much as anyone else, had made inevitable.

Hersh's account of Kissinger's mistakes and malefactions goes on and on. There was a factitious confrontation with the Soviets over construction of a recreational base for Soviet submarines in Cuba, which was supposedly the leading edge of Soviet strategic penetration in the Caribbean. (This at a time when the United States had large bases, thousands of military and intelligence personnel, and electronic spy facilities in Iran and Turkey, which border the USSR.) There was a precipitous and dangerous mobilization of the Sixth Fleet in the eastern Mediterranean during the Jordanian-Palestinian civil war of 1970, on the rash assumption that the Soviets were fomenting a regional crisis. And there was Chile, where Nixon and Kissinger authorized bribery, kidnapping, disinformation, and military coup plotting in order to prevent Salvador Allende's election.

There is farce as well as tragedy in *The Price of Power*. According to John Ehrlichmann, "Nixon would talk about Jewish traitors and the Eastern Jewish Establishment—Jews at Harvard. And he'd play off Kissinger. 'Isn't that right, Henry? Don't you agree?' And Kissinger would respond: 'Well, Mr. President, there are Jews and Jews.'" Nixon calls Kissinger about a foreign-policy paper on Africa: "Is there something in it for the jigs? Make sure there's something in it for the jigs, Henry." Kissinger meets a Southern senator at a White House dinner for African diplomats and mutters, "I wonder what the dining room is going to smell like." At National Security Council staff meetings on Africa, "Haig would begin to beat his hands on the table, as if he were pounding a tom-tom, and make Tarzan jokes." An NSC aide recalls briefings in the Oval Office during the Jordanian crisis: "I'd walk in and begin to give a listing of what happened overnight and Nixon would interject, 'Bomb the bastards' or some other wild remark."

And not only farce but melodrama too. In 1968, jockeying frantically for a job, Kissinger passed on secret information about the Paris peace talks to Nixon's campaign aides, who secretly urged Nguyen Van Thieu to resist any agreement until after the election. The Joint Chiefs of Staff, annoyed by Kissinger's intrigues, planted a spy on Kissinger's staff who stole and photocopied thousands of sensitive documents. In response to press leaks, Nixon and Kissinger had their staffs wiretapped by the FBI and were later blackmailed by J. Edgar Hoover, who himself was double-crossed by an assistant, William Sullivan, who turned incriminating wiretap records over to the White House in order to facilitate a cover-up and thereby secure White House support for his eventual appointment as director of the Bureau. And so on through seven hundred pages: endless sycophancy, posturing, secrecy, and deceit. A former Kissinger aide mused retrospectively: "The essence of all this was betrayal." It sounds like a bureaucratic version of *I, Claudius*.

What do Hersh's revelations amount to? Do they really add up to "something new in American foreign policy," as he claims—new enough to alter our judgment of the already public record? Noam Chomsky once compared Watergate to "the discovery that the directors of Murder Incorporated were cheating on their income tax. Reprehensible, to be sure; but hardly the main point." Next to Vietnam, Kissinger's other transgressions, however staggering, were a sideshow. Above all, he was centrally responsible for carrying on that illegal and brutal war. Recall that from the late 1940s on, as American policymakers privately admitted, the only mass-based political organization in South Vietnam was the nationalist revolutionary movement. To keep this movement from power, the United States financed French colonialism until its demise in 1954; subverted the Geneva Accords; helped organize a campaign of violent repression by its client Diem regime throughout the late 1950s; intervened in force during the early 1960s, after the hitherto nonviolent NLF began resisting the Saigon government's assault; and launched a full-scale invasion in 1965, before there was any evidence of serious North Vietnamese involvement in the conflict. To all this Kissinger never offered any principled objection. (Although, to be fair, neither did his liberal critics, who opposed the war because it could not be won at an "acceptable cost" or because it damaged other, more important American "interests" abroad.)

Not only was the war illegal, by any meaningful interpretation of international law, it was insanely, almost incomprehensibly, destructive. During Kissinger's tenure in office, four million tons of bombs were dropped on Indochina—as much as on all fronts throughout World War II, equivalent to several Hiroshimas per month, and amounting, in South Vietnam alone, to more than sixty tons per square mile and five hundred pounds per inhabitant. More than a million people were killed, and many millions more became refugees. The economy, the social fabric, and even the landscape of the region were devastated, to the point that famine threatened South Vietnam in 1973 and an American AID administrator leaving Cambodia in 1975 predicted that a million people would starve to death in that country within the next year.

This grim record has long been entirely public, and its discovery does not require the talents of a top-notch investigative reporter like Hersh. And if after all this official barbarism Kissinger remained popular, even among liberals, is any useful purpose now served by conclusively demonstrating that, in addition to being a war criminal, he was an egregiously ambitious petty intriguer?

Yes, I think so. But first a word about the demonstration. Hersh interviewed hundreds of former government officials, including aides and close associates of Kissinger (many of whom spoke for attribution), read most of the relevant memoirs of the period, and acquired access to personal files and recently declassified documents. Even this immense research effort cannot ensure definitiveness: his reconstruction of individual episodes will no doubt be challenged. But if even a fraction of Hersh's exhaustive indictment stands, he will have made good his claim that the style, if not the substance, of foreign policy in the Nixon-Kissinger era underwent ominous innovations.

In documenting this mischief, *The Price of Power* raises fundamental questions about American political culture. It does so only indirectly; there is not a speculative word in the book. Yet the density and comprehensiveness of wrongdoing it catalogues cry out for diagnosis.

Perhaps one can understand Kissinger's ascendancy as an expression of the cult of "national security." E. P. Thompson has analyzed "the culture of exterminism," the labyrinth of arguments and rhetoric with which defense establishments generate ideologies that take on lives of their own and provoke responses that seem to verify the need for still more "defense" and "security." The military, the defense industry, and the geopolitical intelligentsia may now be the dominant voices in American foreign policy, outweighing even representatives of non-defense corporations, who own the private economy. Cold War demonology flourishes, and the "Vietnam syndrome" is deplored. Ominous power shifts have occurred: from Congress to the Executive Branch; from the State Department to the National Security Council; from the unionized Northeast to the largely non-union Sun Belt.

The cult of national security has various dangerous corollaries, such as the cult of secrecy. Nixon's fraudulent invocation of "national security" throughout the Watergate cover-up was a reflex of this attitude, and Kissinger's fascination with "back-channels" was merely one of its more outlandish forms. The real enemy was always the rest of us: the supposedly sovereign public. Kissinger's contempt for democratic processes is longstanding: his writings and interviews are laced with references to public opinion as an unfortunate constraint on wise and farseeing statesmen. Foreign policy is, alas, too complex to be left to a fickle, impressionable democratic rabble, who all too often become impatient with the necessary atrocities. We lost Vietnam, Kissinger frequently hints, because we didn't trust our leaders.

Naturally the public, like a child, must be cajoled, diverted, and told only as much as is good for it. This is the premise of Kissinger's memoirs, which skillfully exploit his access to classified materials. Hersh shreds those memoirs, demonstrating dozens of falsifications, distortions, and self-serving half-truths that Kissinger must have thought were forever protected by official secrecy. What has raised that veil, besides Hersh's ferocious persistence, is the Freedom of Information Act—in a sense, the hero of this book. Arguably the most important lesson to be drawn from *The Price of Power* is that without the Freedom of Information Act—currently under assault from the Reagan administration and the intelligence agencies—American democracy, such as it is, is at grave risk.

Another feature of the national security subculture is an obsession with "toughness." Someday, perhaps, a feminist historian will study the cult of toughness in American foreign policy. Kennedy's reckless brinkmanship during the Cuban missile crisis and Johnson's paralyzing fear of being the first American president to lose a war were more than matched in the Nixon White House. That profoundly timid president, who dreaded even the mildest face-to-face confrontations with subordinates, was, as Hersh shows, almost unbelievably truculent in the conduct of foreign affairs. All his advisers had to prove their mettle, particularly Ivy League intellectuals. And so Kissinger (no bleeding heart to begin with) would outdo even Nixon in urging that a "savage, decisive blow" be struck here, there, or wherever: at the North Koreans, Palestinians, Laotians, Cambodians, and—always—Vietnamese. A bureaucratic rival (especially Rogers) who counseled moderation was "soft" or a "fag." Nixon's famous "madman theory"—that the North Vietnamese would give in for fear that Nixon was sufficiently bonkers to drop the Big One if not allowed to have his way—was only the most exotic expression of the security mentality.

Unfortunately, *The Price of Power* does not pursue these questions, or another, more elusive one: the significance of Kissinger's extraordinary celebrity. Kissinger's lionization by the media is one of the most intriguing and dismaying phenomena in recent American cultural history. Hersh has said that one motive for writing this book was his disgust at seeing the press "roll over on its back for so long saying, 'Please scratch my tummy, Dr. Kissinger.'" That is scarcely an exaggeration. Celebrity and power often go together, of course; but Kissinger's prestige is something special, and it can hardly be accounted for even by his masterly manipulation of reporters and columnists.

How else, then, to account for that prestige? It can't have much to do with his writings, which consist essentially of portentous platitudes and ponderous commonplaces, amounting finally to no more than this: powerful states should choose their goals carefully, pursue them unscrupulously, and always employ high-sounding but vacuous rhetoric ("equilibrium," "stability," "world order") by means of which their interests can be disguised as the general interest.

More likely Kissinger owes his vogue to his perfectly representing a new type: the intellectual in (or near) power. As the political scientist Theodore Draper has suggested: "Kissinger as an intellectual in politics captured the allegiance and excited the imagination of a journalistic elite that is itself largely made up of intellectuals *manqués*. By selecting them as his chosen confidants and flattering them with his assiduous attention, he made them feel closer to the seat of power than ever before." Power corrupts—especially journalists, it seems.

The corruption of the Fourth Estate is only one of Kissinger's baneful effects on American life, but one that may now, thanks to Seymour Hersh's splendid indignation, begin to be redressed. Years ago a French democratic leftist, trying to exorcise a long and oppressive legacy, wrote an article consisting wholly of curses and foul epithets directed at Lenin and Stalin. One hopes that *The Price of Power* will initiate a similar, equally indispensable exorcism. For American political culture will not be visibly healthy until entire op-ed pages all across the land are devoted to profane and heartfelt revilement of that depraved mass murderer, that odious war criminal, that contemptible liar, that unctuous fraud, that unprincipled self-promoter, that geopolitical fantast, that contemporary incarnation of the banality of evil, the butcher of Cambodia, the mad bomber of Hanoi, the assassin of Chile, the betrayer of Biafra and Bangladesh: Henry Kissinger. Or at least, no more tummy scratching.

17

THE IMPRESARIO

Irving Kristol

Matisse said he wanted his art to have the effect of a good armchair on a tired businessman. Irving Kristol seems to have wanted his writing to have the effect of a good martini on a beleaguered corporate executive. The executive's prejudices, widely scorned among the young and the educated (in the 1960s and 70s, that is, when Kristol began offering this therapy), were eloquently reaffirmed; his feelings, wounded by impertinent criticism, were tenderly soothed; his conscience, feeble but occasionally troublesome, was expertly anaesthetized. The executive's gratitude knew no bounds; in return, he and his foundations showered their faithful servant with the money and favors that made Kristol so prominent a figure in American intellectual life in the last decades of the twentieth century.

Born in Brooklyn in 1920, Kristol attended City College in the 1930s. There he was part of an unusual cohort of left-wing students, avid readers of Trotsky and *Partisan Review,* an astonishing proportion of whom eventually became leading American intellectuals: Daniel Bell, Nathan Glazer, Irving Howe, Seymour Martin Lipset, and Kristol, among others. After college, he tells us in the engaging "Autobiographical Memoir" that concludes *The Neoconservative Persuasion,* he became an apprentice machinist but did not persevere. (Alas!) A stint in the Army "had the effect of dispelling any anti-authority sentiments" (along with his socialist ideals), since he thought his fellow GIs—representing the common man—pretty mediocre, while Army regulations were generally rational and fair. After World War II he followed his wife (now the eminent historian Gertrude Himmelfarb, who edited this collection) from one graduate program to another until they settled in New York and Kristol became an editor at *Commentary.*

At *Commentary* Kristol found himself in another stellar cohort, this time including Elliot Cohen, Clement Greenberg, Robert Warshow, and Richard Clurman. After a few years he moved on to become executive director of the American branch of the Congress for Cultural Freedom, and then, in 1953, co-editor of the Congress's London-based journal, *Encounter.* The Congress was secretly financed by the CIA. Kristol may not have known that and probably wouldn't have cared. In any case, England seemed provincial after New York, so in 1958 he returned to edit *The Reporter,* the project of a wealthy but imperious European émigré. Soon he found himself an executive at Basic Books.

Kristol had tried to write a book on American democracy but given up. "I was not a book writer. I did not have the patience and I lacked the intellectual rigor." He also lacked the patience for book publishing and was eager to start another magazine. A rich ex-CIA-agent-turned-stockbroker whom Kristol knew from the Congress for Cultural Freedom agreed to finance *The Public Interest,* beginning in 1965. Critical of the Great Society, and particularly of the War on Poverty, *The Public Interest* attracted much interest and support from *The Wall Street Journal,* the Olin, Bradley, and Smith Richardson foundations, and the

American Enterprise Institute. Money was never again a problem, especially once Kristol became field marshal of William Simon's long and devastating march through the institutions of New Deal liberalism on behalf of big business.

Every ism has its truth. What was neoconservatism's? *The Public Interest*'s critique of social policy had a dual thrust: assessment and diagnosis. The bottom line of the assessment was that the more active and interventionist the policy, the less successful. Social Security and Medicare, which simply mailed out checks, worked; more ambitious efforts, such as welfare, education reform, public housing, or juvenile delinquency and prisoner rehabilitation programs, did not. As a first sustained and scholarly review of postwar social policy in America, *The Public Interest* was a genuine public service.

The explanation offered for the failures discovered was another matter. It boiled down to: underreliance on markets and their incentives and overreliance on efforts by a new, self-aggrandizing class of policymakers and service professionals to change attitudes and behavior among the disadvantaged. There were nuggets of insight here, but hostility to the "new class"—a category soon expanded to include practically anyone critical of the status quo—eventually took on an independent ideological momentum. The fact that most of the failed policies had been, as Daniel Patrick Moynihan acknowledged in a burst of candor (or perhaps sheer loquacity), "oversold and underfunded" in the first place was not seriously considered.

Kristol, however, was not a writer to look to for painstaking discriminations. The typical Kristol essay was a relaxed affair—just what the tired businessman required. There are a few long pieces in *The Neoconservative Persuasion,* but most are around two thousand words. First comes the liberal conventional wisdom, laced with scare quotes, about "root causes" or "participatory democracy" or "American imperialism" or "international law." The liberal fantasy in question is refuted by a combination of one-liners, daringly commonsensical contrarianisms, and historical allusions or statistical snippets. By way of conclusion, the deeper, perennial conservative wisdom is restated. It is all genial, effortless, tension-free. Never does Kristol struggle to find his way through some tangled thicket of arguments or to reconcile some apparently contradictory lessons of history. Never does he dive deep into a familiar (or unfamiliar) text, revealing unsuspected patterns, implications, ambiguities. Never does he bring before his readers a sustained procession of historical facts or economic statistics. He appears to write on cruise control.

Kristol's breezy certainty, moreover, is a thing to be envied. His ideological comrade Joseph Epstein wrote wonderingly of Kristol's "commanding tone, supremely confident about subjects that are elsewhere held to be still in the flux of controversy, assuming always that anyone who thinks differently is perverse or inept." In *The Neoconservatives* (1979) Peter Steinfels skeptically remarked "the frequent appearance of 'always,' 'all,' 'ever,' 'whole,' 'only' [I would add 'of course']" in Kristol's prose:

> Indeed, as soon as Kristol announces something as obvious ("Obviously, socialism is an 'elitist' movement") or the plain truth ("The plain truth is that it is these [liberal, individualist] ideals themselves that are being rejected" by the dissident young) or the simple truth ("The simple truth is that the professional classes . . . are engaged in a class struggle with the business community for status and power"), one immediately suspects that the matter is not obvious or plain or simple at all. As soon as he announc-

> es something as demonstrably the case—"the proposition (demonstrably true) that the salaries of professors compare favorably with the salaries of bank executives"; "It is a demonstrable fact that in all modern, bourgeois societies, the distribution of income is also along a bell-shaped curve"—one suspects that the matter is either undemonstrable or demonstrably false.

Kristol led the attack on the "new class." Fundamentally, he charged, liberal and radical intellectuals were an antidemocratic elite, seeking to impose their "ideals" on the sensible, materialistic majority. They did this by capturing the state, expanding its powers, and interfering everywhere. "This movement, which seeks to end the sovereignty over our civilization of the common man, must begin by seeking the death of 'economic man,' because it is in the marketplace that this sovereignty is most firmly established." Keynesian fiscal policy, the consumer-protection movement, and the environmental movement were all aspects of this "reactionary revulsion against modernity," against "the kind of civilization that common men create when they are given the power."

Among the many problems with this theory, one might mention: 1) the assumption of consumer—or any kind of popular—sovereignty in the marketplace (on the contrary, the creation of needs and the management of demand by business are essential to the functioning of a mature capitalist economy); 2) the assumption that demands for reform will never originate among, or strike roots in, a democratic majority; 3) the assumption that government is the natural antagonist of business (this was hardly true in the 1960s and 1970s, and since then the reverse has been so completely and obviously true that only a helpless addiction to Fox News could persuade anyone otherwise). But these objections were beside the point: the "new class" theory did wonders for ruling-class morale. The identification of progressive reform as the project of a scheming, undemocratic elite has proved to be an ideological zombie, impossible to kill.

It is important, in passing, to distinguish the neoconservatives' critique of intellectuals as a new class from the far deeper and richer critique developed by Christopher Lasch. In *Haven in a Heartless World* (1977), *The Culture of Narcissism* (1979), and *The Minimal Self* (1984), Lasch traced the evolution of a new set of functions called forth by the rise of mass production and industrial organization. The new workforce had to be educated; for that very reason, its autonomy and initiative had to be curbed. The varieties of social control exercised by industrial relations specialists, social workers, psychotherapists, educators, public relations and advertising personnel, and numerous other professionals formed, in Lasch's account, a synergy of epic proportions. But Lasch's analysis revealed a profound tension between democracy and corporate dominance, so neoconservatives paid him no attention.

Though Kristol jeered at the supposed idealism of the "new class," he was an energetic preacher of public virtue, notably in "Republican Virtue and Servile Institutions" (1974). Our wise Founders, unintimidated by "democratic dogma," doubted the people's "innate capacity for self-government." They were concerned about what they called "luxury" and we would call affluence—not about the effect of affluence on affluent people's characters but about the effect of the desire for affluence on ordinary people's characters. They conceived of republicanism as "something which involves our making painful demands on ourselves," and of republican virtue as "self-control," a willingness to "subordinate one's own special interests to the public interest," particularly when it came to the "expression of material grievances."

The Founders' stern admonition to popular self-restraint has gone by the board—nowadays we can scarcely even comprehend it, Kristol scoffs:

> Dostoevsky predicted, in *The Brothers Karamazov*, that when the anti-Christ came, he would have inscribed on his banner: "First feed people, and then ask them to be virtuous." We have improved on that slogan to the extent of adding decent housing, good schools, free medical care, and adequate public transportation as necessary preconditions of virtue.

Consider (as Kristol apparently did not) what this sally implies. If we are justified in demanding virtue—"self-control" and self-denial—from people who do not yet enjoy sufficient food, decent housing, good schools, free (or any) medical care, and adequate public transportation, then what painful sacrifices for the common good are we justified in demanding of those who enjoy not merely all these basic goods in superabundance but also riches beyond the dreams of avarice: that is, the 1 percent of the American population who receive 23 percent of the national income and own 40 percent of the national wealth? Colossal sacrifices, beyond a doubt. A serious moralist would treat this question as central to any discussion of public virtue. It seems never to have occurred to Kristol.

"Human Nature and Social Reform" (1978) diagnosed the alleged failure of most social reform in the 1960s and 1970s. Kristol's diagnosis turns on the distinction between "opportunity reforms," like tuition subsidies for night school, which build on existing motivations for self-advancement or on proven traditional motivators like religion or family, and "environmental reforms," like welfare or prison reform, which "enable us (in theory) to change everyone's motivations for the better, through the practical exercise of our unadulterated compassion, our universal benevolence, our gentle paternalistic authority." The former always succeed; the latter always fail. The reason is obvious to everyone but liberal intellectuals: "Our reformers simply cannot bring themselves to think realistically about human nature. They believe it to be not only originally good, but also incorruptible; hence the liberal tolerance for pornography."

Does this analysis hold water? Kristol acknowledged "one important exception": those who are unavoidably dependent—"the old, the halt, the blind, the infirm." Programs that "throw money" (though not "too much money") at such people are "perfectly appropriate." This grudging exception seems to me nonetheless large enough to drive a tank through. For children too are unavoidably dependent, and the environment we collectively provide them (or fail to provide them) will shape their later motivations just as much as their genetic endowment (which is what "human nature" means, if it means anything). In fact, environments shape *everyone*'s motivations, including those of juvenile delinquents, repeat criminals, and welfare cheats, Kristol's prime exhibits of the failure of social reform. Perhaps the most salient feature of the environment in each of these cases, as Michael Harrington pointed out in a reply to Kristol, is the lack of a unionized, full-employment economy. No doubt many people are simply bad eggs, as Kristol is happy to remind us. But the lack of decent employment prospects helps, in many cases, to turn bad eggs into criminals. Full employment constrains profits, however, so attention must be deflected elsewhere, preferably in a metaphysical direction. In debates about social reform (before we decided, as a society, to more or less give up on the whole project), "human nature" was usually the first and last resort of scoundrels. Kristol worked that dodge relentlessly.

It is in foreign policy that neoconservatism has done the most damage with the least intellectual authority. Neoconservatives prided themselves on their moral realism and geopolitical astuteness. But their views—especially Kristol's—on communism and the Cold War were superficial and crudely partisan. Kristol first became notorious for an essay in *Commentary*, "Civil

Liberties—1952." There he argued that because communism was (unlike, say, the U.S. State Department and the CIA under the Dulles brothers) "a conspiracy to subvert every social and political order it does not dominate," there could be no question of "complete civil liberties for everyone." All that Communist Party members and their sympathizers could hope for was some recognition of "the expediency in particular cases of allowing them the right to be what they are."

Himmelfarb bravely and usefully includes this essay in *The Neoconservative Persuasion.* It certainly deserves all the opprobrium it has attracted over the years. Kristol's guiding principle—that a mass political organization may be declared an illegal conspiracy to overthrow the government by force without its having either advocated or attempted the overthrow of the government by force, and that any or all of its members may therefore be denied "complete civil liberties"—is as invidious as it is illogical. Rhetorically, the essay is impressive: a masterly guide to assuming a pose of tough-mindedness while courageously confronting "liberal pieties." But in fact, if your liberal pieties are shaken by Kristol's illiberal blasphemies, they must have been very shaky to begin with.

Kristol's view of the Cold War was about as equally judicious and fair-minded. The Soviet Union was an "immoral, brutal, expansionist power"; it had always been and—given the nature of the regime—could be nothing else. For America, on the other hand, "*realpolitik* . . . is unthinkable": "every American administration has felt compelled to use our influence" to promote "individual rights as the foundation of a just regime and a good society." This benevolence was part of *our* nature, "the very grain of our political ethos." Kristol's superior grasp of the opposing essences of our side and their side made it unnecessary to consider evidence that might have complicated the picture, including American use of atomic weapons at the end of World War II in an attempt to gain leverage over the USSR in negotiating the postwar settlement; American insistence on rearming Germany as part of a hostile military alliance, rather than acceding to Soviet proposals for a neutralized and disarmed Central Europe; and American military intervention or political interference in Western Europe and former European colonies whenever popular movements challenged governments subservient to the United States. "The United States," Kristol wrote, "will always feel obliged to defend, if possible, a democratic nation under attack from non-democratic forces, external or internal." This after the U.S.-supported overthrow of democratically elected regimes in Iran in 1953, Guatemala in 1954, Brazil in 1964, Indonesia in 1965, Chile in 1973, and Argentina in 1976. Is it brazenness or ignorance?

Kristol's pronouncements about international law were likewise simultaneously self-assured and fact free. As expressed in the United Nations Charter, international law was an absurdity, "one vast fiction"; a fiction, moreover, that has been "abused callously, or ignored ruthlessly, by those nations that, unlike the Western democracies, never took it seriously in the first place." Alas, whoever may have taken the United Nations seriously from its inception, the United States certainly did not, consistently ignoring near-unanimous General Assembly resolutions on disarmament, terrorism, South Africa, the Cuban embargo, and an Israeli-Palestinian political settlement, among other issues, and amassing more Security Council vetoes than any other country.

Reared on *Partisan Review,* the neoconservatives naturally took a keen and pugnacious interest in contemporary culture. But while the intellectuals of the 1930s and 1940s were usually concerned to defend avant-garde art and literature against the indifference or hostility of bourgeois society, the neoconservatives were more often concerned to defend bourgeois society against the condescension or contempt of the avant-garde. The root of the problem, as usual for conservatives, was the Enlightenment and the death of God. "The deeper one explores into the self, without any transcendent frame of reference," Kristol wrote, "the clearer it becomes that nothing is there." Hence "utopian rationalism," in the form of socialism, and "utopian romanticism"—the counterculture, including feminism, gay liberation, drugs, loud music, and other perverse forms of self-expression—"have, between them, established their hegemony as adversary cultures over the modern consciousness and the modern sensibility." If everything is permitted, nihilism ensues. Recoiling from this prospect, neoconservatives have discovered the "paradoxical truth that otherworldly religions are more capable of providing authoritative guidance for life in this world than are secular religions." Are any of these very convenient "otherworldly religions" true? Kristol did not say.

Unbelieving conservatives from Plato to Kristol have lamented the political consequences of other people's unbelief. It's an old number, now played out. It is possible to respect those who doggedly defend one or another traditional, supernatural religion, in all its theological rigor. Likewise those who bravely attempt to stammer out the first terms of a new (or recover the lost fragments of an old) non-supernatural religion, well aware that they will probably sound foolish. But those who, like Kristol, merely want the rest of us to accept discipline and obey authority, whatever we believe (they don't really care), deserve no respect. For all his hand-wringing about the dwindling of "the accumulated moral capital of traditional religion," Kristol never gave any indication of what he thought the truth about ultimate matters might really be. He cared about order, not truth.

Kristol was not wrong about everything. In "What Is a 'Neoconservative'?" (1976), he allowed that "neoconservatism is not at all hostile to the idea of a welfare state," including "some form of national health insurance," and that freedom requires only the "right to become unequal (within limits) in wealth . . . and influence." A "ruthless dismantling of the welfare state," he wrote in another essay the following year, is "unthinkable." Who knows why he never repeated these concessions to decency in subsequent decades, when his allies were in power and proceeded to ignore them? Perhaps he forgot he'd made them.

He also, on rare occasions, hit the polemical bull's-eye, wittily skewering left-liberal confusions, as in a speech to foundation executives in 1980:

> Everyone is concerned about youth unemployment in the ghetto, as I am, and I have been involved with various foundations and government as well, over the years, in trying to do something about it. It is astonishing how little has been accomplished. The reason so little has been accomplished is that no one was satisfied with doing a little; everyone wanted to do a lot. For instance, it is a scandal in this country that vocational education is in the condition it's in. It is absolutely absurd. Can you imagine a United States of America where there is a shortage of automobile mechanics, and yet there are "unemployable" kids in the ghetto who can strip an automobile in four minutes flat? But when you try to get a program of vocational education going—and I've tried very hard with various foundations—they say "No! No! We don't want to train these kids to be automobile mechanics. We want to train them to be doctors, to be surgeons."
>
> Let's be reasonable. Not everyone can be a doctor or a surgeon. Some people are going to end up as automobile mechanics. Automobile mechanics have a pretty good life. They make a great deal of money, most of it honestly. But

> the fact is that it has been impossible to get the resources for so limited a goal.

If this is true, it is a far more valuable criticism of political correctness than all of Hilton Kramer's and Roger Kimball's endless fulminations on the subject.

But Kristol was wrong about most things. He was wrong about the Cold War, civil liberties, the "new class," the counterculture, social policy, foreign policy, supply-side economics, religion, and civic virtue. And yet he was perhaps the most politically influential intellectual of his generation. How could that be? Well, as the Old Testament might have said about a false prophet: "He pleaseth the rich exceedingly, and them that have deep pockets he maketh right glad." Sincerely, eloquently, and with an aplomb unruffled by a whisper of self-doubt, Kristol told the rich and powerful exactly what they wanted to hear. They rewarded him in overflowing measure, supporting his ideas, projects, and protégés on a scale unprecedented in American intellectual history. Kristol thought he had left Marxism behind. But he was a living incarnation of Marx's dictum that in every era, the ideas of the rulers are the ruling ideas.

18

ZIPPIE WORLD

Thomas Friedman

In the middle of Thomas Friedman's *The World Is Flat* (2005) is a long quote that towers over the intellectual landscape of the rest of the book like a mountain over low hills. It is Marx and Engels's celebrated prophecy of globalization—"All that is solid melts into air"—from the *Communist Manifesto.* Friedman has apparently just discovered it and is "in awe at how incisively Marx detailed the forces that were flattening the world during the rise of the Industrial Revolution, and how much he foreshadowed the way these same forces would keep flattening the world right up to the present."

Friedman is right to be impressed, however belatedly. After the long detour of Second- and Third-World pseudo-socialism, capitalism has resumed the path Marx and Engels foresaw: toward one wholly rationalized, seamlessly integrated world; with everything for sale; with no one and no activity exempt from the pressure of competition, the risk of obsolescence, the specter of ruin; with no rest, no external haven, no inner sanctuary. A flat world.

This second great age of globalization began, by Friedman's reckoning, on "11/9." (The Berlin Wall came down on November 9, 1989.) "In the Cold War era," he explained in his best-selling *The Lexus and the Olive Tree* (1999), "capital could not move across borders the way it can in today's globalization system." Many national governments did not permit foreign ownership of core industries, foreign speculation in their currencies, or unrestricted foreign access to their domestic markets. (Since the United States was the world's dominant economy, for "foreign" read "American.") They could get away with this because, in the pseudo-socialist bloc, people were not free and in any case did not know what they were missing, and in the Free World the United States was wary of alienating its geopolitical allies. (Though not wary enough to refrain from overthrowing governments in quite a number of them—Argentina, Brazil, Chile, Greece, Guatemala, Honduras, Indonesia, Iran, and others—in order to improve the business climate. Friedman does not mention this.) Friedman's account of "the Cold War system" in *The Lexus and the Olive Tree* is accurate and illuminating, as far as it goes. There is no damned nonsense (or very little) about "freedom"—except for the freedom of those with a lot of capital to do anything they pleased with it. That is indeed what the Cold War was about.

The end of the Cold War made it politically feasible, and computerization made it technically feasible, to move capital around the world at dazzling speeds and staggering volumes without interference from any but the most determined governments. This allows large investors to buy control of a country's key resources, industries, and infrastructure, to put intense upward or downward pressure on its currency, and thereby to influence, or even dictate, its fiscal, environmental, labor, and tax policies. These new masters of the universe, gathered around computer screens in New York, London, Frankfurt, and Tokyo, are the subject of the most memorable of Friedman's many piquant coinages: the Electronic Herd.

What lures the Herd to graze in an economy is a favorable investment climate; or, in another charming Friedmanism, the Golden Straitjacket. Donning the Straitjacket means low social-welfare expenditures, low or no tariffs or subsidies to protect domestic industries, no barriers to foreign ownership, currency speculation, or profit repatriation, and a flexible labor market, that is, no unions. (If you want to know more precisely what a "favorable investment climate" looks like, study the decrees of the Bush administration's post-invasion Coalition Provisional Authority, which were designed—without consulting any non-rich Iraqis—to fit post-Saddam Iraq for the Straitjacket.) All this is bitter medicine, but salutary. "Governments which deviate too far from the core rules will see their investors stampede away, interest rates rise, and stock market valuations fall. The only way to get more room to maneuver in the Golden Straitjacket is by growing it, and the only way to grow it is to keep it on tight. . . . The tighter you wear it, the more gold it produces and the more padding you can then put into it for your society."

Such is the canonical view of globalization. Friedman is exceptionally, exuberantly in-our-face about it, insisting that its harsh discipline is not merely a necessary evil but also fair, economically rewarding, and in fact democracy-enhancing. You can rail at the stampeding Herd for leaving your country's social safety net in tatters, your unemployment rate several points higher, and many people's life savings diminished as the currency plummets. It's no one's fault, though, but yours and your spendthrift government's. "There's no one in charge!" Friedman admonishes. Capital attraction and capital repulsion are neutral processes, like gravitation.

And playing by the "core rules" will not only make your society richer; it will also make you freer. (Friedman's boosterish, lapel-grabbing use of the second-person pronoun is contagious, I'm afraid.) "The democratizations of technology, finance, and information," he enthuses, "are at the heart of the globalization system." You can't keep your population down on the farm, politically speaking, once they've plugged into the Net. Moreover, corruption, nepotism, bureaucratic incompetence, and arbitrary power (unless it's awfully secure—more secure than despots tend to be these days) are bad for business; the rule of law, a professional civil service, accurate and accessible statistics, and a stable, legitimate government are good for business. If your society wants to prosper, it will shape up. This "revolution from beyond" Friedman calls "globalution."

The World Is Flat is an updated report from the field. Whatever one thinks of Friedman as a thinker (I'm afraid there's only one possible opinion of him as a prose stylist), he's an energetic reporter and a good storyteller. His new book teems with interesting anecdotes about innovative companies, technologies, and business processes. Everyone's heard by now of the book's opening gambit: his wide-eyed tour of the call centers of Bangalore, India, where adolescents re-christened "Derek" and "Daisy" practice saying "Thirty little turtles in a bottle of bottled water" in order to communicate with Americans frantic about lost luggage or frozen computers. There's also a brief history of open-sourcing: of how Linux and Apache grew, on virtually pure anarchist principles, to become the backbone of the Internet. In counterpoint, one learns how Walmart, with decidedly non-anarchist principles, conquered the world by becoming "the best supply-chain operator of all time," in the words of an awed business consultant.

Supply-chaining is one of the world-flattening forces that are kicking globalization up another level. Outsourcing, offshoring, work-flow software, digitization—every new organizational and technological development tends to divide, isolate, simplify, and cheapen the production process. An old friend of Friedman's used to be an illustrator. Now, thanks to computer design programs like Quark and Photoshop, he's JAFA (Just Another Fucking Artist). His skills have become "vanilla"—Friedmanese for expendable, a mere commodity—so he has "transformed himself into an ideas consultant," supplying drawing concepts that are outsourced for production. This is the fate of a good half of the characters who crowd Friedman's pages. While unassumingly making a living, they are overtaken by labor-saving technology and turned into inexpensive vanilla custard. Fortunately, they somehow manage to reinvent themselves as a pricier "chocolate sauce" or "cherry topping," and the GDP continues its steady ascent.

The book's other characters include dynamic executives who are sponsoring all this outsourcing, offshoring, and vanillaization. The go-go chairman of Rolls Royce Ltd. (which naturally doesn't make cars anymore—too vanilla) spouts this choice bit of New Economy–speak, which greatly impresses Friedman: "We own the ability to identify and define what product is required by our customers, we own the ability to integrate the latest science into making these products, we own the route to the market for these products, and we own the ability to collect and understand the data generated by those customers using our products, enabling us to support that product while in service and constantly add value." Can you guess from that babble what Rolls Royce *does* make now?

Perhaps most impressive and intimidating are the "zippies," the alpha fauna of Friedman's brave new flat world. Zippies are "the huge cohort of Indian youth who are the first to come of age since India shifted away from socialism and dived headfirst into global trade and turned itself into the world's service center." An Indian magazine calls them "Liberalization's Children," and they rule: "young city or suburban resident, between 15 and 25, with a zip in the stride. Belongs to Generation Z. Can be male or female, studying or working. Oozes attitude, ambition, and aspiration. Cool, confident, and creative. Seeks challenges, loves risks, and shuns fear . . . destination-driven, outward-looking, not inward, upwardly mobile, not stuck-in-my-station-in-life." An even bigger cohort of Chinese zippies, Friedman promises, are only a few years behind them, and together they are going to blow their lazy, spoiled American contemporaries away.

It's tempting to smirk at this ad-copy prose and at the rest of Friedman's hymn to the Grand Global March of Productivity. There are serious empirical and analytical questions about it all, too. As Doug Henwood in *After the New Economy* and Eamonn Fingleton in *Unsustainable* have shown, prophecies of permanent, turbocharged, cyber-digitally-driven prosperity look pretty dubious. Real pay for most U.S. workers, Henwood notes, is lower than in 1973; and as Fingleton points out, "with almost no exceptions, manufacturing-oriented economies have outpaced the United States in income growth" in the 1980s and 1990s. And that income growth was more evenly distributed: it's highly plausible that the growth of the digital economy has contributed to America's notable income inequality. In fact, virtually the only industry in which information technology has made an unquestioned and substantial contribution to productivity is financial services. And that, from society's point of view, may well be no more beneficial than gains in the gaming industry would be—of which, arguably, the capital markets deserve to be considered a part.

Bringing the blessings of capital markets to the rest of the world was one of the chief benefits of globalization in the 1990s, Friedman wrote in *Lexus*. In one of that book's most obnoxious passages he announced: "I believe globalization did us all a favor by melting down the economies of Thailand, Korea, Malaysia, Indonesia, Mexico, Russia, and Brazil in the 1990s, because it laid bare a lot of rotten practices and institutions in countries that had prematurely globalized." Apart from its callousness, this and Friedman's other comments on the Asian financial crisis of 1997–98 made clear that he had misunderstood its lessons: that someone *is* in charge of the Electronic Herd and the capital markets; that it's the IMF (which takes its orders from the U.S. Treasury); and that following the IMF's prescriptions had left countries more, not less, vulnerable to being whipsawed.

Still, Friedman is far from heartless. There's a frank recognition of the pain of globalization in *Lexus,* and even the surprising statement that "you dare not be a globalizer today without being a social democrat." In *The World Is Flat* he writes: "The social contract that progressives should try to enforce between government and workers, and companies and workers, is one in which government and companies say, 'We cannot guarantee you any lifetime employment. But we can guarantee you that government and companies will focus on giving you the tools to make you more lifetime-employable.'" In a flat world, "the individual worker is going to become more and more responsible for managing his or her own career, risks, and economic security, and the job of government and business is to help workers build the necessary muscles to do that."

Friedman offers three simple, sensible muscle-building proposals: portable-pension legislation, portable health insurance (with plans negotiated by government, not individual employers), and two years of government-subsidized tertiary education for everyone. (He might, if he were a bit braver, have emphasized that all this and much more like it could have been accomplished for a fraction of the amount wasted on the richest 1% by the Bush tax cuts.) He even has a suggestion for the anti-globalization left, whose idealism he professes to admire: form NGOs in Africa, India, and China that will "promote accountability, transparency, education, and property rights" and help "ensure that the poor get the infrastructure and budgets to which they are entitled."

After all, the poor, too, yearn to join the flat world. "The wretched of the earth want to go to Disneyland, not to the barricades."

I wouldn't presume to badmouth Disneyland to the poor. But one may well feel a bit uneasy about the quality of life in the flat world. Thoreau is said to have replied, when informed excitedly by a mid-nineteenth-century Thomas Friedman that Maine and Texas could now communicate: "But what if Maine and Texas have nothing to say to each other?" History does not record Friedman-then's reply, but Friedman-now would have absolutely no idea what Thoreau was talking about. That information technology might have the effect of making life, at least in some respects, less gracious, subtle, sensuous, and profound, but instead more sterile, frenetic, shallow, and routine—there is no inkling of this in *The World Is Flat.*

"If you are a little too slow or too costly—in a world where the walls around your business have been removed and competition can now come from anywhere—you will be left as roadkill before you know what hit you." It sounds like the war of all against all—"turbocharged," to use one of Friedman's favorite adjectives; and the ultimate weapon, the focus of creativity, the highest achievement of this new stage of civilization is apparently . . . ever-newer operations flow software, to optimize your business process. Except for those Third World NGOs, no one in the flat world seems to be doing anything of loftier significance than getting Walmart's suppliers to make deliveries just a few minutes nearer to ship-time or inventing a new radio-frequency identification microchip to track its inventory.

Well, it will be the zippies' world, not mine. I'm sure they will be fully as cool, confident, and creative, as ambitious, aspiring, and attitudinous, as Friedman promises. I only hope they'll have enough imagination to be bored.

PART III

GLIMMERS OF UTOPIA

19

CROWDS AND CULTURE

A few years ago, I spent two weeks in Italy. According to guidebooks and friends, April should have been ideal: after the rains, before the summer heat and the tourist season. In the event, it rained every day, and the churches, museums, markets, gardens, ruins, and temples were thronged with tourists. Disappointment makes one philosophical, so I began to reflect on the crowds.

I had prepared for the trip by reading *Twilight in Italy* and *Sea and Sardinia* by D. H. Lawrence and *Old Calabria* by Norman Douglas. Lovely books all and written, apparently, just before the Flood. Trains and boats were crowded in these books, but with Italians (the authors traveled second or third class), not tourists. Cultural sites and picturesque scenery were not, as now, overrun. Only artists and the upper or upper-middle classes either wanted or could afford to visit; and as a result, those who came found what they were looking for. Unlike me.

In 1930 Ortega y Gasset published *The Revolt of the Masses,* whose opening pages announced a momentous phenomenon, which he called "plenitude" but might have called "crowdedness." For the first time in Europe, Ortega wrote:

> Towns are full of people, houses full of tenants, hotels full of guests, trains full of travelers, cafes full of customers, parks full of promenaders, consulting-rooms of famous doctors full of patients, theaters full of spectators, and beaches full of bathers. What previously was, in general, no problem, now begins to be an everyday one, namely, to find room.

Ortega was ambivalent about all this. No one, he admitted, could begrudge the people more pleasures or better medical care. But culture was another matter. He thought that while formerly most travelers were prepared, by training or inheritance, to appreciate art and historic places, the new crowds were not. The latter had come to assert themselves rather than submit themselves; or else—most often, in fact—for no definite purpose. The masses "have decided to advance to the foreground of social life, to occupy the places, to use the instruments, and to enjoy the pleasures hitherto reserved for the few." Though this sounds unexceptionable, "it is evident that these places were never intended for the multitude, for their dimensions are too limited, and the crowd is continually overflowing."

I must confess to similar retrograde feelings, especially about tour groups. Swarms of Spanish and Swedish high-school students pinned my companion and me against the wall at the summit of St. Peter's. Everywhere we turned in the Boboli Gardens, we encountered chattering clumps of Italian junior-high-school students. We dashed from room to room in the Pitti Palace, trying to stay ahead of a German group with a very loud guide. The mosaics at Sicily's Piazza Armerina were splendid even in the rain—but only because the many groups present were mostly sheltering in the gift shop and cafeteria. And so on, everywhere.

All this may sound so commonplace, so predictable, so taken-for-granted a travel hazard that there's not much point complaining about it. Actually, I'm not sure I'm complaining. Perhaps the crowd is even a cause for—guarded—celebration, for a muffled cheer. In theory, after all, the cultural landmarks of Europe are everyone's heritage. Better a single confused, brief, distant glimpse of them than yet another generation of ignorance for half the population or more. Many of the crowd will have come for no reason they can articulate; but for others, out of a daily round of routine labor and consumption, the trip may be a shy, wistful homage to the higher life. And even if barren for the traveler, the trip may have a residual effect, may water a seed, blow on a spark, transmit a message to a child, neighbor, or co-worker.

In any case, isn't the increasing activity of the masses—even if painfully inept at first—virtually the definition of political progress? To a democrat and egalitarian, can this publicizing of culture, this subversion of elite privilege, be anything but good? And isn't this large-scale economic and cultural democratization what made possible my own pilgrimage, the child and grandchild of poor, uneducated southern Italian immigrants?

True . . . and yet. Something's not right. It's not a happy match; the places themselves are, in a sense, frustrated. A half-empty theater or sports stadium is a waste; when they're full, both performers and audience are exhilarated. But the Farnese Gardens, the Cappella Palatina, the Greek temples of Sicily can only work their magic on a few visitors at a time. And no doubt they would prefer some visitors to others: erudite old friends and ardent neophytes rather than the dutiful, the acquisitive, the ignorant, or the naively curious.

It doesn't matter, I tell myself; such distinctions are politically invidious. The culturally well-prepared are disproportionately the socioeconomically advantaged. Even if it were feasible, as of course it's not, would I really want to penalize the disadvantaged, to compound injustice by restricting their access to what

Ortega called "the best places, the relatively refined creations of human culture"?

No, I guess not. Anyway, my purpose here is not to propose a policy, which is a complicated and detailed matter, but merely to sort out my feelings. Am I glad or not that those crowds were there; or, better, why am I ambivalent about them? I'm glad that—to put it crudely—the masses are being made aware of culture. But I'm sorry that this awareness is first awakened through the medium of advertising and therefore perceives culture, at least at first, as an object of consumption. Whether active (reading their guidebook) or passive, few tourists seemed (I'm speculating, I admit) to recognize that there might be any other qualification for being where they were—in the holy places of European culture—than having paid.

I've quoted Ortega's complaint that the "places hitherto reserved for the few" are now being occupied by "the multitude." Ortega was a Nietzschean conservative and had his own, nonpartisan idea of who such places ought to be reserved for: "those who make great demands on themselves" rather than those who merely "float on the waves." Is this a valid distinction? Yes, I believe it is. But Ortega's mistake—what made him a conservative—was his assumption that this distinction between high-quality and low-quality human beings, between creative and critical people on the one hand and passive consumers and conformists on the other, was a metaphysical distinction, was just a fact of human nature. He never considered that increasing the number of the responsible, the cultivated, the noble from generation to generation might be possible through a supreme effort of democratic pedagogy.

If such a pedagogy is feasible—unfortunately, the experiment will not be made anytime soon—there may be just as many visitors on an average day then as now to the great artistic shrines and historic places, or even more. But they won't be crowds.

20

THE POWER OF NEGATIVE THINKING

Russell Jacoby

"If you can't say anything nice," my mother used to admonish, "don't say anything at all." Presumably Russell Jacoby's mother told him the same thing. Fortunately, he disobeyed her and has written some of the most useful, acerbic, and entertaining cultural criticism of recent decades. *Social Amnesia* (1975) traced the Americanization of psychoanalysis, in the course of which it lost sight of how society constrains subjectivity and hence lost its critical edge. *Dialectic of Defeat* (1981) surveyed the "Western Marxist" tradition of Lukács, Korsch, et al. His best-known book, *The Last Intellectuals* (1987), deplored the extinction of independent intellectuals with wide interests and a broad general readership, and their replacement by academics and journalists housed in institutions and writing primarily for peers. *Dogmatic Wisdom* (1994) blasted both sides in the culture wars—militant multiculturalists and apocalyptic neoconservatives—for "litigating over property lines when the house is on fire"; that is, while liberal education "shatters under the weight of commercialism" and while "the irresistible power of advertising and television" produces a "monoculture of clothes, music, and cars." Jacoby's arguments were often original and were unfailingly astute, though not always couched in the gentlest, most collegial tones. One finished these books with a heightened appreciation of many intellectuals' capacity for vapidity, trivialization, and self-importance.

The End of Utopia: Politics and Culture in an Age of Apathy is another of Jacoby's broadsides against contemporary intellectuals, particularly those on the left. Their horizons have shrunk, he charges; explicitly or implicitly, they have acquiesced in the general conviction that "this society is the only possible one." Critics of the political economy take for granted competition and commodity production, timidly suggesting only minor modifications in the operation of markets. Multiculturalists absurdly equate their demands for increased turf, pelf, and status with a program for radical social transformation. The "idiom of pluralism and rights" bounds the imagination of philosophers. Whether or not the "end of ideology" and the "end of history" correctly describe the world, they all too aptly characterize the left's worldview.

> Today socialists and leftists do not dream of a future qualitatively different from the present. . . . Almost everywhere the left contracts, not simply politically but, perhaps more decisively, intellectually. . . . At best radicals and leftists envision a modified society with bigger pieces of pie for more customers. They turn utilitarian, liberal and celebratory. The left once dismissed the market as exploitative; it now honors the market as rational and humane. The left once disdained mass culture as exploitative; now it celebrates it as rebellious. The left once honored independent intellectuals as courageous; now it sneers at them as elitist. The left

> once rejected pluralism as superficial; now it worships it as profound. We are witnessing not simply the defeat of the left, but its conversion and perhaps inversion.

Much grapeshot follows, trained on an impressively wide range of targets for so short a book: Robert Kuttner's *Everything for Sale,* Michael Sandel's *Democracy's Discontent,* Michael Tomasky's *Left for Dead,* Ralph Miliband's *Socialism for a Skeptical Age,* John Roemer's *A Future for Socialism,* Michael Albert's *Looking Forward,* Lawrence Levine's *The Opening of the American Mind,* Charles Taylor, Nancy Fraser, Homi Bhabha, Gayatri Spivak, Jonathan Culler, Tony Judt, Edward Said, Stanley Fish, Clifford Geertz, bell hooks, *Social Text,* Toffler-style futurism, mass-culture studies, and sundry other persons, texts, and discourses. Here, in Jacoby's mordant asides, is the chief fun and profit of the book. Some comfortably tenured leftists, he remarks, "see themselves as outsiders, blasting the establishment. Like uptown executives cruising around in pricey jeeps and corporate lawyers in luxurious utility trucks, they pose as rugged souls from the back country; they threaten the seats of power as they glide into their reserved parking spots." The radical program on multiculturalism "might be characterized as jargon attached to an air compressor." Three bemused paragraphs contemplating a Foucauldian critique of the Santa Cruz municipal anti-discrimination ordinance are a stitch. Like Dwight Macdonald (one of the few intellectuals he admires), Jacoby is important above all as a cultural hygienist, scouring verbal plaque and conceptual decay with his high-powered electric-sarcastic drill.

To deal the zeitgeist a box on the ear is one thing, however; to account for it is another. What explains the eclipse of utopianism? In a sense, the answer is obvious: utopia lies buried in the rubble of Stalinism and Maoism. As Jacoby points out, Cold War thinkers consistently equated utopia with totalitarianism and liberal pluralism with democracy; and they carried the day. There were undoubtedly good counterarguments: in particular, that Stalinism was not in the least a utopian experiment but was more like czarism plus electricity. But arguments are no defense against plausible and politically convenient simplifications. For every pundit, editorialist, and politician in America since roughly World War II, the automatic qualification of "utopia" as impractical and/or dangerous, and probably un-American, saved thought.

Still, one must give the zeitgeist its due: what most people believe is not invariably false. There is a rational kernel within the shell of anti-utopian prejudice. It is simply this: We all want to see the plans. And there are no plans. A century or more of resonant but empty slogans urging revolution, liberation, the abolition of money, the end of scarcity, a world without work (or conflict or hierarchy or alienation or authority or force) has at last produced widespread skepticism about all fundamental criticism and exalted aspiration.

Utopian slogans have worked much mischief. (Jacoby himself is not wholly innocent. Scoffing at mundane social democratic talk about full employment and retraining the workforce, he reminds us loftily that "once upon a time leftists and radicals talked of liberation and the abolition of work." So they did; but what, if anything, did they mean by it?) The remedy is not to give up on utopia but to stop sloganizing. To begin with, what does "utopia" mean? Jacoby, like the "negative thinkers" of the Frankfurt School, whom he quotes approvingly, is not generous with specifics, apparently as a matter of principle. But he does offer a helpful definition. The core utopian conviction is "that the future could fundamentally surpass the present . . . that the future texture of life, work and even love might little resemble that now familiar to us . . . that history contains possibilities of freedom and pleasure hardly tapped."

Utopia, then, is in the *future*. Why is this worth emphasizing? Revolutionists and abolitionists, utopia's false friends, insist that it can be constructed out of present materials through a heroic act of will. This is to underestimate recklessly the depth and subtlety of the necessary changes and the intricacy and inertia of every moral culture. Utopia is impossible unless, among an overwhelming majority, solidarity and trust are nearly instinctive; responsibility, self-reliance, initiative, honesty, and other civic virtues are practiced much more widely than now; and democratic habits of self-confidence, candor, and tact are far better developed. Channels of communication and public information are as yet rudimentary. And let's not forget rhetorical skills like wit, fluency, and concision: without a vast improvement in the general level of these, attendance at all the necessary meetings on the way to utopia will result in an epidemic of premature brain death. With all these moral and psychological changes in place, we can make a start on the technical problem—no less complex, probably—of reconciling equity and efficiency in production and distribution.

Obviously such drastic and intimate changes, on the requisite scale, without undemocratic coercion or divine intervention, cannot be accomplished in a generation, or probably even in a few generations. Carrying off a general strike may be a fine thing, but creating a new moral ecology is an infinitely more difficult and valuable thing. In the *Fabian Essays*, defending gradualism against the revolutionists and abolitionists of his day, George Bernard Shaw wrote:

> The right is so clear, the wrong so intolerable, the gospel so convincing, that it seems to them that it must be possible to enlist the whole body of workers, soldiers, policemen, and all—under the banner of brotherhood and equality; and at one great stroke to set Justice on her rightful throne.

> Unfortunately, such an army of light is no more to be gathered from the human product of nineteenth century civilization than grapes are to be gathered from thistles.

Ditto for the human product of twentieth-century civilization. And even an army of light won't be enough, if a majority or a substantial minority remain benighted. The whole society, more or less, must see the light, or it isn't utopia.

The foregoing would be a counsel of despair if the human race were only going to last for a few generations. But utopia's enemies must, if they're logical, deny that such changes are possible in *any* number of generations; must assert, in essence, that humankind has already attained its farthest point of moral development and that our present level of social virtue cannot be substantially improved on *in saecula saeculorum*. This is even more implausible than revolutionism. The wisdom and generosity of the corporate boardroom and the *Wall Street Journal* editorial page may be the best we can do today. But by 2500? Surely it's more likely that we'll all be as gods by then than that we won't have evolved beyond Jack Welch and George Will. Today half the human race has no sanitation, one-fourth has no clean water, one-fifth no adequate housing, and one-sixth no basic health services, while the amount Americans and Europeans spend annually on pet food, cosmetics, and ice cream would supply all those necessities, plus basic education, to everyone in the world who lacks them, with a great deal left over. Do anti-utopians really believe that this disgusting state of affairs will persist until 2500 and beyond? It's too fantastic.

Moral progress is not inevitable, but it is not impossible. It is slow, painful, and uncertain; this is another way of putting the tragic view of life. That view is noble and true, but it is not the same as the lazy, self-serving conservative assumption that things can never be radically better and so there's no point racking one's brains to come up with any possible steps in that direction.

What steps, for example? Here I have some differences with Jacoby. He thinks modest reform schemes like Kuttner's and Roemer's—involving corporate tax incentives, citizen "policy juries," asset redistribution by means of coupons, and the like—are part of the problem and warms instead to the turgid deliverances of Bloch and Marcuse and the inspired rants of Fourier. I suppose there's no harm in the latter, but I find the former more useful by a long shot. Kuttner, Roemer, Alec Nove, et al. leave you feeling that they understand capitalism every bit as rigorously as its defenders, yet are convinced it's a long way from the best that can be had, even if they can't fully articulate that "best." Suitably modest but sufficiently roused: this seems the right frame of mind just now for twenty-fifth-century utopianism.

I think, too, that a return to metaphysics, which Jacoby seems to favor, is not a step in the right direction. He finds in Rousseau, Whitehead, Marcuse, and other thinkers a "logic of negativity," according to which oppressive empirical reality is denied and transcended by means of a liberating metaphysical ur-reality. "Metaphysical universals inhere in the world, but transcend it," he explains. "An individual event may be 'untrue' in that it is contradicted by reality, but this untruth expresses its achievement or different truth, its basis in metaphysical principles." Hmm. Jacoby and his postmodern, antimetaphysical antagonists seem to be making symmetrical arguments. His syllogism runs: "Only metaphysical principles can generate utopian ideals; utopian ideals are indispensable; hence metaphysical principles are valid." Their syllogism runs: "Only metaphysical principles can generate utopian ideals; metaphysical principles are invalid; ergo, utopian ideals are a fraud." But the shared major premise is wrong: utopian ideals do not depend on metaphysical principles. Ideals are not propositions; they are expressions of what the eighteenth century called "sympathy" or "benevolence" and what we may simply call moral imagination. The capacity to envision a more decent world is like the capacity to imagine beautiful forms. Both require a native endowment of sensibility, moral or aesthetic, cultivated by training and experience and not choked off by pressing personal burdens or insecurities. Screw "metaphysical principles." Besides, the historical evidence is mostly the other way. Priestley and Diderot, Hazlitt and Shelley, Mill and Morris, Shaw and Wells, Russell and Dewey were all metaphysical skeptics and utopian radicals. Were they all merely confused?

One of my favorite utopians is Matthew Arnold, to whom Jacoby devotes several eye-opening pages. Though hijacked by conservatives, Arnold belongs in the pantheon of the left. He championed high culture: nearly everyone knows that, and that is all nearly everyone knows. But he was also, consistently and emphatically, an egalitarian. He thought the most important thing in life was the free development of one's highest faculties, to which everyone had a right; that this was only possible in a society without gross material and educational inequality; and that the best way to correct such inequality was democratic state action. His defense of tradition was not in the least antidemocratic; on the contrary.

Arnold mostly kept his distance from the politics of his day. He called himself a "Liberal of the future": it was essential, he believed, to keep alive a sense of large and distant possibilities and to leaven the quotidian with it. A gracious life, a life of "sweetness and light," with ready access to "the best that has been thought and said in the world" and the resources and leisure to assimilate it: no society could be considered just in which all this was not universally available. The "secret of the life of the future," he wrote, is "civilization made pervasive and general." But that will require much slow effort, as he reminded radicals, and a lot of money, as he warned conservatives.

Arnold's "Liberalism of the future" seems to me the very pattern of an intelligent utopianism. If alive today he would, I have no doubt, sympathize with single-payer universal health care and a rise in the minimum wage and deprecate a reduced capital-gains tax and across-the-board deregulation. But mainly, he would gently insist that this society is not "the only possible one." To cowed leftists and smug rightists he would repeat, in the name of the best that has been thought and said in the world, that "the ideal life is, in sober and practical truth, none other than man's normal life, as we shall one day know it."

21

GRAND DISILLUSIONS

Nicola Chiaromonte

The disintegration of the Old Left in the first half of the twentieth century produced an engaging and, on the whole, admirable type: the "virtuous" intellectual. Disillusioned by first-hand involvement with wars and totalitarianisms, undeceived by the ideological enchantments of left or right, these writers undertook to preserve an amateur, nonpartisan status and to bring Cold War controversies before the bar of common sense and uncommon candor. One might say—though the phrase is a trifle ambiguous—that they made a career of honesty. For this they were rewarded with widespread affection and loyalty, if not quite celebrity, during their lifetime and a sort of minor immortality afterward. I'm thinking of Orwell in England, Camus in France, Dwight Macdonald in the United States, and Nicola Chiaromonte in Italy.

Chiaromonte was born in southern Italy in 1905. He joined a libertarian socialist group, Giustizia e Libertà, in his twenties and fled Mussolini's regime in 1934. He later fought in the Spanish Civil War (he appears, as the philosophical Scali, in Malraux's *Man's Hope*). During World War II he came to the United States; he moved in *Partisan Review* circles and contributed to Dwight Macdonald's *Politics,* where the ingenuous activist socialist radicalism of the early twentieth century was metamorphosing into disenchanted humanism with ambiguous political implications. He returned to Europe after the war, wrote essays and theater criticism (occasionally for *Dissent* and other American journals), and co-edited *Il Tempo Presente* with Ignazio Silone. He died in 1972. *The Worm of Consciousness,* a collection of his best-known pieces—among them the graceful, searching meditations "Modern Tyranny" and "The Mass Situation and Noble Values"—came out in 1976. *The Paradox of History,* given as the Christian Gauss Lectures at Princeton in 1966, was published in England in 1970 and appears now, for the first time, in the United States. Summing up as it does a life full of both action and erudition, it is an unusual, and intensely interesting, testament.

There is a passage in *The Paradox of History,* on the aftermath of World War I, that very well describes the "virtuous" intellectual and at the same time sounds the central theme of Chiaromonte's book:

> The individual who has lived through a great historical upheaval has not only been dispossessed of his beliefs. He has found himself face to face with a reality that goes far beyond him and everyone else. He has discovered that one cannot be satisfied with substitutes for truth, and that one cannot at will believe in anything or nothing at all. He has seen that in the relations between man and the world something exists that cannot be changed. At the same time, he has sensed the reality of a Power which nobody can control. Finally, he has found himself personally in question, and he knows that, under any circumstances whatsoever, there is only one thing that matters: the relation between

individual conscience and the world. This is something that cannot be counterfeited.

The "Power which nobody can control" is Fate. Chiaromonte proposes to trace "the resurgence of the idea of Fate in a world . . . dedicated to the idea of progress."

Autonomy, self-confidence, mastery of the environment—these notions are the essence of cultural modernity. Through a complex alchemy presided over by nearly all the modern masters, these ideas were transmuted into a kind of philosophical precious metal, a key to interpretation and action: History as Progress. The strands of this concept are various, but they include at least two chains of reasoning. First, the physical world is intelligible and, to some extent, controllable; contrary to religious cosmology, human beings are part of the physical world; therefore, human relations are also, at least in principle, intelligible and controllable. Second, each individual life involves a progression, mediated by education, from helplessness to self-control; so, too, humankind is bound to grow into control of its collective destiny. The story of this growth is History. Obviously the cornerstone of this optimism is Reason; or rather, faith in Reason. Understanding means mastery; as Bacon said, knowledge is power.

All of this is familiar enough, as are the main historical objections to modern optimism: the theological-conservative doctrine of Original Sin; the Romantic idea of organic hierarchy; and the neo-Marxist critique of Enlightenment as instrumental reason. Chiaromonte's objection is different. It is an intuition derived from the shadowy but powerful Greek notions of Moira, Ananke, and Nemesis, jointly interpreted by Chiaromonte as Fate. What these notions have in common is a suggestion that the reach of rationality is limited, because physical nature is full of unforeseeable accidents and human nature of incomprehensible impulses. To describe those limits precisely is impossible; to defy them, even for noble purposes, entails tragedy. Chiaromonte's explanation of Fate is at times obscure and unsatisfying; but at its most lucid, it conveys some of the cosmology behind the tragic spirit.

As befits its imaginative and mythical origins, Chiaromonte's argument takes the form of a commentary on a body of fiction: the novels of Stendhal, Tolstoy, Roger Martin du Gard, Malraux, and Pasternak. "Only through fiction and the dimension of the imaginary," he writes, "can we learn something real about individual experience." What we learn is that "individual experience" perennially refutes historical optimism. Chiaromonte contends that the works of Stendhal et al. make up a tradition: the antihistorical novel, in which the idea of History as rational and progressive, as the working out of an intelligible human Destiny, is shown to be an illusion. As far as I know, no one has ever before linked these authors in quite this way; whatever the merits of Chiaromonte's argument as political philosophy, it is, as literary criticism, a brilliant conception.

In *The Charterhouse of Parma* the ardent, empty-headed young Fabrizio del Dongo sets out to join Napoleon's army. What ensues is farce: he is robbed by the first people he meets, thrown into jail as a spy, taken in by a worldly woman, an army provisioner, who outfits him in a dead hussar's uniform and sends him off to the great battle at Waterloo. Fabrizio wanders around the battlefield, alternately delighted and horrified, but always uncomprehending. And in fact the event as Stendhal describes it is largely incomprehensible—even, it seems, to Napoleon and his marshals, who gallop to and fro to little purpose and less effect. The scene is a masterly deflation of martial heroics, and especially of Napoleonic mythology. Hegel is supposed to have called Napoleon "the Idea on horseback." Stendhal's exquisite mockery is the antithesis of this apotheosis.

Tolstoy avowed that the antiheroic philosophy of *War and Peace* had its source in Stendhal's irony. *War and Peace* and Isaiah Berlin's essay on its epilogue, "The Hedgehog and the Fox," are the center of gravity of Chiaromonte's book. According to Chiaromonte (and Berlin), Tolstoy's antipathy to the "great man" theory of history stemmed from a profound skepticism that anyone—great or ordinary, individually or collectively—could control, or even comprehend, the direction of history. In the novel, those who pretend otherwise, whether French or Russian, are shown to be either deluded or self-serving. Wisdom comes only to those who, like Pierre and the dying Prince Andrei, are forced to recognize the insignificance, the radical contingency, of their grandest projects. After such an awakening, one can only abandon the unreal hope of making history. "Real" life is rooted, intractable, impervious to abstractions.

It is a commonplace to compare Homer and Tolstoy, for their "epic" scope and vivid descriptions of nature, ritual, and warfare. Chiaromonte points out a deeper resemblance. Simone Weil called the *Iliad* "a poem of force." She meant that, more than anything else in Western literature, the *Iliad* insists on the futility of attempting to use force "rationally," as a means. Chiaromonte suggests that *War and Peace* is a second "poem of force," because it depicts world-historical ambition as hubris, the willful disregard of human limitations.

Chiaromonte's chapters on Malraux, Pasternak, and Martin du Gard's magnificent, neglected *Summer, 1914* extend his argument that "individual experience" undermines ideology. The Second International, the Russian Revolution, the Spanish Civil War, the Communist movement in China appear in these novels not as stages in the progress of Absolute Spirit or the Dialectic, but as so many installments of chaos. Disillusionment is the lot of every honest, undoctrinaire character. What they all learn is not so much that power corrupts as that large-scale historical designs necessarily transgress a certain limit—the limit of human predictability, the horizon of free will. Ideologies ignore "the irrational forces hidden in society, in nature, and within the individual himself" (the Greek word for "divine," *theion,* originally meant "hidden"). They are guilty, according to Chiaromonte, of "cosmic impiety."

The "mystery" of free will is at the core of his critique of historical determinism; it is in terms of free will that he formulates the "paradox" of history. "If we could get to know all the consequences of our actions, history would be nothing but an idyllic and constant harmony of free wills, or the infallible unfolding of a rational design. We would then always act rationally, that is, we would not act at all, since we would simply follow a preestablished and sterile pattern. But then we would not be free. We are free, however, and that means literally that we do not know what we are doing." He is taking aim at dialectical materialism; but if true, his thesis discredits every utopia, William Morris's no less than B. F. Skinner's.

One can quibble with Chiaromonte's "paradox" on logical grounds. His equation of freedom with uncertainty is dubious: freedom is not indeterminacy, but self-determination, for which knowledge is not an obstacle but a prerequisite. And anyone who harbors the slightest strain of residual positivism will find it flaring up when Chiaromonte prescribes humility before "the eternally impenetrable whole" and "all that is ineffable, arcane, and secret in the world" as a cure for "the sickness of our times."

But these objections miss much of the point and all the undeniable power of Chiaromonte's warning. What he meant, I believe, is not that an "idyllic and constant harmony" among human beings would be sterile or oppressive, but that it is unattainable; that perfectibility is the premise of utopianism, a premise empirically disproved by fascism, Stalinism, and mechanized global war. In *Summer, 1914* the pragmatic businessman

Antoine Thibault exclaims, with love and exasperation, to his brother Jacques, a socialist dreamer: "You will not succeed in changing man!" Jacques trembles with defiance and doubt—for these characters, the question of Progress is still open, which is why Chiaromonte calls *Summer, 1914* "the last great novel of the classical nineteenth century." For Chiaromonte in 1966, after half a century of barbarism, the question is closed. Utopianism in the late twentieth century is at best contemptible naïveté, at worst a murderous pretext. The party of humanity has been reduced, for the time being, to chastened silence.

Do these dark counsels represent the beginning of wisdom or a failure of nerve? Perhaps both. The quality of Chiaromonte's thinking (not to mention his biography) inspires immense respect, even trust. And anyone who could live through the horrors experienced by Chiaromonte's generation without an occasional loss of nerve must simply have lacked imagination. Mass murder is awful enough; mass murder rationalized by appeals to science and socialism—this must have seemed to "progressive" intellectuals like the death of all hope.

Hope is irrepressible, though. Two years after Chiaromonte traveled to the New World to deliver his gloomy meditation on the necessity for limits, an ebullient revolution broke out in the Old World, tossing off, among innumerable impudent slogans, "All Power to the Imagination" and "Love Without Limit, Play Without Restraint, Live Without Dead Time." To his credit, Chiaromonte met the French student revolt with the wisest, most generous response of any from his generation. He challenged the students to adopt a "nonrhetorical form of 'total rejection' "; that is, to

> detach themselves without shouting or riots, indeed, in silence and secrecy; not alone but in groups, in real 'societies' that will create, as far as possible, a life that is independent

> and wise, not utopian or phalansterian, in which each man learns to govern himself first of all and to behave rightly toward others, and works at his own job according to the standards of the craft itself, standards that in themselves are the simplest and strictest of moral principles and, by their very nature, cut out deception and prevarication, charlatanism and the love of power and possession.

This is a skeptical voice, but not a cynical one. It is, at any rate, a far cry from neoconservatism. The twentieth century hurt Chiaromonte into metaphysics, but not into despair, and still less into callous chauvinism.

Camus is not mentioned in *The Paradox of History,* but I suspect Chiaromonte's book was written under the influence of *The Rebel.* There is the same rejection of ideology, concentration on art and literature, impossibly high-flown prose style, distaste for programmatic detail, and stress on limits and Mediterranean *mesure.* Both are unforgettably eloquent about what must not be done and irritatingly vague about what, if anything, should be done. They are, in their way, the dernier cri of twentieth-century literary radicalism, by which I mean the attempt to derive from art a criticism of politics and an explanation of the apparently inexplicable history of this century. Nowadays their legacy has been claimed by the Parisian "new philosophers"—a sad dénouement to an honorable enterprise.

Chiaromonte was no Cold Warrior—nor were the rest of the "virtuous" cohort. They were not any sort of warrior, except insofar as they proposed, in Camus' words, "to fight within History to preserve from History that part of man which is not its proper province." What this meant was not a retreat from politics into art, but a desire to infuse politics with the values of art: intellectual detachment, emotional honesty, imaginative fullness. That was, and remains, a radical program.

22

THE REALM OF NECESSITY AND THE REALM OF FREEDOM

Lewis Hyde

Lewis Hyde, a gifted poet and translator, has had trouble making a living. This experience has led him to reflect on our current social arrangements, in which to do one's best work—to offer one's most precious gifts—may bring no return. The irrationality of these arrangements—of competition and commodity production—has occurred to nearly everyone, if only in passing, and has goaded a great many people into print. Yet Hyde has original and fruitful things to say in this wise, charming, wide-ranging book.

The Gift: Imagination and the Erotic Life of Property (1983) is in part a history of the world we have lost, the world before the hegemony of the market. From ethnography and folklore, Hyde has reconstructed the economics and ethos of societies based on gift exchange. Trade is immemorial, of course; but production for a market, as an organizing principle of society, is new, as is the ethos of such a society: possessive individualism. Far more typical of human history is the circulation of goods and services on something like the following principles. First, social status is conferred not by wealth accumulated but by wealth disbursed. The "big man" is the one who throws the biggest parties, or whose ceremonial gifts are of exceptional quality and quantity. Second, "the gifts must always move": the reception of gifts or favors creates reciprocal obligations, though not exclusively to the donor. Everyone is embedded in a network of such obligations, so that in fact, as well as in theory, everything everyone possesses is owed to everyone else. Third, the material basis of the group's life—game, fish, fruit, trees, children—is considered a gift, for which mythical explanations, rites of thanksgiving, and rules of use must be formulated and administered, usually by priests. And so on, with all such principles giving expression to the primacy of the collective.

The anthropological record is sparse, so Hyde reconstructs a good deal of the ethos of premodernity from fairy tales. In the relevant tales, a magical gift is given to one person, it is hoarded, and disaster ensues; a similar gift is given to a second person, it is shared, and that person is superabundantly rewarded. The many variations on this theme occasionally hint at different attitudes toward giftedness and gratitude, but the morality of the tales is invariable: the generous are disproportionately rewarded and the selfish are disproportionately punished.

Hyde then offers a history of humankind's fall from grace: a history of usury. Usury—lending at interest—contravenes the ethics of a gift society: wealth must not be removed from circulation; all wealth belongs to the group; no person's gift may become another person's capital. The prohibition of usury was virtually unanimous in both religious and early civil society. But by the middle of the nineteenth century, nearly all usury laws had been repealed and the theology of usury, at least in industrial societies, had altered drastically. Somehow, the possessive individualism on which capitalist ideology is based had crept into Protestant theology and become ethical individualism, with its radical devaluation of the spiritual authority of the church. It is a fascinating chapter of intellectual history, masterfully narrated.

And yet the material Hyde has culled from ethnography, folklore, and religious history is open to a very different reading. On his own evidence and that of his main sources (in particular, Marshall Sahlins's *Stone Age Economics*), gift societies were—to exaggerate only slightly—Hobbesian societies. Gift exchange was, at least in part, a way of keeping the war of all against all in abeyance. Hyde understates the element of involuntary obligation and implicit sanction in the "institutions of positive reciprocity" he praises. Gift exchange among the Kwakiutl sounds a lot like hug exchange in California: something you do not out of spontaneous affection, but because if you don't, you're considered antisocial. Arguably, the purpose of gift-giving in premodern societies is not to bear witness to a lively sense of loving community but to create a plausible appearance of it and to shore up that facsimile against the dimly sensed disintegrative possibilities of individualism: envy, possessiveness, self-aggrandizement. Like the practices of Christian asceticism, the rituals of gift exchange are, to some extent, defenses.

Moreover, fairy tales embody some of the worst as well as the best wisdom of the race. In the tales Hyde cites, the victims—those who are too insecure and unhappy to give freely, to part with the gift—are blamed and further deprived, while the emotionally rich get richer, as if their generosity were not, like all virtue in a world of scarcity, an accident of temperament and upbringing. Considerations like these keep one from romanticizing premodernity.

In a chapter titled "The Gift Community" and thereafter, Hyde begins in earnest to grapple with the tensions that give his subject point and poignancy. Like all ancient institutions, gift exchange embodies hopes of rootedness, connectedness, mutuality, spontaneity, surrender—the benefits of *eros*. Market exchange, for all its world- and soul-destroying irrationality, embodies complementary hopes: mobility, separateness, individuality, self-possession—the benefits of *logos*. And these polarities suggest others: criticism/myth, innovation/conservation, rights/responsibilities, masculine/feminine. Hyde skillfully elicits one set of meanings after another from historical changes in modes of production and exchange, reckoning psychic loss and gain with keen discrimination.

But what is to be done? Gift exchange, or primitive anarcho-communism, is no longer a possible form of social organization; it could flourish only within small, self-sufficient groups. In industrial society, one can try to draw boundaries, to mark off privileged spheres—friendship, family, art, collective political work—within which commodity logic may be suspended and something like gift relations may operate. But commodity logic is relentless; in the end, someone must enter the market economy in order to support the privileged sphere.

How much of the spirit of the gift can be preserved? Hyde suggests that we look for an answer in the psychology of creativity and in the social relations of art and science. *The Gift* contains an exquisite evocation of what Hyde calls "creative commerce" and the "labor of gratitude." Among colleagues, inspiration and example are paid for not by a fee but by the self-transformation of the recipient. The distributional premises of a competitive market economy are scarcity and the zero-sum. But to the extent that ideas circulate as gifts, the "wealth" of every individual in a co-operative creative "economy"—in an art or science—increases simultaneously. And so, in a limited and fragile way, it really is true of the community of scientists and artists that "the free development of each is a condition of the free development of all."

This is an idealized portrait, of course; the egotism of actual artists and scientists is familiar enough. But that idealization at least suggests the right questions. What are the material conditions of creative freedom? Are freedom and justice best conceived as rights to full membership in a creative community? How would a world of artists, respectful of one another's gifts, organize their collective subsistence labor? This is what formal political theory is about on those rare occasions when it's about anything at all.

The Gift has no theoretical pretensions. It is no more than a sustained meditation, full of gaps and perplexities, intriguing hints, tentative suggestions, and above all, generous hopes. Still, if only as a memory and a prophecy, a glimpse from the realm of necessity into a realm of freedom, it is, like the best of gifts, good beyond expectation, beyond desert.

23

THE PRICE OF EVERYTHING AND THE VALUE OF NOTHING

Michael Sandel

Perhaps each of the seven deadly sins must have its day, politically. "Lust is good" might have been the rallying cry of the 1960s and 1970s counterculture. Gordon Gekko announced earnestly in the 1980s that "greed is good," ratifying the Reagan Revolution and boosting the morale of the One Percent. Let us hope that envy and anger will soon become our ruling sins. American society today needs nothing more urgently than a growing and passionate conviction among the bottom 99 percent that the gross economic inequality currently prevailing is unfair, undesirable, and unnecessary.

As Gramsci observed (and Hume before him), power in every society—not only in democracies—rests on consent. "Acceptance" or "resignation" may actually be a less misleading term, since "consent" implies an active, explicit affirmation, whereas all Gramsci and Hume meant was that if a large majority of the population ever became sufficiently fed up to withdraw from participation in a society's dominant institutions, the society would cease to function, at least along the old lines. This suggests that the analysis of any drastically unequal, obviously unjust society like ours should begin with the question "Why do most people put up with it?"

The legitimating ideology of contemporary America is complex, but one main element of it is represented by the phrase "free market." That phrase stands for something like this: Except when fraud or violence is present, every economic transaction among adults is morally permissible, and any interference with it is unjust. Shorter version: Everything's for sale.

Michael Sandel in *What Money Can't Buy: The Moral Limits of Markets* (2012) went far to document the extent to which that radical proposition has penetrated everyday life. Honor is for sale: university buildings used to bear the names of great scholars or administrators, sports arenas the names of the teams that played there or the community that rooted there; now they are named after donors or sold to corporations. The environment is for sale, in the form of a market for pollution permits, as well as the sale to rich sportsmen of the right to kill endangered species. Citizenship may soon be for sale: influential economists have proposed selling immigration visas at auction or for a set price, say $50,000. (Of course, this may require changing the inscription on the Statue of Liberty to "Give me your rich, looking for tax havens.") Sandel does not mention *Citizens United;* perhaps he thinks the fact that political office and influence are for sale in the United States is too obvious to need pointing out.

Money buys other privileges. "Concierge medicine," the practice of putting doctors on lucrative retainers, assures the rich of immediate and individualized medical care. "Line-standing" companies take hefty fees for holding places in a queue for events like congressional committee hearings, Supreme Court sessions, or "Shakespeare in the Park," which in theory are free and open to the public, first come, first served. Ticket scalping, corporate skybox seats, express-lane highway passes and exemptions from speed limits, bypassing lines to board airplanes—ever more fine-grained varieties of differential treatment are being priced and sold.

There are many more examples. "Legacy" admissions: a fair number of less qualified applicants to prestigious universities are admitted each year in the hope that their alumni parents will become donors. There is the sale of organs: increasingly, kidneys are sold and wombs are rented out, generally by people who are economically insecure, even desperate. There is the outsourcing of national security to private companies: in effect, the defense of the country by mercenaries rather than citizens. Public buses and even police cars are covered with ads. Apologies, wedding toasts, birthday gifts: no rich person need waste time personally attending to any of these social amenities; all of them can be taken care of by strangers for a fee.

Well, so what? According to neoclassical economic theory, markets maximize human welfare. They ensure that what is produced or done is what is wanted, and that what is wanted is what is produced or done, in just the right proportions, as nearly as any earthly institution can. But every theory rests on simplifying assumptions. Neoclassical economic theory rests on assumptions about behavior, institutions, and information—the motives of agents, the prerequisites of production, and the conditions of exchange—that once may have seemed like plausible simplifications, at least to those people who were happy with the policy implications of the theory: namely, that government action to increase employment, redistribute income, or protect workers and the environment was likely to be counterproductive.

It has become increasingly clear over the last couple of decades, however, that the assumptions of neoclassical economics are not in fact plausible, though because of the political power of those who oppose government action, free-market fundamentalism retains considerable prestige. *What Money Can't Buy* does not take on the theory directly. It asks, rather: What is the moral character of a society in which everything is for sale? Should everything have a price? Is there a difference between the price and the value of a thing?

Most of us undoubtedly believe that there are things that money can't, or shouldn't, buy—love, devotion, and trust, for example. Not everyone believes this; the famed neoclassical economist and Nobel Prize winner Gary Becker thinks otherwise:

> A person decides to marry when the utility expected from marriage exceeds that expected from remaining single or from additional search for a more suitable mate. Similarly, a married person terminates his (or her) marriage when the utility anticipated from becoming single or marrying someone else exceeds the loss in utility from separation, including . . . separation from one's children, division of joint assets, legal fees, and so forth. Since many persons are looking for mates, a *market* in marriages can be said to exist.

Perhaps, but few people would admit unblushingly to marrying chiefly for "expected utility."

Likewise, most of us would say that everyone ought to have a fair chance in life, that those who are suffering most should be cared for first, that the best education should go to those who can make the best use of it, and in general that need or desert should be taken into account in the distribution of scarce resources, not merely the ability to pay. Skillfully, Sandel parses this popular intuition into two distinct sources of unease about the commercialization of everything. "The fairness objection asks about the inequality that market choices may reflect; the corruption objection asks about the attitudes and norms that market relations may damage or dissolve." Without minimizing the first objection, Sandel concentrates on the second.

If we pay students to read books and mercenaries to fight the country's wars, then we risk forgetting (or not teaching the next generation) what it is to love learning or love one's country. If it became common to rent poor women's wombs because the legal mother is too busy or lazy or vain to carry the baby, we would risk diluting the intensity of maternal love. If we sell naming rights to academic and athletic buildings, we risk forgetting that it is intellectual excellence and community spirit that we should want to foster among the people who frequent those buildings, not merely reverence for wealth. It's not inevitable, perhaps, that thoroughgoing commercialization will crowd out nonmarket values. But it's a grave risk. Bad currency drives out good; weeds smother more delicate growths; and in general, coarse, grasping, self-regarding behavior, when unchecked, undermines civic virtue.

Most practices beyond straightforward commercial transactions have social meanings and moral purposes, Sandel reminds us. Financial incentives alone cannot sustain a society of any complexity or richness. Shared values are indispensable; deliberation must supplement—indeed, must structure—markets. "Such deliberations," he writes,

> touch, unavoidably, on competing conceptions of the good life. This is terrain on which we sometimes fear to tread. For fear of disagreement, we hesitate to bring our moral and spiritual convictions into the public square. But shrinking from these questions does not leave them undecided. It simply means that markets will decide them for us. This is the lesson of the last three decades. The era of market triumphalism has coincided with a time when public discourse has been largely empty of moral and spiritual

> substance. Our only hope of keeping markets in their place is to deliberate openly and publicly about the meaning of the goods and social practices we prize.

Secular liberals have been criticized, with some justice, for their reluctance to discuss abortion, divorce, pornography, promiscuity, and other sexual and family matters on their merits rather than strictly in terms of privacy rights. Privacy is not the only value worth taking account of in social and cultural debates, any more than efficiency is the only value worth taking account of in political and economic debates. Sandel is right: vigorous (though courteous) and continuing argument about the good life, however difficult to maintain, is essential to a healthy democracy. Perhaps it is not too much to ask that presidential and other campaign debates include some such argument, at least occasionally?

24

ENOUGH . . . FOR NOW

Bill McKibben

I once thought the most troubling book I had ever read was *The End of Nature* (1989), Bill McKibben's searching meditation on humankind's definitive eclipse of our nonhuman context. That book was not primarily a catalogue of likely environmental disasters, imminent or eventual, though there was more than enough of such worrisome news. What mainly troubled McKibben was that we have, without forethought, passed a momentous limit. By the end of the twentieth century, the scale of human activity had grown so rapidly and enormously that the nonhuman world now exists on our sufferance—not this or that niche, but the character of the whole.

The resulting loss, McKibben suggested, cannot be gauged. In the last two centuries we Americans have destroyed many of the wonders of the world: the Colorado River and its sublime canyons (very nearly including the Grand Canyon), the California redwoods, the tall-grass prairie, the bison herds, the grizzlies. Each disappearance has occasioned much anguish among those who loved those places and creatures, at least in imagination. But in each case the idea of nature survived: our confidence, however feckless, that we might disfigure the planet here or there but could never overwhelm it; that we might misuse it, or even use up this or that aspect of it, but that as a whole it would endure, essentially as it always had, mute, unmasterable, sovereign in its indifference to us.

No longer. The increase of carbon dioxide and other "greenhouse" gases in the atmosphere, and the associated long-term climate changes, are capable of altering the distribution of life forms on earth so profoundly that the distinction between natural and artificial is imperiled. If "natural" means what happens without human intervention, outside human control, then the natural world has, in effect, disappeared. Even if global industrial activity is henceforth curtailed, which is hardly likely, we have already gone too far. We may yet avoid ruining the world, but we have already shrunken it drastically, with unpredictable—and probably not very healthy—effects on our collective psyche.

McKibben's next book, *Hope, Human and Wild* (1995), reported on some comparatively sane ways of living within this shrunken world. It described the resourceful city administration of Curitiba, Brazil, with its ingenious low-tech solutions to flood control, garbage collection, and public transportation; the Indian state of Kerala, comparable to the United States in literacy and life expectancy with only one-seventieth the per-capita income; and, surprisingly, the northeastern United States, where forests and wildlife have made an unexpected recovery in recent decades and communities have begun to defend themselves against industrial predation. Whether enough people will decide soon enough, as McKibben urged his readers, "to slow down, to reduce expectations, to undevelop" is highly uncertain. Still, the book left one with a chastened, tentative hopefulness about nature's prospects.

About the human prospect, however, it is hard to feel anything but terrified after reading *Enough: Staying Human in an*

Engineered Age (2004). As most people know, the genetic modification of many plants and animals—not by traditional crossbreeding but by directly inserting or altering individual genes—has been attempted, with much controversy about the results. According to one eminent scientist (James Watson, who discovered the structure of DNA), we are "at the beginning of a great GM [genetically modified] plant revolution," which will "ensure that crops contain a fuller array of nutrients . . . hold the key to distributing orally administered vaccine proteins . . . [and] provide ways as yet unimagined to preserve the environment." According to another (Harvard professor Richard Lewontin), the new technology merely "provides a powerful tool for the control of agricultural production by monopolistic producers of the inputs into agriculture, with no ultimate advantage either to farmers or consumers and with the possibility of destroying entire national agricultural economies."

An even more fateful controversy is just getting under way. It looks, many scientists claim, more and more likely that humans too can be genetically modified by such means, whether to prevent disease or to enhance desired traits. Some diseases, like cystic fibrosis, sickle-cell anemia, and Tay-Sachs disease, require the presence of a single defective gene. If a couple conceives several embryos in vitro, one without the disease-carrying gene can be chosen and implanted in the mother's womb. Such genetic screening is already available and is not particularly controversial.

But what if genes for IQ, physique, memory, musicality, et cetera can be isolated and modified? What if a future child's character and personality can, to an initially limited but slowly increasing extent, be predetermined? Would such genetic interventions be morally right? And even if most people believe they wouldn't be, should they nevertheless be legal for those who believe otherwise?

Before approaching these questions, a factual caveat. Some scientists object that it does *not* look very likely that human behavior can be genetically modified. Steven Pinker, for example, writes that "not only is genetic enhancement not inevitable, it is not particularly likely in our lifetimes. . . . The human brain is not a bag of traits with one gene for each trait. Neural development is a staggeringly complex process guided by many genes interacting in feedback loops." Richard Lewontin likens the genetic code to a complex ecosystem: "You can always intervene and change something . . . but there's no knowing what the downstream effects will be or how it will affect the environment." Barry Commoner declares flatly: "By any reasonable measure, the findings [of the Human Genome Project] . . . destroy the scientific foundation of genetic engineering."

Still, it seems wise to consider ahead of time what we should do if genetic enhancement turns out to be feasible. If we are to pass this even more momentous limit, to alter human nature as we have always known it, let us at least not do so without forethought. And so: even if someday we can safely intervene in the biological mechanism of inheritance and get the results we want, ought we to do it? *Enough* is McKibben's answer, an unequivocal no.

In the first place, genetic enhancement is un-American. The essence of Americanism is found in that bold and noble sentence from the Declaration of Independence: "All men are created equal." As with all great truths, precisely what this statement means has been disputed. But it has been sufficiently well understood throughout the last two centuries to serve as the foundation of equality before the law and the basis of American democracy, which is perhaps humankind's grandest (however imperfect) political achievement.

Whatever "all men are created equal" may mean, exactly, it will no longer be true after a few dozen or a few hundred generations of genetic enhancement. As McKibben points out, like most technological advances in an already drastically unequal society, "designer" genes would benefit the rich far more than the poor:

> They would take the gap in power, wealth, and education that currently divides both our society and the world at large, and write that division into our very biology. A sixth of the American population lacks health insurance of any kind—they can't afford to go to the doctor for a *checkup*. And much of the rest of the world is far worse off. If we can't afford the fifty cents a person it would take to buy bed nets to protect most of Africa from malaria, it is unlikely we will extend to anyone but the top tax bracket these latest forms of genetic technology.

These are not mere Luddite mutterings. According to Princeton geneticist Lee Silver, a prominent advocate of the new technology, "emotional stability, long-term happiness, inborn talents, increased creativity, healthy bodies—these could be the starting points chosen for the children of the rich," while "obesity, heart disease, hypertension, alcoholism, mental illness—these will be the diseases left to drift randomly among the families of the underclass." The "GenRich" (genetically enhanced) minority, Silver continues, will control "all aspects of the economy, the media, the entertainment industry, and the knowledge industry." Eventually, "the GenRich class and the Natural class [that is, the rest of us] will become . . . entirely separate species with no ability to crossbreed, and with as much romantic interest in each other as a current human would have for a chimpanzee."

Surely this is un-American. As if to explicate the Declaration of Independence, Thomas Jefferson, its principal author, later wrote: "The general spread of the light of science has already laid open to every view the palpable truth, that the mass of mankind has not been born with saddles on their backs, nor a favored few booted and spurred, ready to ride them legitimately, by the grace of God." But one must ask, what science once gave, is science now about to take away? "The ultimate question raised by biotechnology," concludes Francis Fukuyama in his very astute *Our Posthuman Future,* is: "What will happen to political rights once we are able to, in effect, breed some people with saddles on their backs, and others with boots and spurs?" What will happen, pretty clearly, is the end of democracy and the American ideal. A modest proposal, therefore: Shouldn't we get a little closer to attaining those things before we risk losing them forever merely in order that a privileged minority can ascend to superhumanity (and, not incidentally, so that a powerful industry can reap enormous profits)?

This is assuming we have some choice in the matter. Perhaps, after all, we won't. "Whether we like it or not," Lee Silver admonishes, "the global marketplace will reign supreme." There you have it—the antagonism between democratic deliberation and free-market fundamentalism could not be more forthrightly, even contemptuously, expressed. There's a lot of money to be made in biotech, as there was in generating greenhouse gases, even if those activities turn our inner and outer worlds upside down. Get over it.

The political argument for restraint is straightforward and, it seems to me, unanswerable. But most of *Enough* is devoted to making a deeper, more ambitious, more difficult argument against human genetic engineering: an argument from meaning. The promise of the new technologies (McKibben also discusses robotics and nanotechnology, the use of molecules for computing, manufacturing, and more) is fabulous. Newly formulated gene packages will improve our every physical, emotional, and intellectual capability, eventually without limit. Beginning with the more directly gene-dependent ones, every disease will be eradicated, including cancer—even including aging; immortality too is part of the program. Nanobots (contingents of molecule-size robots) with unimaginable information-processing capacity will synthesize food, assemble consumer goods, and clean up waste, thereby eliminating hunger, poverty, and pollution. And in the fullness of time, they will construct a vastly superior species, thereby eliminating us.

Some of these, as McKibben shows, are false promises. To take a longstanding one: the Green Revolution in agriculture has, it is true, invariably increased plant yields, but it has also invariably increased micronutrient deficiencies and small-farmer indebtedness as well. The latest genetically engineered miracle, "golden rice," is a will-of-the-wisp. Biotechnology is not the solution to world hunger; biodiversity is. Low-tech solutions are also readily available for Third World poverty and disease; though since they are less profitable than high-tech solutions, they require a little disinterested First World support. The brand-new promise of nanotechnology is also dubious, even if feasible: nano-weapons, or even nano-accidents, would be far more devastating than present-day biological or chemical weapons.

But whether feasible or not, post-humanity is, McKibben argues, a poisoned gift as long as we have not yet achieved humanity. All the proposed new technologies aim at a fundamentally similar result: more. They aim to make our genetic hardware, our resources, our actions in some way larger or faster or easier. More computational power or muscle mass or dexterity or serotonin or orgasmic potency; faster communication or transportation or food preparation; easier work or no work. More lifespan, sensory inputs, entertainments, et cetera ad infinitum. More and faster and easier are not, in general, bad. On the contrary, they are, other things being equal, good. But sometimes—as in the near future, perhaps, when a flood of new stimuli and experiences may overwhelm our sensory and imaginative capacity to assimilate them, not to mention our political capacity to keep them from rending humankind's already precarious community—the good can be the enemy of the best.

What then, if not more, is best for human beings now? McKibben bravely faces this all-important question and throws out some fruitful hints. He cites some fascinating psychological research on joy, in particular the "almost trance-like state" the subjects entered when their work was going especially well. In this state, "fatigue, hunger, or discomfort ceased to matter." This ecstatic experience seems to derive from "the intense concentration that risk and adversity entail"; it "arises more from sensory focus than sensory overload"—from going inward, that is, rather than simply adding on, whether data, circuits, or genes. The world, the research subjects testify in a striking formulation, "falls away." This sounds a good deal like the peak experiences described by mystics and meditators. It also bears some resemblance to the "deep time" of fully engaged reading, evoked memorably by literary critic Sven Birkerts in *The Gutenberg Elegies*. It even (or so it seems to me) remotely echoes Nietzsche's enigmatic allusions to "self-overcoming."

McKibben's point is that there's an inner world as well as an outer world, and penetrating the one may be as essential to human fulfillment as conquering the other. The new hypertechnologies will facilitate the latter but not the former. Since our inclination is usually to evade what's difficult, we may find an increasing disproportion between our power and our depth. If there really is, as he speculates, a "strange connection between effort and joy and pride and reward," then perhaps limitless abundance would be less satisfying than the techno-utopians suppose.

It is perfectly true, of course, that inwardness—or self-cultivation or self-overcoming or whatever you like to call it—requires a sufficiency of material goods. Underfed and overworked people should not be asked to forgo further calories or conveniences. But as McKibben tirelessly reiterates, we in the developed world are already pretty close to the "enough" point. "We have reached a point of great comfort and ease relative to the past. The real question is whether, having reached that point, we want to trade it in for something essentially unknown." Turning back technologically, or even standing still, is no more desirable than it is possible. But it's at least thinkable that "the rush of technological innovation that's marked the last five hundred years can finally slow, and spread out to water the whole delta of human possibility." And to begin, for decency's sake, with those who are now much farther from the "enough" point than we are would provide a pretty challenging technological agenda for the rest of this century, at least.

Heartily as I agree with McKibben, I am tempted to amend his battle cry to "Enough . . . for now." We can't really know, after all, how a grown-up human race would regard this question. Perhaps someday in the distant future we will want, as a species, to assume a new form of life. Perhaps we will have together come to fruit, reached an unsurpassable ripeness, a stable equipoise of individuality and community, solidarity and self-assertion, such that nowhere on earth remained large pools of unnecessary pain or ignorance, such that all or most possible harmonies within us and among us had been sounded and danced to. Then, not from fear that one's future child may be left behind in a hectic competition for top preschools, or from any such desperately sad motive, but instead with a grateful reverence for the rounded humanity and exquisite comity we will by then have perfected together, some may volunteer to renounce that perfection and be tinkered with.

If that's how it happens, then so be it. But we today should leave to those who will be, by our own lights and through our own efforts, wiser than us, a decision that is beyond our present wisdom. We should, for the future's sake, acknowledge the limits of that wisdom. We are not wise enough—not now, not for a long time—to justify abdicating our specieshood, renouncing our humanity forever in favor of post-humanity. We are wise enough, though, to make a good life for our species now and to see a few steps in the direction of a better one.

At least, I hope we are.

25

MORE THAN HUMAN?

Progress and decline are spatial metaphors; they suggest a curve headed upward or downward over time. The more points through which a curve is plotted, the better defined it is; so the farther backward and forward we can plausibly—without floating away in fantasy—extend the temporal axis, the better we'll understand cultural tendencies like the decline of verbal literacy.

Backward, then, into the prehistoric mists. What was it like before there was writing? Whatever other categories may be useful for imagining the differences between then and now, surely immediacy is. Between perception and reaction, between stimulus and response, there lay no shadow, no complex processing, no translation of cipher into referent into meaning. The large parts of our neurophysiology that are needed to decode, store, and retrieve written information went instead to speed and intensify the reflexes of pre-literate man. No writing meant fewer options to search out and compare before any decision (and fewer decisions, naturally); fewer competing perspectives or frameworks to choose among. Instinctual conflict, sometimes; but no pale cast of thought. I would guess that Homeric, or at any rate Neanderthal, heroes really did "leap" into battle, really did "embrace" death. Imagine their orgasms.

But this was not an entirely benign, nobly primitive condition. Humankind has not evolved biologically very much since the invention of writing, so pre-literate people had roughly the same neurophysiological capacity, the same quantity of imagination, as us. But since they were forced to deploy it within very much narrower dimensions, the results were exotic, even bizarre. They didn't just charmingly endow snakes, trees, and waterfalls with personality, and sometimes divinity. They often heard them speak, and sometimes died of fright. Nearly every oral culture seems to have been a theocracy, and an amazing number of them (on the evidence of Julian Jaynes's *Origin of Consciousness in the Breakdown of the Bicameral Mind*) were based on hearing the voices of gods—that is, on mass delusion. Imagine their terrors.

Loss and gain, then. The things that matter most to us, the terms in which we tell our life stories—loves, beliefs, tastes, ambitions—presuppose a degree of vicarious experience, an extent of information, inconceivable fifty thousand years ago; while our ancestors' significant life-experiences—to have lived among intimately familiar and subtly discriminated flora and fauna; to have enjoyed or endured sensations and enacted impulses with a vividness, spontaneity, and intensity unattainable now—involved a radically different balance of direct and vicarious experience, of intensive and extensive information. Our existence is immeasurably more mediated, less immediate, than theirs.

Sven Birkerts's essay "Into the Electronic Millennium" plausibly described a transition to an era in which most people's experience will be still more vicarious and less direct, their information more extensive and less intensive. This may seem an oddly neutral way to characterize the chilling prospects the essay holds out. I do indeed share Birkerts's unease about the near-to-medium term. But something at the margin of his vision, and in particular his allusion to the eclipse of individuality, calls for comment as well.

Let me try for a moment to disconnect the what from the how; the evolutionary process from its political context; what Birkerts calls "electronic collectivization" from the fact of its design and exploitation by business, the media, the entertainment industry, and the state. Let's disregard, in imagination, these extrinsic, distorting influences on cultural development and suppose that we the people freely, democratically, and wisely controlled our cultural evolution. What difference would this make to the fate of writing?

Every text, we know, has a context; and the more artful the text—whether poem, tale, picture, argument, or equation—the larger the relevant context. Texts of sufficient richness we call ineffable: the body of direct and vicarious experience, of extensive and intensive information, needed to register their whole force and depth is unattainable for beings with our capacities.

Depth is not the only dimension in which our aesthetic and intellectual reach exceeds our grasp. An aspiration to breadth or universality—to "all-sidedness," to assimilate the best that has been thought and said and be one of those on whom nothing is lost—became a cultural ideal only in modern times, just as its realization began to be impossible. The impulse to master the still (barely) masterable corpus of mid-eighteenth-century knowledge produced the *Encyclopédie,* which is, in respect of this ideal, the high tide of modernity. After the confidence of the *philosophes* comes the titanism (and ultimate resignation) of Goethe, the exquisite melancholy of Matthew Arnold and Henry James, the delirium of Pound and the High Modernists, and the white noise of postmodernism.

Along with the marketing requirements of late twentieth-century capitalism and the (related) spread of a narcissistic or pre-Oedipal character structure, one contributing cause of postmodernism may be despair over the impossibility of assimilating more than a fraction of the best that has been thought and said "on all the matters which most concern us," of achieving "a harmonious perfection, developing all sides of our humanity," as Arnold put it in *Culture and Anarchy* (1869). To know even a single branch of culture both intimately and exhaustively will soon exceed the capacity of just about anyone. In the arts as in science and politics, the division of labor has made available an abundance and variety of experience and information that are no longer merely stimulating but arguably overstimulating, even overwhelming. We can try, as Richard Rorty urges, "to admire both Blake and Arnold, both Marx and Baudelaire, both Nietzsche and Mill, both Trotsky and Eliot, both Nabokov and Orwell"; we can hope to understand "how these men's books can be put together to form a beautiful mosaic." But it's a stretch. Add to this list Wittgenstein, Bartók, Rilke, Balanchine, and Lévi-Strauss, and we begin to stagger. Add further—and who could bear to omit?—Duke Ellington, Robert Bresson, Jasper Johns, Frank Lloyd Wright, Martha Graham, Michel Tournier, and we have long since passed a limit. Though we may know enough to admire, we cannot really comprehend, cannot possibly devote to all these masters and masterpieces the patient, deeply informed attention they require.

And if *per impossibile* we could, we would scarcely have begun to do justice to "all the matters which most concern us." I'm helpless to evoke, can't even properly name, the beauties of science and mathematics. But no one, I suppose, believes they're inferior to those mentioned in the preceding paragraph? Look steadily and whole at the misery for which, as an American citizen, one bears one's mite of moral responsibility, and an interior voice sounds: You must change your life. But where to find the time, the energy, the spare imagination?

It's too much. "Harmonious perfection" is out of the question. We must either accept cultural overload, partial vision, mutual incomprehension, or else find some way to extend our range, augment our capacities, enhance our neurophysiology. Actually, there's a good deal to be said for the first alternative. Why does there need to be anybody who can "put together" all of culture? If print remains our principal medium of expression and communication, we can hold on, at least for a while, to the present rhythms and grain of our mental life, the architecture of our selves. "Privacy" and "autonomy" may be only names for our current balance of direct and vicarious experience, of intensive and extensive information. But it is *our* balance; it is us. No doubt our way of life will continue to change. I can no more imagine the cultural primacy of books lasting another fifty thousand years than, say, theism or meat-eating or the nuclear family or private ownership of the means of production. But—for reasons I'll explain in a moment—I'm more than ambivalent, I'm positively alarmed, about beginning the transition now.

Still, the transition will begin someday, and should. The ideal of universality—that there needs to be someone (or something) that can put together all of culture—is deep-seated, perhaps ineradicable. Birkerts invokes a figure-ground analogy for human identity. It is an apt analogy; but in the limit case, when the ground—the sheer scope of cultural possibilities, even considering only those available in traditional forms—alters drastically, qualitatively, then the implications of the analogy cease to be conservative. The figure must change dimension, perhaps radically, in order to maintain differentiation.

If this requires a new neural network, perhaps one extending outside our skin, then sooner or later, evolved or constructed, we will have one. Networks can embed hierarchies, temporal as well as logical: memory, tradition, culture itself are such networks. Organic rather than electronic ones, to be sure; but then, it's synergy rather than substitution that I look forward to.

Of course memory can be constricted and history flattened by commissars, spin doctors, or profit-maximizing advertising executives and media managers. The design of a culture, the shape of a species's collective sensibility is a political question. Right now that question is being begged, whence my alarm. Ideally, verbal literacy would be subsumed or transcended in the course of cultural evolution, not simply eroded. The attrition of civic memory and craft knowledge, a reduced attention span and loss of discrimination, the attenuation of nuance and the homogenization of vocabulary—in all these ways the decay of literacy currently serves both the manufacture of consent and the accumulation of capital. A populace that cannot recognize rhetorical devices, make moderately subtle verbal distinctions, or remember back beyond the last election or ad campaign is defenseless against official propaganda and commercial hype. Only rootedness makes sustained resistance to the modern Leviathan—state, corporations, and media—possible. And an important form of rootedness is our internalization of the Word in one form or another: sacred scripture or poetic tradition or civic mythology or family lore. Benign cultural evolution, genuine emancipation, would lead us to work through such traditions, preserving even while going beyond them. As it is, we are merely being distracted from them.

The deepest and bitterest of all current disagreements is about whether modernity itself is an example of benign cultural evolution. In the creation of modern cultural and economic individualism, premodern communal traditions were similarly undermined without being worked through. For the most part, the people of Europe did not make their own painful way beyond village, kin network, handicraft, and local religion into a brave new world of mobility and rationality, city and factory. By and large, they were bulldozed. In that case as in this, the transition was shaped and paced, though not entirely motivated, by the needs of elites. True, a democratic transition to modernity in Europe would have taken centuries longer and might not even now be consummated. But it would not have given rise to the twin specters of antimodernist fundamentalism and postmodernist nihilism.

Marx and Freud made parallel and profoundly true observations, one about social practices and the other about individual beliefs. If a practice or belief is overthrown prematurely, is repressed rather than outgrown, the result is pathology. To suggest that humankind is now ready to leave behind verbal literacy, when only a tiny, fortunate fraction have savored its pleasurable possibilities to the full, is not hubris. It is fatuity; worse, cruelty. At this stage of our political and cultural development, electronic collectivization would produce not new, marvelously complex and efficient forms of cognition and communication but historical amnesia and mass manipulation.

If I may hijack one more of Birkerts's inspired metaphors, that of language as a kind of ozone: someday, perhaps, we will no longer need an ozone layer. Of course we must immediately stop depleting atmospheric (and linguistic) ozone or else face catastrophe. But eventually we will decipher the genetic code and redesign our skin, our immunological system, and probably much more. I hope, though, that it takes a few millennia. To think what the "free" market or the authoritarian state would do with genetic engineering is awful, just as it's awful to see the transformative possibilities of electronics squandered on weapons production, law enforcement, advertising, the credit industry, and the entertainment industry.

That our organic senses, including memory, will someday be joined, in a way we cannot now conceive, to electronic ones is something I certainly can't prove, yet don't really doubt. Our perennial desire to integrate and master all knowledge can no longer be accomplished with our present sensorium. But we will not get there by continuing to dissipate our linguistic heritage. We are not transcending verbal literacy; we are merely forgetting it. Contemporary postmodernism is a false dawn because the finest possibilities of modernity have not yet begun to be realized. For the same reasons, the electronic millennium is now a threat rather than—what it may yet prove to be, in the farther reaches of cultural evolution—a promise.

Envoi

WHAT WERE WE THINKING?

Unless we have reached the end point of humankind's moral development, it is pretty certain that the average educated human of the twenty-third century will look back at the average educated human of the twenty-first century and ask incredulously about a considerable number of our most cherished moral and political axioms: "How could they have believed *that?*" We do this ourselves every time a movie like *Twelve Years a Slave* or a novel like *The Handmaid's Tale* or a play like *Angels in America* or a work of history like *Bury My Heart at Wounded Knee* or of journalism like Michael Harrington's *The Other America* prompts us to ask, "How could decent, intelligent people have believed they were entitled to treat other human beings like that?"

So let's interrogate some of our beliefs about political morality with the eyes of our descendants. Two four-letter words lie at the heart of contemporary America's public morality: "free" and "fair." "It's a free country" is every American's boast; "I only want a fair shake" is every American's plea. I doubt I need to remind my readers of the more flagrant forms of unfairness in our national life—that one American child in five lives below or near the poverty line; that somewhere between 80 and 90 percent of our economy's productivity gains since 1980 have gone to the top 10 percent of the income distribution; that the top twenty-five hedge-fund managers earn more than all the nation's kindergarten teachers combined; that one hundred thousand Americans will die for lack of health care over the next ten years in order to give a large tax cut to Americans with incomes above a half-million dollars; and so on and on, down the long and shameful catalogue. Our twenty-third-century descendants may ask—they *will* ask—how we could have tolerated such unfairness; but they won't ask how we could have believed such inequalities to be fair, because we don't, most of us, believe them to be fair. Let's instead consider a different question: whether our present-day ideals of fairness and freedom, even if we lived up to them, would satisfy our descendants.

The average CEO now earns around three hundred times as much as the company's average employee. Many people are dismayed at the contrast with the good old days of the Eisenhower administration, when CEOs earned only 30 times as much as their average employees and paid a far higher tax rate, and yet the country didn't seem to be going to the dogs. But let's put aside our reaction to this striking change and ask more generally whether and why some people ought to earn more than others.

The usual answer, I suppose, is that people deserve whatever they get through the operation of supply and demand. The competitive marketplace quantifies the value that one's efforts have for others. Some people (like doctors) employ vital skills; some people (like baseball players) give exceptional enjoyment; some people (like corporate executives) assume extra responsibilities; some people (like investors) forgo luxury consumption. All such people are rewarded in proportion to the satisfaction they furnish others, as measured by others' willingness to pay, directly or indirectly, for those satisfactions. No payment, no service. As Adam Smith wrote: "It is not from the benevolence of the butcher, the brewer, or the baker that we expect our dinner, but from their regard to their own interest."

Of course it's not that simple. Consider those doctors, baseball players, and executives I used as examples of economic agents who exchange services for money. In fact, they—like you, like me—live with only one foot in a market economy and the other in a gift economy. Any doctor or scientist or athlete or nurse or teacher or carpenter worth her salt feels at least occasionally that she is making a gift of her best efforts; and as with all such gifts, the chief reward is internal: the pleasures of giving and of exercising one's faculties at their highest pitch.

Nowadays, the gift economy leads a precarious existence, appearing mostly in commencement-day addresses in which graduates are exhorted to follow their dreams, while most of them are worrying frantically about how to pay their debts. The family is a gift economy, and so is culture, including both the arts and the sciences, as well as the shrinking public and nonprofit spheres. But ever since industrial mass production—that most fateful of innovations—became virtually universal, the market economy has progressively squeezed out the gift economy. In a mature capitalist society, competition grows in both extent and intensity, that is, both between and within economic units. Creativity and generosity are not forbidden, but they are no longer self-justifying; they are, on the contrary, subordinated, like all activity in the non-public sphere, to the goal of increasing shareholder value. In the private economy, you can do whatever you like—create beauty, pursue truth, help others—as long as what you like to do makes someone a profit.

I said earlier that people in a market economy are rewarded in proportion to others' willingness to pay. That willingness to pay is the measure of value in a market economy; and so, to say that a person deserves what she earns is to say that there is at least a rough correspondence between the value of what she produces and the value of what she receives. As Milton Friedman, the high priest of American capitalism, put it: "The ethical principle [underlying] the distribution of income in a free-market society is, 'To each according to what he and the instruments he owns produces.'"

This notion of desert relies on two distinctions: first, that one person's input—to any output or outcome at all—can be sharply distinguished from all other inputs; and second, that merit can be distinguished from luck: that is, that diligence, good judgment, and other productive qualities and character traits, as well as talent, are not fully attributable to biological endowment, early environment, education, and other contingent and therefore morally arbitrary sources. I don't believe those distinctions hold up.

Let's take that CEO, and let's assume we know somehow that she produces thirty or three hundred times as much as her average employee. Causation is a transitive relation. If A is a cause of B, and B is a cause of C, then A is a cause of C. If A contributes to the production of B, and B contributes to the production of C, then A has contributed to the production of C. Now, who has contributed to the production of our CEO, and therefore to the production of whatever she produces? Clearly, her parents, spouse, teachers, fellow students, predecessors, colleagues, rivals, and friends, along with all *their* parents, spouses, teachers, fellow students, predecessors, colleagues, rivals, and friends, along with all those who created the physical, organizational, and cultural resources employed in the production of whatever our CEO produces, along with all their parents, spouses, teachers, fellow students, predecessors, colleagues, rivals, and friends, and, it goes without saying, all *their* parents, spouses, teachers, and so on through what is, if one wants to insist on the point, an infinite chain of causes.

I do want to insist on the point. Einstein famously wrote: "I have all along been standing on the shoulders of giants." So has our CEO. Exceptional contributions, whether to art, science, or the gross national product, are prepared for by the whole previous development of the field. People who make brilliant, courageous, and illuminating mistakes, which may be indispensable to the ultimate success of a rich and famous artist, scientist, or entrepreneur, are not, in a competitive market system, retrospectively and proportionately rewarded for their contributions, even though Friedman's definition of justice would seem to require it.

My point is that all production is social production. The productive assets of every age are the joint product of all preceding ages, and all those born into the present are legitimately joint heirs of those assets. And the same arguments for joint rather than individual inheritance of wealth created in the past apply to the distribution of income in the present. If this seems counter-intuitive, it is perhaps because there persists a deep and ancient distinction between luck and merit, according to which we deserve praise and reward for our good actions, though not for our good fortune. But what if our good actions are the results of our good fortune?

Philosophy assimilates scientific discoveries slowly, so it is usually riddled with archaic concepts and images, survivals from an earlier scientific epoch. One such survival, it seems to me, is the concept of merit. It has always been partly recognized (it is, indeed, implicit in the word "gifted") that talents and aptitudes come under the heading of luck rather than merit. But the inescapable implication of modern genetics, neuroscience, and psychiatry is that character, no less than talent, is inherited or else formed by very early experiences. Diligence, decisiveness, initiative, coolness under pressure—all these entrepreneurial virtues are, no less than intellectual or manual abilities, part of one's natural endowment. And from a strictly moral point of view, no one deserves a reward for being born luckier than someone else. I imagine the twenty-third century will ask: "Why did you make talent and character the measure of an individual's desert rather than of her duty? How could you have overlooked what is to us the obvious and elementary principle of fairness: from each according to her abilities, to each according to her needs?"

I suggested earlier that causation is potentially an infinite regress. If that's true, does anyone deserve anything? In fact, potentially infinite regressions are perfectly commonplace and don't normally defeat us. We call a halt to them wherever seems appropriate. Every parent has to decide when a child is genuinely curious and when it keeps asking "Why?" just to put off going to sleep. Every conscientious judge has to decide when to stop applying the maxim "To understand all is to forgive all," even though it's undoubtedly true. The point about these decisions is that they are arbitrary and fallible—in making them we rely on prudence rather than principle. So that when we decide to ignore the infinite chain of causes that produced the output of the CEO and pay her the whole market value of it, our decision is not a matter of justice, as Milton Friedman claimed it was.

I said "our decision" just now, but of course you and I don't have anything to say about the just distribution of income and wealth. Indeed, the purpose of definitions like Friedman's is precisely to prevent such distributions from becoming a matter of public decision. In the 1940s, an influential senator, trying to stifle criticism of Harry Truman's Cold War policies, demanded that "politics should stop at the water's edge." It worked then, and the proponents of the economic class war have had a similar success in preaching that democracy should stop at the economy's edge. In principle, the state is governed according to the rule of one person, one vote. Economic enterprises such as corporations are not even democratic in principle: there the rule is, one dollar of shareholder value, one vote. In both areas, it hardly needs pointing out, principle counts for very little. None but the largest investors have any influence with corporate management; while in politics, rich donors in effect have many votes, the rest of us none.

The case of politics is particularly egregious. Two political scientists, Martin Gilens of Princeton and Benjamin Page of Northwestern, recently summarized years of detailed statistical research into the relation between what voters want and what we get:

> In the United States, our findings indicate, the majority does not rule—at least not in the causal sense of actually determining policy outcomes. When a majority of citizens disagree with economic elites and/or with organized interests, they generally lose. Moreover . . . even when fairly large majorities of Americans favor policy change, they generally do not get it. . . . For Americans below the top of the income distribution, any association between preferences and policy outcomes is likely to reflect the extent to which their preferences [happen to] coincide with those of the affluent. Although responsiveness to the preferences of the affluent is [not] perfect, responsiveness to less-well-off Americans is virtually nonexistent.

If democracy means one person, one vote, in what situations is democracy morally obligatory? Here is an answer from Robert Dahl, perhaps the most eminent American political scientist of the twentieth century. According to Dahl, members of any association are entitled to insist that it be governed democratically when the following conditions hold: the group must reach some decisions that are binding on all members; discussion and collective decision-making are feasible; membership is stable, so those who make the decisions will be subject to the consequences; and there is a rough equality of competence, meaning that members are capable of judging their own interests and also of judging which decisions they must delegate to experts.

Now, why don't these conditions hold for corporations as well as for political communities? One possible objection might be that, unlike laws, management decisions are not binding—employees can quit. The answer to this objection is that in the real world, unlike the world of smoothly clearing labor markets and other fantasies of neoclassical economics, the costs of renouncing employment are frequently as great as the costs of renouncing citizenship. Another possible objection is that management requires special skills, which workers may not possess. But surely workers are no less capable of hiring and supervising managers than shareholders are, and probably more so. Still another objection is based on the notorious "iron law of oligarchy," according to which any sizable association tends to be dominated by those with the most aptitude and ambition. But the same holds for political democracy, which no one proposes abandoning on that account. Finally, there is the moral objection: aren't shareholders entitled to control the firms they invest in? For the same reasons that entitlement theories fail to justify large inequalities in income—namely, that wealth is a social product and that differences in ability and character are morally arbitrary—they fail to justify large differences in the power to control our common economic destiny. And more: since one requirement of fair political competition is that all group members have equal access to relevant information about group decisions and equal opportunity to place items on the agenda for decision, it follows that in a society like ours, where economic resources translate into political resources, economic inequality must result in political inequality, a conclusion that is obvious to everyone except the conservative majority on the U.S. Supreme Court. Political democracy requires economic democracy; indeed, the distinction between the political and the economic is altogether artificial. How, our twenty-third-century descendants will ask us politely, but perhaps with a tinge of exasperation, did you manage to overlook *that?*

If you have the misfortune to be a left-wing social critic, the most galling part of each day is encountering the ubiquitous self-designation of apologists for capitalism as champions of freedom. One day a MAGA congressman introduces the Economic Freedom Act, which would free the four thousand or so people who pay it from the estate tax and liberate the rest of us from Social Security and the minimum wage. The next day some foundation with "freedom" in its name gives an award to Charles Koch for his stalwart defense of Koch Industries' freedom to render sizable areas of West Virginia, Arkansas, and Louisiana uninhabitable. And every day the Congressional Freedom Caucus warns sternly that it will not rest until the tens of millions of Americans who cannot afford proper health care without assistance from the rest of us are finally free to go without it.

The primitive intuitions about freedom to which defenders of laissez-faire capitalism appeal are widespread and at least superficially plausible. No one makes you shop at Walmart, after all, or work there either. If you don't like it where you live, you're free to move. If you don't like what you're hearing, change the channel. If you don't like Fords, buy a Chevy. This model of life as a series of discrete purchases and of citizens as sovereign consumers seems to lie in the background of many Americans' conviction that, whatever its other virtues or defects, capitalism relies exclusively or primarily on free choice and that regulations or taxes or public provision, even if sometimes justified, necessarily diminish freedom.

This everyday, rough-and ready understanding of freedom was more or less adequate once, back when America was, uniquely in its time, neither a feudal nor a capitalist society. For a couple of centuries, because the land was so rich and was empty of any inhabitants whose rights white men felt obliged to respect, economic autonomy—the ability to make a living without selling one's labor—was very widely, almost universally possible. Those two centuries formed the American imagination, which has not yet adjusted to the traumatic fact that the possibility of individual self-reliance, and therefore of economic autonomy in the sense presupposed by laissez-faire ideology, is gone forever. When the means of making a living were largely unowned and available to all, economic agents could confront one another as equals, capable of entering into genuinely voluntary agreements and morally binding contracts. Today, by contrast, employment contracts typically involve members of two groups that are radically unequal, since one group has control over something the other must have access to in order to survive, but not vice versa. That is just another way of saying that we live in a class society. Our individualistic political rhetoric, appropriate to the frontier period but now a century and a half out of date, serves only to conceal the one-sided class warfare that its victims stubbornly refuse to acknowledge.

Those victims have some excuse; they are daily bombarded by laissez-faire ideology. Intellectuals, on the other hand, really ought to know better. The structural unfreedom inherent in class relations was authoritatively described by an early critic of capitalism and champion of labor unions. I'm referring to Adam Smith, who wrote in book I of *The Wealth of Nations* that in disputes between masters and workmen

> it is not difficult to foresee which of the two parties must [ordinarily] have the advantage . . . and force the other into compliance. The employers, being fewer in number, can combine much more easily; and the law, besides,

> authorizes or at least does not prohibit their combinations, while it prohibits [or strictly regulates] those of the workmen. . . . Employers are always and everywhere in a tacit but constant and uniform combination [to keep down wages].
>
> [Moreover,] in [general,] the employers can hold out much longer. [A master], even if he did not employ a single workman, could generally live a year or two on [his accumulated capital]. Many workmen could not subsist a week, few could subsist a month, and scarcely any a year without wages.

Smith, unlike his descendants from Ricardo to Milton Friedman, was a friend of the workingman.

If we could speak with our nineteenth-century counterparts, we might ask questions like "Why did you believe it legitimate for one person to own another? Why did women seem to you incapable of self-determination? Why did you consider that political authority could be inherited, for example by monarchs or aristocrats?" If our imaginary nineteenth-century interlocutors defended their morality against ours, we might learn a good deal by trying to rebut them and vindicate our own moral intuitions.

Similarly, we should try to imagine which of our current beliefs will seem benighted to our twenty-third-century descendants. I suspect they will want to ask us questions like "Why did you base desert on performance, which can't be measured and is in any case a function of one's endowments? After all, no one deserves her endowments. Why did you make that strangely artificial distinction between the political and the economic? It looks as though your only purpose was to prevent economic democracy. Why did you define freedom so narrowly, as the absence of constraints on one person's right to employ her capital but not on another person's right to realize her capacities? Why did you assume that contracts between parties with radically unequal resources could be free and fair?"

Freud wrote, in a rare hopeful vein: "The voice of the intellect is a soft one, but it does not rest until it has gained a hearing. Ultimately, after endlessly repeated rebuffs, it succeeds. This is one of the few points on which one may be optimistic about the future of humanity, but in itself it signifies not a little."

The human intellect is already more than adequate to dispose of apologetics for greed—it is the human heart that needs instruction. In Edward Bellamy's *Looking Backward* (the second-best-selling book, after *Uncle Tom's Cabin,* in the nineteenth century), Julian West, the nineteenth-century Bostonian who wakes up in the twenty-first century, is told by his guide, Dr. Leete, that in this new world the helpless and disabled receive exactly the same income as everyone else.

> "The idea of charity on such a scale," I answered, "would have made our most enthusiastic philanthropists gasp."
>
> "If you had a sick brother at home," replied Dr. Leete, "unable to work, would you feed him on less dainty food, and lodge and clothe him more poorly, than yourself? More likely far, you would give him the preference; nor would you think of calling it charity. Would not the word, in that connection, fill you with indignation?"
>
> "Of course," I replied; "but the cases are not parallel. There is a sense, no doubt, in which all men are brothers; but this general sort of brotherhood is not to be compared, except for rhetorical purposes, to the brotherhood of blood. . . ."

> "There speaks the nineteenth century!" exclaimed Dr. Leete. "Ah, Mr. West, . . . If I were to give you, in one sentence, a key to what may seem the mysteries of our civilization as compared with that of your age, I should say that it is the fact that the solidarity of the race and the brotherhood of man, which to you were but fine phrases, are, to our thinking and feeling, ties as real and as vital as physical fraternity."

This passage is a bridge to what is surely a very remote utopian future. But it also echoes a distant and yet very familiar past: the Sermon on the Mount, with its promise that "Blessed are those that hunger and thirst for justice, for they will be satisfied," and a little later in the same gospel, the parable of the sheep and the goats, where Jesus almost seems to have been admonishing Julian West and his hard-hearted contemporaries: "Whatever you do to the least of my brothers and sisters"—to the poorest of the poor—"you do to me."

Those who hunger and thirst for justice won't be satisfied for a long while yet, except in imagination. But even that, as Freud said, signifies not a little.

PUBLICATION HISTORY

Agni

Closing Time (originally "Demos and Sophia," September 1988)
"No, in Thunder!" (Fall 1991)

American Prospect

Democracy-Proof (July 2002)

Boston Phoenix

Corruption, Cruelty, Cant (July 1983)

Boston Review

More Than Human? ("Extrasensory," December 1996)
Enough . . . for Now (October 2003)
Reasons and Passions (September 2012)

Christianity & Crisis

Solidarity Ever? (October 1989)

Commonweal

The Price of Everything and the Value of Nothing ("Market Mania," November 2012)
What Were We Thinking? (January 2023)

Dissent

Can We Be Good Without God? (September 1990)
The Dandy ("The Lady and the Luftmensch," Spring 1994)
Requiem for the Enlightenment (September 1996)
Premature Anti-Utopians ("Partisan Responsibilities," Spring 1997)
The Power of Negative Thinking (Summer 1999)

Grand Street

The Contradictions of Conservatism ("Privilege and Its Discontents," Fall 1989)

Harvard Review

Crowds and Culture (October 1992)

Los Angeles Review of Books

Democratic Vistas ("Plutocratic Vistas," July 2012)

n+1

Farewell, Hitch (Winter 2005)

Nation

Zippie World (May 2005)
The Logic of Mass Destruction ("A Parade of Arrogance," April 2011)
The Impresario (May 2011)

Where Has Our Virtue Gone? ("Damage," May 2015)
The Hedgehog and the Fox ("Liberalism's Two Sides," May 2023)

Village Voice

The Realm of Necessity and the Realm of Freedom (August 1983)
Grand Disillusions (December 1985)

ACKNOWLEDGMENTS

Thanks to Jessie Kindig, my editor at Yale University Press and Verso; to my agent, William Callahan of Inkwell; to Matt Boudway of *Commonweal,* for keeping me in work; to Eleanor Hobbs, Askold Melnyczuk, Brian Morton, Jim Sleeper, and John Summers for long and steadfast friendship; to Freddie de Boer, brilliant and fearless; to CrookedTimber.org, a model of intellectual community; and to my comrades at The Alcove, for their wit, erudition, and charity.

INDEX